THE MAKING OF A PEACEMONGER

THE MEMOIRS OF
GEORGE IGNATIEFF

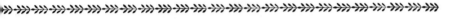

The Making of
a Peacemonger

Prepared in association with Sonja Sinclair

*To Ruth and Alex Fordyce:
with memories of Lake Simcoe
George Ignatieff*

UNIVERSITY OF TORONTO PRESS
Toronto   Buffalo   London

© University of Toronto Press 1985
Toronto   Buffalo   London
Printed in Canada
Reprinted 1985

ISBN 0-8020-2556-0

Canadian Cataloguing in Publication Data

Ignatieff, George, 1913 –

The making of a peacemonger

Includes index.
ISBN 0-8020-2556-0.

1. Ignatieff, George, 1913 –   . 2. Diplomats –
Canada – Biography. 3. Canada – Foreign
relations – 1945 –   . I. Title.

FC601.I45A3 1985   327.2'09'24   C85-098036–4
F1034.3.I45A3 1985

Photo on jacket and p. xx by Robert Lansdale

This book has been published with the assistance of the Canada Council and the
Ontario Arts Council under their block grant programs.

Contents

֎֎֎֎֎֎֎֎֎֎֎֎֎֎֎֎֎֎֎֎֎֎֎֎֎֎֎֎֎֎

Illustrations

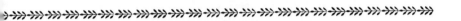

Preface

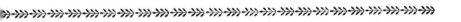

According to Goethe, 'you cannot understand history unless you've lived through history yourself.' True. But it is equally true that, having been intimately involved in some of the cataclysmic events that have transformed the world since my childhood in pre-revolutionary Russia, I would find it difficult if not impossible to pose as a detached, dispassionate observer of the international scene.

This book therefore does not attempt to be a history in the scholarly, totally objective sense of the term. Instead it is a personal account of those events in which I have participated or which I have witnessed, with only enough background information to place these events in their proper context. While I have tried, to the best of my ability and with the help of many friends, to ensure historical accuracy, I have felt free to interpret events and describe my reactions to personalities the way I saw them.

These recollections and impressions have been organized and recorded by Sonja Sinclair, after countless interviews and discussions, and I am deeply indebted to her for the perception and patience with which she tackled the project. Any faults of memory or interpretation are mine; the literary qualities are entirely hers.

This book would never have been written without the encouragement and support of the Gordon Foundation. I wish I knew how to express adequately my gratitude to Walter, Duncan, and Elizabeth for their boundless kindness towards me and my literary efforts.

A number of friends have read or advised me on the manuscript. My particular thanks are due to John Holmes, who was my colleague during much of my foreign service career and whose history of Canadian diplomacy is, I believe, the definitive work on the subject. All John's comments and suggestions proved tremendously helpful. I am also indebted to Jane Barrett, head librarian at the Canadian Institute of International Affairs, who used her vast knowledge and her access to the pertinent documents to check the text for historical accuracy. Basil Robinson, surely the ultimate expert on the relationship between Prime Minister Diefenbaker and the Department of External Affairs, brought that expertise to bear on the chapter which deals with the Diefenbaker years. Professor Helen Hardy read an early draft and helped to point me in the right direction.

My wife, Alison, and my sons, Michael and Andrew, encouraged me throughout this project and offered comments which were invariably constructive and helpful. To them, my grandson, Theo, and those who may come after him, this book is dedicated.

Toronto, June 1984

My grandfather, General Nikolai
Pavlovich Ignatieff: 'A remarkably
brave, astute, and fiercely patriotic
individualist whose public service
career was as colourful and controversial as any to be found in Russia's
diplomatic history'

LEFT: Nanya Manya, my devoted nanny,
who made her way to England to be
close to her 'foster-son'

My mother, Princess Natalie Nicholayevna Mestchersky, at the time of her marriage in 1903

My father, Count Paul Nicholayevich Ignatieff, minister of education under Tsar Nicholas II

Refugees in England: my mother with her five sons: (*left to right*) Leonid, Nick, Alex, George, Jim

Governess Peggy Meadowcroft with her young 'English gentlemen': (*left to right*) Jim, George, Nick, Leonid, Alex

'The Douk' (*left*) with CPR survey party team-mates in British Columbia

University of Toronto graduate and Rhodes scholar, 1936

Alison and I, following our wedding in the Russian Orthodox Cathedral in Montreal

During a 1949 meeting of the UN General Assembly, in conversation with
General McNaughton (*right*) and Dr Luis Padila Nervo of Mexico (UN Photo)

Assisting Mike Pearson in laying a wreath on a war memorial in Stalingrad
(now Volgograd). On the right are Ambassador John Watkins and then-CBC
correspondent René Lévesque.

Smiling approvingly as Mike and Maryon Pearson admire a gourd for wine presented to them during a visit to an agricultural exhibit in Moscow

Presenting my credentials as ambassador to Marshal Tito, president of Yugoslavia

At a 1965 North Atlantic Council meeting, checking a point with Paul Martin (*centre*), external affairs minister, and Paul Hellyer (*left*), minister of national defence (NATO Photo)

As ambassador to NATO, with Alison in our Paris residence, 1966 (NATO Photo)

As acting president of the UN General Assembly, with the UN secretary general, U Thant (*left*) (UN Photo)

Provost of Trinity College: trading the protective but confining cocoon of
bureaucracy for the free world of academe

THE MAKING OF A PEACEMONGER

ONE

In the service
of the tsars

Long before multiculturalism became part of Canada's political and social vocabulary, the humorist Stephen Leacock developed his own formula for helping immigrants adapt to their new homeland. Leave them alone, he suggested in a story about Ukrainians, and pretty soon they'll think they won the Battle of Trafalgar.

Judging by my own experience, Leacock was only partly right. True, I consider myself just as Canadian as those of my fellow citizens who were born in this country or who belong to the so-called founding races. Though I was born in Russia, went to school in England, and didn't set foot in Canada until I was fourteen, with two or three exceptions, none of the people with whom I came into contact during my thirty-three years of public service seemed particularly conscious of my foreign origin or treated me differently because of it.

Yet, without ever questioning my Canadian identity, I have also been acutely aware of the influence which my family background and my childhood experiences have had on my personality, my outlook on life, and my interpretation of history. Even had I wanted to forget my ancestry and the fact that I was descended from three successive generations of prominent Russian public servants, I would have found such oblivion impossible. Time and again during my diplomatic career, my name triggered memories among the people with whom I came into contact. Depending on their nationality and their political persuasion, being an Ignatieff turned out to be either an asset or a liability.

Though both my parents could trace their ancestry back to the Middle Ages, the first Ignatieff to emerge from relative obscurity was my great grandfather, Paul Nikolayevich Ignatieff. During the Decembrist uprising in 1825, when ideas spawned by the French revolution were sweeping across Europe and some Russian officers were siding with the rebels, he made sure that the company of guards which he commanded stood firm in defence of the tsar in front of the Winter Palace in St Petersburg. This service launched him on a series of promotions which culminated in his appointment as president of the Council of Ministers and his elevation, along with all his descendants, to the rank of Count of the Russian Empire.

His son and my grandfather, Nicholas Pavlovich, was a soldier and a diplomat whose exploits became legendary both within and outside Russia. His talents were put to their first major test in 1859, when, as a 27-year-old colonel, he led a mission to the Far East to deliver military supplies to the Chinese government and supervise the training of their armed forces. This was in keeping with a treaty whereby the Chinese had agreed, in a moment of weakness, to extensive territorial concessions on their border with Siberia. After a hazardous three-month journey grandfather rode into the capital of the Celestial Empire, attired in a dress uniform specially made for the occasion, only to discover that the Chinese had changed their minds. Not only did they have no intention of ratifying the border settlement or of accepting Russian arms and instructors. At a time of rapidly deteriorating relations with the British and French, they viewed the arrival of yet another European emissary with considerable suspicion, to the extent that they urged grandfather to turn around and go home. For almost a year he tried in vain to persuade them to reconsider. But the situation changed drastically when British troops under the command of Lord Elgin and their French allies decided to compel the Chinese by force of arms to grant them the trading privileges to which their governments considered themselves entitled. It turned out to be a one-sided conflict. Setting out from Shanghai the European armies, backed by a fleet of some two hundred vessels, occupied Tsien-Tsin, stormed and looted the Imperial Palace, and were about to attack Peking when the city capitulated.

At this point grandfather decided the time had come for him to intervene. He offered the belligerents his services as mediator and managed to negotiate a peace treaty that was acceptable to the French and the British, while leaving the Chinese deeply indebted to their Russian benefactor. So much so that an emissary from the emperor came to thank grandfather for his services and apologized for the long delay in settling the border dispute. Negotiations now proceeded rapidly though with the utmost secrecy, so as not to arouse any suspicions on the part of the British and French, who would presumably oppose any border settlement that threatened their naval hegemony in the Pacific. Within three weeks all details had been settled and the Treaty of Peking was signed on 2 November 1860.

In years to come the Chinese were to resent bitterly this 'unequal treaty' which presented Russia with the rich Ussuri region, gave it access to the Sea of Japan, and enabled it to establish a naval base at Vladivostok. More than a hundred years later, when rumours were circulating in Ottawa that I might be appointed Canada's first ambassador to the People's Republic of China, the ambassador of Taiwan made a point of informing me, in the presence of a Canadian cabinet minister and several high ranking officials, that no emissary by the name of Ignatieff would ever be acceptable to a Chinese government, regardless of its political complexion.

But in the heyday of European imperialism, grandfather was clearly convinced that it was his duty to assert Russian interests, whenever and wherever the opportunity presented itself. Indeed he had good reason to believe that, once the western powers found out what had happened, they would try to dissuade the tsar from ratifying a treaty which was contrary to their interests. Fortunately it would be months before the British and French fleets reached home, and without telecommunications they had no way of informing their governments about the treaty. If grandfather could get back to St Petersburg fast enough, the tsar might agree to ratify the Treaty of Peking before the western powers knew it existed.

He left Peking on 8 November and rode on horseback all the way across Mongolia and Siberia back to St Petersburg, which he reached on 1 January 1861. When he finally reached home, he got into a hot bath fully dressed in his travelling clothes, because he figured that was the only way to get rid of all the vermin he had collected during his two-month ride. The following day he was received by the tsar, who personally awarded him one of the country's highest decorations, the Order of St Vladimir. The Tsar commented that the motto of the order seemed particularly fitting: 'Service, Honour and Glory.' The French and the British navies were still at sea.*

Alexander II was so impressed with grandfather's accomplishments that he appointed him head of the Asian Department at the Foreign Office and four years later sent him to Constantinople as ambassador to the Ottoman Empire. He was accompanied on this mission by his bride, the former Princess Golitzina, whose great-grandfather, Marshal Kutuzov, commanded the Russian forces during the Napoleonic wars.

Being a stauch imperialist as well as a slavophile, grandfather took advantage of his position in Constantinople to champion the freedom aspirations of the Bulgarians and the Serbs, who were looking hopefully to the tsar as a liberator from Turkish domination. The way grandfather saw it, if he could hasten the demise of the Ottoman Empire and replace it with friendly governments in the Slavonic portions of the Balkans, Russia would gain access to the Mediterranean, with everything that implied in terms of trade advantages and naval power.

*The account of grandfather's mission to China is based essentially on a speech delivered by one of his colleagues, K.A. Gubatsov, at a meeting of the Slavonic Benevolent Society dedicated to the memory of the society's recently deceased president, Nicholas Pavlovich Ignatieff. According to the text of the speech, to be found in the Lenin Library in Moscow, the author based his remarks on material assembled by my grandfather and published in a limited edition of a hundred copies. The same material was also used in 1902 by Lieutenant Buksgevden as a source for part of his book entitled *The Treaty of Peking*.

Predictably enough, grandfather's plans ran head on into those of another imperialist, Benjamin Disraeli, who was busy propping up Turkey in an effort to safeguard Britain's sea routes to the Far East and reinforce Queen Victoria's claim to the Indian throne. So it is hardly surprising that British historians by and large take a dim view of my grandfather's role and personality. 'Clever, unscrupulous, amusing, ingratiating and dangerous' is how Robert Blake describes him in his biography of Disraeli.

My own mental picture of grandfather was and remains much more attractive. Though he died before I was born, everything I know about him leads me to believe that he was a remarkably brave, astute, and fiercely patriotic individualist whose public service career was as colourful and controversial as any to be found in Russia's diplomatic history. His attempts to change the map of Europe and to cast the tsar in the role of liberator of the Balkan peoples almost succeeded. During the Russo-Turkish war, the tsar's forces had fought their way to the gates of Constantinople when Britain, alarmed by the prospect of a Russian victory and its likely impact on British sea lanes to India, mobilized the fleet and threatened to intervene on the side of the Turks.

The result was a hastily drawn up peace treaty which my grandfather carried from St Petersburg to San Stefano, where it was to be signed. He was in such a hurry to get to his destination and forestall any further untoward developments that his coach plunged over a precipice while negotiating a snow-covered turn in the road through the Shipka Pass in the Balkans. Grandfather managed to save himself by hanging on to a tree and completed the journey on horseback. He had lost his plenipotentiary papers in the accident, but apparently he was such an awe-inspiring character that no one dared to ask for them and the Turks signed the treaty. Under its terms Turkey recognized the independence of Romania, Serbia, and Montenegro, while Bulgaria was to become an autonomous principality with an outlet to the Mediterranean via Salonika. But the tsar later let himself be persuaded by his advisers to yield to pressures from Britain and Germany and agree to extensive revisions of the treaty. As a result, Germany's already considerable power was greatly enhanced. As for Britain, she got from Turkey a typically imperialist reward for her assistance: the island of Cyprus.*

Some ninety years later, when I was representing Canada at NATO and the United Nations and when we dealt with recurring crises in the Middle East, in Cyprus and in Czechoslovakia, I couldn't help wondering what would have happened had my grandfather's ideas prevailed rather than those of Disraeli, Bismarck, and their friends in St Petersburg. No doubt history would have taken a different turn; and it seemed to me at least conceivable that, without the strengthening of an increasingly militaristic Germany at the expense of Russia, without the artificial life support systems administered to a disintegrating Ottoman Empire and the denial of freedom to the Balkan peoples, the world might have been spared the horrors of two world wars.

As it was, grandfather was discredited, and though he later served for a year as minister of the interior under Alexander III, he once again ran afoul of the tsar's advisers, this time for urging the sovereign to summon a consultative assembly in order to bring him closer to the people. This advice was denounced as 'criminal folly' by the tsar's entourage and spelled the end of grandfather's public service career before he reached his fiftieth birthday. Strangely enough, premature retirement was to become a recurring theme in the history of the Ignatieffs. Though the circumstances were vastly different in each case, both my father and I eventually chose to leave public service rather than remain under conditions which we considered unacceptable.

My father, Count Paul Nikolayevich, spent the early years of his adult life managing the family estates in the Province of Kiev (now the Ukraine), where he became increasingly involved in local government. In pre-revolutionary Russia, whose population was pre-

---

*Grandfather's original dispatches and other papers are in the Lenin library in Moscow. Photocopies of some of these papers, presented to me by my hosts during my 1983 visit to the Soviet Union, will serve as source material for the forthcoming history of the Ignatieff family, being written by my son Michael.

dominantly rural, regional councils called *zemstvos* handled land claims, road and school construction, soil improvement, and most of the other matters which directly affected the lives of the people. Father's commitment to the *zemstvo* movement and his work first at the grassroot and later at executive levels led to a rapport with the peasant population which was unusual, to say the least, among members of the aristocracy.

It was during this period that he married my mother, the youngest of eight children of Prince and Princess Mestchersky. Though the family traced its name and title as far back in Russian history as did the Ignatieffs, they were involved in the intellectual and social life of the country rather than public service. Mother was born and raised on the beautiful country estate of Dugino near Smolensk, in a home which, with its hundred rooms, was more a palace than a house. She used to recall with nostalgia the natural beauty which surrounded her during her happy childhood. Like many similar manifestations of the old regime, Dugino was burned to the ground during the revolution.

My parents met at the home of a mutual friend in St Petersburg late in 1902 and renewed their acquaintance a few weeks later in southern France, where the Mestcherskys had a winter home. They were married in April 1903 in Nice, and in spite of their brief engagement, my mother's trousseau left nothing to be desired. As she described it, 'thick woollens and suits, including for some reason a riding habit I never wore, were bought at the best shops in Nice and Paris.' As for household effects, 'the linen came from Rouffes in Nice, and bed linen with lace embroidery was ordered from Brussels; table linen was always ordered from a certain shop in Dresden, where our family crest was reproduced on the tablecloths and napkins. I was given more than enough to last the fifteen years before we were to lose all our belongings to the Bolsheviks.'*

After a honeymoon at Cap d'Antibes the newlyweds headed for the Ukraine and a memorable welcome for the young bride. 'All the

*My mother's unpublished recollections are being used by Michael Ignatieff for his forthcoming history of the family; so are my father's memoirs, quoted later in this chapter.

Ignatieff family were at the railway station to greet us,' she recalled later. 'After we had all hugged and kissed one another on the platform, we stopped at practically every home in the village to receive bread and salt, the customary greeting for new arrivals in the Ukraine.' That same evening they were serenaded with folk songs sung by the village choir outside the window of their home.

By 1906 father's reputation had reached the central government, and when unrest swept the country in the wake of Russia's defeat in the Russo-Japanese war, he was appointed governor of the Province of Kiev. He knew only too well the problems he was going to face. Having chosen to live in the Jewish district of the city, my parents had seen with their own eyes the horrors of the anti-Jewish pogroms perpetrated by the 'Black Hundreds' (a reactionary anti-semitic group that supposedly acted on behalf of the tsar) and condoned by authorities who were only too glad to divert attention from their own shortcomings and the poverty of the people. In the words of father's diary, 'When I took office anti-Semitic propaganda in Kiev was at its height and some of the monks had joined the movement; one old priest in particular stirred up the populace by preaching against those who had, as he put it, crucified Christ.'

Father decided that the first thing for him to do as governor was to put an end to this search for scapegoats and incitement to violence. He summoned the old monk, accused him of preaching a doctrine which was contrary to the basic tenets of Christianity, and insisted that he make a public confession of his error. The following Sunday the monk begged a packed congregation to forget all that he had preached 'under the guidance of evil forces.'

Father then informed the leaders of the Black Hundreds that they would be held personally responsible and punished for any further anti-Semitic disturbances. He also asked the commander of the Cossack division, who rode every morning through the city on his white charger, to make frequent appearances in the Jewish districts of Kiev, and to inform his officers that the governor had requested the assistance of the entire division in the maintenance of order. In the event of renewed disturbances, any failure on the part of an officer to take appropriate action would result in instant dismissal. Word soon got around that the governor meant business, and there was no further trouble.

In 1912 father was appointed assistant minister of agriculture, and three years later he crossed the dividing line betwee administration and politics when he accepted the education portfolio and joined the tsar's Council of Ministers. His was one of several wartime appointments made in a belated attempt to appease public opinion. As news of the defeats of the Russian army filtered through the curtain of censorship, there was growing evidence of popular unrest and demands for a less autocratic form of government. The tsar apparently let himself be persuaded that he could defuse the situation by replacing some of the incompetents and reactionaries in his entourage with more liberal-minded men.

Father accepted the appointment with great reluctance. Indeed, according to his testimony before the provisional government's Commission of Inquiry,* he pleaded with his sponsor, Alexander Krivoshein, who was the minister of agriculture, to let him go back to Kiev, where he could apply his expertise to local government issues, among people who knew and respected him. He clearly suspected that there was little he and a handful of colleagues would be able to do to influence the character of an administration which seemed totally impervious to change.

But in the final analysis his misgivings were outweighed by his lifelong commitment to the monarchy and his personal allegiance to the tsar. He had first met Nicholas II many years earlier, when the monarch was still heir to the throne and he and my father were both undergoing military training with the Preobrazhensky Guards – the future tsar as battalion commander, father as officer cadet. Grand Duke Nicholas, the heir's uncle and commander of the regiment, was on an inspection tour with his nephew when they smelled the aroma of coffee coming from father's tent. They stopped to have some, and the grand duke asked father, as a teaser, to

---

*This commission was set up in 1917 by the provisional government to enquire into the events that led up to the abdication of the tsar; my father was one of many witnesses it summoned.

explain to them why autocracy was so unpopular in Russia. Coming to attention as behooved a cadet, father replied that Russians did not resent the personal authority of their sovereign: 'What we in Russia do resent,' he continued, 'is the autocracy of the policeman, the governor, the bureaucrat, and, indeed, the minister.'

This outspoken reply apparently made an impression on the future tsar because he referred to it some thirty years later when he summoned father to his first audience following his appointment to the government. Had he changed his mind about the autocracy of ministers now that he was one himself, Nicholas asked. Father replied that he had not. However, father requested and received an assurance from the sovereign that he would have a free hand in reforming Russia's educational system. There certainly was plenty of scope for improvement. The country suffered from widespread illiteracy, and although universal elementary education had been introduced in 1908, its administration remained centralized under the Department of Education in St Petersburg. The first thing father did was transfer responsibility for elementary education to local governments, which were equipped to deal with the tremendous variety of ethnic and economic needs to be found in the country. He felt very strongly that, in a multicultural empire such as Russia, children should not be forced into a single mould, particularly if they came from parts of the country such as the Ukraine or Georgia which had their own history and literature.

Years later, when my parents settled in Canada, multiculturalism was one of the features that appealed to father about his new homeland and one of the reasons why he chose to live in Quebec. In the nineteen-twenties and thirties, when the so-called élite in Quebec was English-speaking and would not dream of associating with French Canadians, father went out of his way to assure his neighbours that he considered himself part of the community. I remember being impressed, when my parents died, by the number of their French-speaking friends who came to express their sympathy.

As minister of education, father also broadened the curriculum of secondary schools to include vocational training for those students whose talents were manual and technical rather than academic. At the university level, he set out to free academic appointments from political interference and racial discrimination. Up until then, Jews had been barred by law from becoming university professors; father not only did away with all such restrictions but also made sure that a number of Jews were actually appointed to university faculties.

Father's determined fight against anti-Semitism, both as governor of Kiev and as minister of education, is difficult to reconcile with the allegation, made by both Soviet and Jewish historians, that his father was responsible for confining Jews to ghettos and depriving them of their civil rights. I suppose it is possible that, during his brief term as minister of the interior in 1881, my grandfather may have been persuaded by the tsar's advisers to sign such an edict. But I find it hard to believe that he could have been the instigator of an anti-Semitic policy, particularly since it is a matter of record that he was dismissed because of his supposedly democratic tendencies.

Yet misconceptions die hard, and as I was to discover years later at the United Nations, father's anti-discrimination policies failed to dispel completely the stigma which some Jews associated with the Ignatieff name. Among the many Israeli statesmen and officials who were Russian-born, those who had been students at the time father was minister of education saw in me a natural ally; but members of the previous generation did not hide their distrust of a man whose grandfather they believed had been responsible for their persecution. There have been times in my life when being an Ignatieff was a decidedly mixed blessing.

Though father's educational reforms and anti-discrimination measures were nothing short of revolutionary, his downfall after two years in office was due to a fundamental disagreement over political and military rather than educational matters. Along with two or three of his fellow ministers, he repeatedly tried and failed to persuade the tsar that the answer to the growing popular discontent lay not in shoring up the autocracy but rather in closer co-operation with the legislative assembly (Duma) and with local government agencies.

Father was equally unsuccessful in explaining his reasoning to Empress Alexandra, with whom, according to custom, he requested an audience at the time of his appointment to the government. The fact that she did not receive him until eight months later was in itself an indication that he was not one of her favourite ministers, and judging by father's memoirs the feeling was mutual. Like many Russians, he resented the way the tsar had fallen completely under the influence of his wife and her friend, the notorious Rasputin. She in turn clearly opposed father's attempts to steer the government away from arbitrary decisions and into closer co-operation with the Duma.

Predictably enough, the meeting was not a success. The empress accused father of wanting to replace the elderly prime minister, who was her protégé, with one of several men who, according to her, were disloyal to the tsar. The way she saw it, the solution to Russia's problems lay in even stricter censorship of the press and more rigid exercise of central power. Father protested that, even if dictatorship were desirable, it could not be effective without the backing of unconditionally loyal troops. 'But such an army no longer exists,' he pointed out in words that, in retrospect, seem almost prophetic. 'The army now is an armed populace, the old regiments have fallen in the fields of East Prussia, Galicia, and Poland. No dictator could rely on this army in a struggle against the popular trends that are sweeping the nation.'

The interview ended on an icy note, with a barely concealed threat by the empress. Officers who fail to follow their commander must expect to be dismissed, she told father.

More military defeats at the front, food shortages at home, and successive cabinet crises all contributed to growing unrest throughout the country. Late in 1916 the tsar decided to apppoint a highly unpopular minister of the interior, known to be one of the empress' nominees and a devotee of Rasputin's, and put him in charge of the distribution of food. As far as father was concerned, this was the last straw. During a meeting at the military headquarters where the emperor had personally assumed command of the troops, father pleaded with him to let him resign rather than force him to be party to a 'crime.' Early next morning, a special train arrived with the empress and her children, and at a chance meeting later in the day, all the tsar said to father was,'I think we have talked about everything there was to discuss.' The appointment of the minister of the interior was confirmed, and so was his responsibility for the distribution of food.

Exactly a month later, during a special audience on 3 January 1917, father handed his letter of resignation to the tsar. While assuring the sovereign of his unconditional allegiance to 'the fundamental principles of unity of Tsar and the people,' the letter asked Nicholas II 'to relieve me of the unbearable burden of having to serve against the dictates of my conscience.' The tsar seemed moved by the letter and told father to go on with his work; but six days later a newspaper reporter telephoned to inform him that he had been dismissed.

They met for the last time on 22 January, when the tsar bestowed on father the rank of privy councillor at an audience at Tsarskoye Selo, the imperial residence. It was an emotional meeting during which father expressed once again his concern that the crisis was getting out of hand. The tsar's last words to him were, 'Thank you for telling me the truth – as you saw it.' They embraced and father said, 'God have mercy on your soul.' Less than two months later, on 15 March 1917, the tsar was forced to sign the instrument of abdication. As father had predicted, the 'armed populace' was about to take over the destiny of Russia.

TWO

Luck on our side

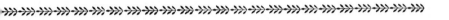

I was born in St Petersburg on 16 December 1913, just in time to witness the Russian revolution and civil war, become a refugee, experience the loss of the wealth and privileges enjoyed by previous generations of Ignatieffs, and begin to sink roots in a new environment. It could be argued that the upheaval in my early life was reflected in the names by which I was called during various stages of my childhood and adolescence. Count Georgi Pavlovich became plain George on the ship that carried me and my family from our homeland, Bolshie and Ignateeth at school in England, Bohunk and The Douk while working on the railway in British Columbia, and Ig at university in Toronto and Oxford.

My first childhood recollection is being told by my nanny – Nanya Manya, as I called her – to lie down on the nursery floor so I'd be out of the line of fire of the demonstrators who were streaming past our house on their way to the Duma. I was barely three years old in February 1917 when the unrest that had been brewing in Russia for years erupted in rioting and armed insurrection. Living as we did just around the corner from the Duma, we had ringside seats for a spectacle which became more threatening with each passing day. According to my mother's recollections, 'lorries of wild, half-drunk soldiers and sailors with red flags went by firing rifles indiscriminately; it became impossible to move in the house, for fear of being hit by a bullet or a bomb while passing a window.'

Though I must have sensed that lying flat on the floor and listening to the sound of shooting implied danger, I don't remember being particularly frightened. Security at that stage in my life was personified by my parents, my four older brothers, and, above all else, a nanny for whom I was the centre of the universe. As the wife of a cabinet minister, my mother had to lead a life in keeping with her husband's status and responsibilities. There were school and university receptions she had to attend, hospitals she was expected to visit, a large house and a flock of servants to be supervised – not to mention an almost continuous string of pregnancies to keep her occupied. In the first thirteen years of her marriage she had given birth to seven sons and seen two of them die: Paul fell victim to a typhoid epidemic and baby Alexander survived only a few days following his premature birth in 1916.

It was a matter of both custom and necessity that mother turn over the care of her children to members of the household staff. Manya came to us at the age of eighteen, and since I was her sole responsibility, I soon became the focus of all the love and attention she might have lavished on a child of her own.

My parents were not molested in those early days of the revolution, but life in St Petersburg did become increasingly difficult. Food was scarce, and though my aunt sent us generous supplies of milk from her country estate, father's valet took considerable risks by going every day to the railway station to pick it up. We also had our two cars confiscated, though the indomitable valet managed to find one of them in a St Petersburg garage, repaired it, and arranged to have it sold back to my parents.

What was more serious was my father's failing health. For many months he had lived under the strain of a heavy workload combined with the growing sense of impending catastrophe. At that time, many of my parents' friends still believed that the disturbances would eventually die down and that Russia would settle down to an orderly form of government. Father had no such illusions; in fact, mother recalled later that she had never seen him in such a state of utter despair. Yet he went on testifying before the provisional government's Commission of Inquiry, received deputations from the factories that still belonged to him, and agreed to serve as president of the Russian Red Cross. On top of all that, there were (according to mother) endless revolutionary deputations which insisted on seeing father at any time of day or night.

Presumably because of this physical and mental strain, he developed such debilitating pains that he became a virtual invalid. We children saw next to nothing of him during this period; we were told that he was not to be disturbed under any circumstances. At first mother could not even persuade a doctor to come and see her sick husband; they were all afraid of having their cars confiscated by the mob if they ventured out on the street. Eventually she did succeed in contacting a doctor who was the personal physician of Kerensky, the head of the provisional government, and who therefore enjoyed greater freedom of movement than most of his colleagues. He examined father and recommended that he recuperate in Kislovodsk, a spa in the Caucasian Mountains famous for its medicinal waters.

And so we left St Petersburg on 16 July 1917, supposedly for a short holiday. Several of father's former colleagues from the Ministry of Education were at the station to see us off. One of them, a specialist in Russian folklore, presented father with a walking-stick made of birch, Russia's national tree. Attached to it was a letter which said that the stick was a symbol of the reforms father had launched in his country's educational system; they had taken root and would continue to grow.

All I remember about the long journey to Kislovodsk is father singing nostalgic folk songs and Nanya Manya covering the seats in our compartment with sheets to protect me from the all-pervasive dirt which was already becoming the hallmark of a rapidly disintegrating society. Nevertheless, there was nothing to suggest that we were about to become refugees or that Russia was in the throes of a revolution. Though the tsar had abdicated the country did have a government, the war was going on, the trains were still running. We were accompanied on our journey by two nannies for the two youngest children, a maid for the three older ones, an English governess, a French and a Russian tutor, a chef, an assistant cook, and Katya, my mother's faithful lady's maid. Included in our luggage were a silver basin and pitcher, so Katya could bring mother hot water every morning and help her wash and do her hair. Years later mother admitted that the summer of 1917 was an odd time to be travelling across Russia with such a 'circus.' But her brother, who had preceded us to Kislovodsk, had warned her to bring all the loyal servants she could because she'd have a hard time finding any locally. Besides, she said, she was too distraught to give the matter much thought.

At Kislovodsk, life seemed remarkably peaceful at first. We stayed in a pleasant rented house with a garden and there was plenty of food, even such delicacies as meat and fresh fruit. Though the Bolsheviks seized power in October 1917, the full impact of this second revolution did not reach Kislovodsk until the following spring. That is when the searches began. The way my mother described it, 'Bands of ruffians either under-dressed in dirty rags, or over-dressed in stolen clothing' came time and again to our house, equipped with search warrants, and claimed they were looking for arms or counter-revolutionary literature: in fact, they took whatever valuables they could find.

During one of these searches, which lasted five hours, two armed men stood guard over father and the English governess while a third tried to frighten mother into divulging the hiding place of any valuables; if she failed to confess and they ended up finding something, he said, the consequences would be terrible. But she just stared at the huge diamond ring on his finger and asked him if he had no shame or respect for her age. They turned the house inside out, particularly my parents' bedroom; but they never did find the vase that contained our money and mother's jewelry, hidden under a floor board in the bathroom. For me, the most precious possession in that vase was the golden chain and Orthodox cross given to me at my baptism by my grandmother, who was also my godmother. Inscribed on the cross are Constantine's words which can be roughly translated as 'With this cross you shall overcome.' I wear it constantly to this day.

The searchers departed empty-handed except for a seal with the Ignatieff coat of arms and five volumes of a special edition of a biography of Alexander I. It was typical of my mother's indomitable spirit that she marched to the bolshevik headquarters the next day and the day after and demanded the return of her property. Incredibly enough, she did get back the books, though not the seal.

During this period our staff gradually dwindled. The first to go were Katya and the chef, Kulakov, who, as my mother so delicately put it, 'had behaved badly and had to get married in a hurry.' Mother was deeply attached to Katya – so much so that Katya was the first person to whom she ran for advice some time later when father was arrested; nevertheless, it was apparently unthinkable that the two culprits should remain under my parents' roof. One by one the rest of the staff disappeared, mainly because we could no longer afford them, until the only ones left were the English governess, Peggy Meadowcroft, the Russian tutor, Georgi Alexandrovich, and my beloved nanny. It was at this point that I suffered the first traumatic shock of my life. Unbeknown to me, Peggy had persuaded mother that having one child so totally dependent on someone who was not part of the family was unhealthy and might become dangerous if we were forced to flee. Besides, there were too many mouths to feed. Manya would have to go.

To spare my feelings, mother and Manya agreed that she would make her exit at night, while I was asleep. When I woke up the following morning, my brothers' tutor informed me that I was now a big boy and that I'd be eating with the rest of the family. Nobody told me where Manya had gone or why she had deserted me, and my immediate reaction was panic. I tried to hang on to my bed for security, and as Georgi Alexandrovich yanked me away my head hit the floor and I was knocked unconscious. I woke up in Miss Meadowcroft's room, with a big bump on my head and the realization that something fundamental had gone out of my life. It was the end of my pampered childhood, and the end of whatever subconscious notion I may have had that I was entitled to a privileged existence. In a sense, I had been dragged kicking and screaming into the twentieth century.

Manya was just as devastated about leaving me as I was about losing her. Later she somehow managed to make her way to England so she could be near me, and became a trained nurse. I didn't know she was there; mother and Peggy decided to keep her away from me. It wasn't until I returned to England as a Rhodes scholar that we finally got together, and she proudly introduced me to her bewildered friends as her foster-son. In the 1960s, when I went to Paris as Canadian ambassador to NATO, she came to stay with

Alison and me and joined us for the 14 July march-past in celebration of Bastille Day. We were sitting right behind Madame de Gaulle, and I remember how horrified I was when Manya started making uncomplimentary remarks about the general, who, she said, was being mean to the British by keeping them out of the Common Market. However, her opinion of de Gaulle took a right about turn when she found that he had provided me with a guard of honour during a visit to the Ecole Militaire. At last, she said, her foster-son was getting the kind of respect that was his due.

The next traumatic event during our stay in Kislovodsk was the arrest of my father. It happened in the middle of the night in August 1918 when, according to mother, 'there came a thunderous banging at all the doors of the house.' Seventeen armed men burst into the house, told father that he was being charged with sabotage, and led him away. One of the men wore the uniform of a Moscow University student, and when father said to him, 'What a strange meeting, colleague,' the young man looked down and didn't reply. Father was still a virtual invalid, and mother ran after him to put a coat over his shoulders and press some medicine into his hands. 'Where will I see him again?' she cried as she heard the waiting truck start its engine. 'At the railway station tomorrow,' came the reply.

Mother went to the station the following morning, found father inside a cattle car, and though some soldiers tried to stop her, she managed to break loose and give him some food she had brought. She tried to see him again the day after, but this time the soldiers intervened and she got so upset that she threw the yogurt she had brought at them. When she found out that father was being taken to Piatigorsk, a neighbouring town where a revolutionary tribunal was busy meting out death sentences, she spent half the night and most of the following day at the bolshevik headquarters, pleading with the authorities to release her husband or at least let her accompany him. They refused.

In the end, it wasn't mother's pleas but rather father's reputation as a public-spirited individual that saved him. According to his own account, one of the men who had come to arrest him asked him that same night whether he was the former minister of education. When father replied that he was, the soldier said, 'None of the students want this to happen to you.' In Piatigorsk he was marched to the local jail and locked in a cell which he shared with two former governors. There was no furniture, and they had just started investigating the insect life on the dirty floor when father was summoned to the presence of an elegant-looking man by the name of Alexandrov. Speaking flawless French – apparently the chairman of the tribunal was a Swiss communist – he told father that members of the Red Army who had been students at the time he was a minister had heard about his arrest and had tlreatened trouble unless he was released. He was therefore free to go home. Father replied that he had been arrested without reason, and that he was now being turned out into the street, no doubt to be killed by the mob; he demanded that his family be informed he was safe, and that he be provided with an escort. Alexandrov complied, and father was in fact brought home on the last train before communications between Piatigorsk and Kislovodsk were severed by the advancing White Army.

The day after father's release there was a mass execution of prisoners in Piatigorsk. Among those who died was the former minister of justice and a general of Bulgarian origin who happened to be vacationing in the region when he was arrested. The names of the victims were published in the newspapers, and father's name was among them. His escape was doubly miraculous considering that the White Army, after it had occupied Kislovodsk, found among captured bolshevik documents a list of those who were to be executed in case the town had to be evacuated. Apparently the entire Ignatieff family was on that list, including the children; it was the unexpectedly rapid advance of the White Army that saved our lives.

I was by now five years old, and though I didn't understand what the civil war was all about, I could see with my own eyes the horrors that were being perpetrated in the name of supposedly just causes. I must admit that, in terms of man's inhumanity to man, there was little to choose between the two sides. When the Whites came, we saw from our windows people being hanged from lampposts for having allegedly sided with the Bolsheviks, and I remember a man screaming pitifully while he was dragged to death behind a horse. Mother actually pleaded for the life of one of my brothers' teachers who was to be executed by the Whites, until she was told to stop meddling or she too would be beaten up. As for father, he had been convinced all along that no matter what happened in the civil war, people who thought they could turn back the clock and undo the revolution were daydreaming. When he was approached by a spokesman of General Denikin, one of the White Army commanders, to see if he would be prepared to serve as minister of agriculture in a government committed to the restitution of land to its former owners, father refused on the grounds that such plans were totally unrealistic.

Next thing we knew, the Reds were back, and we were once again being subjected to constant searches and threats. I have no doubt that, had we stayed much longer, none of us would have survived. Civil war is always gruesomely cruel, but in the Caucasian Mountains it was possibly worse than anywhere else. On the White side there was a Cossack general whose atrocities were legendary, while the Red Army in that part of Russia included wild tribesmen for whom killing seemed to be a normal pastime. By the end of 1918 my parents were the only members of the aristocracy still living in Kislovodsk, and when the Whites once again occupied the town in January 1919, father let himself be persuaded by mother and Peggy that, no matter how reluctant he was to leave Russia, he could not keep on risking the lives of his wife and children. Somehow, the family would have to try to escape.

Just how was another question. There were after all seven of us, eight counting Peggy Meadowcroft, who was the only member of the original ménage still left. Transportation in Russia was either non-existent or chaotic, and those trains that were running were crawling with vermin and subject to attacks by whichever army happened to be near by. But luck was on our side. General Wrangel, the White Army commander in the south, came to Kislovodsk to recuperate from a bout of typhus which was raging in epidemic proportions at the front. When his wife heard that my parents were in town, she offered them the use of the general's armoured train, which had to go back to Novorossiysk on the Black Sea. There was a flotilla of British warships in Novorossiysk at the time, and the idea was that one of them would take us aboard and help us get out of Russia.

So we packed all our possessions into the trunk that had at one time contained mother's trousseau, and all of us piled into a horse-drawn droshky intended to hold a maximum of four people. I still remember that ride to the railway station: I was perched on my mother's lap and hanging on for dear life to the mudguard because I was convinced I was going to fall out. The journey to Novoros-siysk, which would normally take a few hours, lasted two days. The train kept stopping for unknown reasons, and as we stood on a siding I could see only a few feet away a freight car full of dead or dying men – whether Red or White we couldn't tell. That sight, particularly one man whose emaciated arm seemed to be stretched out towards me as though pleading for help, is indelibly etched in my memory. Even though this was February 1919 and World War I had been over for four months, Russians were still killing and maiming one another, or dying from starvation and disease. If I have seemed at times obsessed with disarmament and accused of being a 'peacemonger,' it's partly because I learned at an early age what war can do to people and to their country.

Novorossiysk was a kind of no-man's land at that time. The White Army had pretty well been defeated in the south, but British war-ships in the harbour were shelling the bolshevik positions and pre-venting the Reds from entering the city. We found shelter with a Russian family who put us up in two of their rooms; father and mother slept in one, the five boys and Peggy Meadowcroft in the other. We were crowded but, compared with most refugees, re-markably comfortable. I was happy because there was no time for lessons except in such simple tasks as tying my own shoes. We were kept busy fetching drinking water from a nearby hospital (the municipal water supply had been polluted by the fighting in the hills) or buying food in the port, which could only be reached by boat. To this day I associate motor launches, particularly decrepit ones, with our stay in Novorossiysk. Peggy, who had wasted no time getting to know the British naval officers, took us boys on board to meet her new-found friends; they in turn introduced us to the joys of football and the mysteries of the English language, the latter made more palatable with tea and chocolate biscuits.

But most of the time Peggy was fully occupied trying to get us all the permits required by both the British and White Russian authorities if we were to be allowed to leave the country on a British ship. This was where Peggy was at her best: in the midst of civil war and with thousands of refugees clamouring for help, she simply refused to take no for an answer. Arrangements were made for us to leave on the *Huanchaco* of the Pacific Steamship Navigation Company; but two days before she was due to sail we were informed that Russians were no longer allowed to land in England. It seemed that the *Huanchaco* would have to leave without us. Peggy promptly took an overnight train to Ekaterinodar, the headquarters of the White Army some 120 miles away, managed to get the destination on our exit permits changed from England to France, and was back in Novorossiysk the following morning, a matter of hours before the *Huanchaco's* scheduled departure.

We had been warned that we had to be on board before 4.00 p.m., but even at such a crucial milestone in the family's fortunes father did not lose sight of fundamental priorities. When the ship's chief officer arrived with a truck and half a dozen Turkish prisoners to help us load our belongings and hurry us on our way, he was amazed to find the family assembled in the presence of the local priest, who had been summoned to sing a *molieben* for our safe journey. 'I do wish these people would quit singing psalms and get going,' he said to Peggy while the Orthodox service proceeded in its typically leisurely way.

Finally we were all on board, watching our native country recede on the horizon. The date was 13 May 1919, and the *Huanchaco* was leaving Russia for the last time. Had she sailed without us, I doubt whether we would ever have managed to get away. The ship was bound for Constantinople, but we took three weeks getting there because of a number of stops along the way. When we docked in the Bulgarian port of Varna, local officials who heard about father being aboard wanted to arrange a public reception for him, because he was the son of the man who had negotiated the Treaty of San Stefano and whom they therefore considered a national hero. In fact my grandfather Ignatieff's lifesize statute stood in front of Varna Cathedral, with the inscription 'Liberator of Bulgaria.' Father refused the reception because, he said, Russia and Bulgaria were still technically at war, and such a ceremony would therefore not be appropriate. However, several Bulgarian generals called on him informally on board ship and told him in the presence of the ship's officers that they regretted having fought on the wrong side.

For us boys, the sea voyage and the stay in Varna were better than a tonic. We played on Varna's beautiful beach, and occasionally some of the officers took us sailing or fishing. They also changed our Russian names to the English equivalents Nick, Jim, Alex, Lionel, and George; except for Leonid, who didn't like the anglicized version, that is what we have been called ever since. Before we landed in Constantinople, all of us tried to find among our modest belongings something we could give to the crew as a token of appreciation. The chief officer was surprised when Alex produced a brass chain with a Swiss coin attached to it and handed it over as though he were parting with Russia's crown jewels. Only when Peggy explained to him that Alex had clung to this treasure throughout the revolution and concealed it from bolshevik searches did he realize what a compliment the boy was paying him.

In Constantinople, mother left all of us sitting with our meagre luggage on the dock while she set out, on foot, in search of accommodation. This was the city where father was born, where his father had spent many years as Russian ambassador, so presumably he could have found someone who knew the family and might be willing to help; but he refused to ask for charity. Eventually, mother found a poor, kind-hearted Armenian woman who took pity on us and agreed to put us up. Her drunken husband beat her up when he found out what she had done.

Constantinople was decidedly the low point in our fortunes. I remember sleeping in a chest of drawers and being hungry most of the time. At least in Russia we usually had milk or stale bread to eat, while here we lived mostly on greasy broth and locust beans which fell off the carob trees. Father had a little tsarist and some

Kerensky money, but it was difficult to exchange either, because the Bolsheviks were flooding Turkey with currency of their own in an effort to obtain foreign exchange. As though things weren't bad enough, a pickpocket stole all the tsarist money that father had hoped to put aside for future emergencies. I don't know what we would have done if mother had not run into a woman whom she had known slightly in Kiev, and who insisted on loaning her two thousand francs. Mother accepted on the understanding that she would repay the loan to the woman's daughter, who was living in England, at the earliest opportunity. Even so, they agreed that it might be best not to tell father about the transaction.

After two weeks in Constantinople, we were informed by the French embassy that we had visas for France and that we could embark on a ship called *Flandre* which was about to leave for Marseilles. After years of service as a transport for soldiers and war materials, the ship was filthy; but at least we got decent food, and though I can't claim to remember the scenery, the cruise through the Aegean Islands and past Sicily and Stromboli must have been beautiful. From Marseilles we proceeded by overnight train to Paris, where mother installed us in the station restaurant. She herself stopped only long enough to fortify herself with French coffee and brioches before boarding the Metro in search of accommodation.

I think by now I was beginning to realize what an extraordinary woman my mother was. She had lost her home, her country, two of her sons, and many dear friends. She had stood up to the Bolsheviks when they arrested her husband and tried to deprive her of her remaining possessions. Through all the time when father was a virtual invalid, she had held the family together, drawing on inner resources which she couldn't have suspected she had or would ever need during her sheltered childhood and early years of married life.

In Paris mother found a modest pension near the Place St-Martin and, dauntless as ever, proceeded to take advantage of the opportunity to show us the city. Every morning, whether we felt like it or not, we set out on a sightseeing expedition. An obviously foreign woman with five children in tow, trudging on foot through the streets of Paris, must have been a strange sight; so much so that total strangers occasionally came up and asked could they be of any

help. One day I remember telling mother I was simply too exhausted to go, so she agreed to leave me at the pension under the
supervision of my brother Jim; Peggy Meadowcroft had gone ahead
to England to make arrangements for our arrival there. I forget
what happened but I started to cry; Jim got mad at me and threw a
pail of water over me. The water seeped through the floor into the
room of the concierge, who promptly called the police, and when
mother returned, she was threatened with eviction. However, she
managed to calm the concierge down and we were allowed to stay.

In a sense France would have been a logical place for us to stay
since my father, like many Russian aristocrats, had been educated
bilingually in Russian and French. However, our parents decided
otherwise, and after a few weeks we left for London, where Peggy
was waiting to transform me and my brothers into English gentlemen.

THREE

Down on the farm

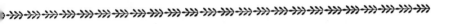

We reached London in July 1919 just in time to see a triumphant Lord Haig ride through the city at the head of a parade which marked the victory of British forces over their World War I enemies. Among the nations represented at that parade, the only one missing was Russia. By signing a separate peace treaty, the Bolsheviks had excluded their compatriots from those celebrations even though millions of Russians had fought and died to bring about the Allied victory.

'Remember, Paul, that Russia is a defeated nation,' Peggy Meadowcroft said to my father shortly after our arrival. Those few words summed up the change in the relationship of the Ignatieffs with our governess and the new role she was about to assume in our lives. A few months earlier it would have been inconceivable for her to call my father by his Christian name. But she was now our saviour, no longer our employee. More than that, she also personified to an extraordinary degree the spirit of British supremacy which permeated post-war England. It was no accident that the first English song I was taught to sing was 'Rule Britannia.'

We believed ourselves to be penniless until father read a notice in *The Times* to the effect that Count Ignatieff should get in touch with the Midland Bank, where he would find information to his benefit. What he found was thirty thousand pounds sterling, a very handsome sum in those days. The money had been deposited by an English broker who handled the foreign sales and shipping accounts for a crystal factory and some cotton mills father had inherited shortly before the war. When these properties were seized by the Bolsheviks, the broker completed all outstanding transactions and then launched a search for the rightful owner of the proceeds. Part of this unexpected windfall was invested in a Sussex farm, where my parents and some of their relatives could recuperate from their ordeal; the rest went to pay for our education.

While my two oldest brothers went off to school, Alex, Leonid, and I were left at the mercy of Peggy Meadowcroft's crash course in Victorian manners. She obviously believed that children should be brought up to give the least possible trouble, and that the best way to achieve this noble objective was by way of a routine which would keep them occupied every minute of the day. In the suburban flat which we shared with Peggy and her mother, we had to get up at seven and go to bed at seven – promptly. Immediately after breakfast we had to practise various musical instruments before going to our day school. Games were strictly forbidden, and so was any socializing with schoolmates. Indeed Peggy did not even allow us to do homework, since this would interfere with her routine and her carefully structured system of punishments, meted out for the most minuscule infraction of the rules. One of my early recollections is being made to write out countless times 'I am a bad boy' for failing to take off my hat when I stepped inside a house.

Indeed anything Peggy perceived as disobedience inevitably led to a spanking or pages of writing, or both. Even bowel movements could not be left to take nature's course; unless they performed according to Peggy's bidding, there was a penalty to be paid. Since our escape from Russia had left me with a mild case of malnutrition, Peggy decided that I should be made to eat fat bacon, and she actually found a Harley Street specialist to subscribe to this monstrous therapy. 'What did Dr. Batteshaw say?' she would ask whenever I seemed a bit slow swallowing. 'Fat, Peggy,' I had to reply, choking on tears and bacon.

The only times I escaped from this treadmill regime was on Sundays when I went to church and during school holidays which I spent on the family farm. Just as I associated Peggy with everything that had gone wrong in my young life – loss of country, loss of security, loss of status – so the Orthodox church gave me a sense of belonging, of being in touch with my roots, of safety and stability in an otherwise confusing world. Even in early childhood I derived great comfort from prayer and from the familiar Orthodox liturgy, and I have remained a devoted member of the church ever since.

In spite of the force-feeding to which Peggy subjected me, I continued to suffer attacks of weakness, and one day I fainted in church. When I woke up in a luxurious Daimler with beautiful fittings, I thought for a moment that I had died and gone to heaven. But the liveried chauffeur explained to me that I was in Queen Mother Alexandra's limousine, in which he had conveyed to church Her Majesty's sister, the Dowager Empress of Russia. 'You'll find her inside if you go back,' he said. I did, but I can only assume that the car made more of an impression on me than its royal occupant. Though I understand that I was introduced to the mother of the murdered tsar at the end of the service, I have no recollection of the meeting.

On the other hand, I have very vivid memories of the odd cluster of friends and relatives whom my parents had assembled on the Sussex farm. There was my father's younger brother, Nicholas, formerly a general and commander of the Preobrazhensky Guards during the war. Short and stocky with a bald head and a massive beard, uncle Kolya practised his military skills on the farm by re-enacting on the dining room table the battles he had fought. All the cutlery would disappear to his end of the table to be converted into regiments, divisions, and army corps deployed in mortal combat. We children had to wait for these manoeuvres to end before we could retrieve our forks and knives. Then one day Alex, looking the picture of innocence, inquired just whom or what the Preobrazhensky Guards were supposed to guard. 'The life of His Imperial Majesty the Tsar, of course,' replied uncle Kolya. 'Then why didn't they?' asked Alex with indisputable logic. There was an ominous hush before the general drew himself up to his full five foot four inches. 'If you were an officer and a gentleman rather than an impertinent boy,' uncle Kolya spluttered, his beard bristling, 'I would challenge you to a duel.'

The general's aide-de-camp during these table-top war games was his son-in-law, Colonel Malevsky, who was also an ex-officer in the guards regiment. Two other members of the ménage were mother's sister Princess Wassilchikoff, and her husband, Boris, desperately ill from tuberculosis he had contracted in a Soviet prison. Then there was a judge by the name of Mezetsky, whose father had been our priest in Kislovodsk; a Miss Adams-Brown, formerly my aunt Katherine's lady companion, who sold corsets, practised Christian Science, and gave advice on how to run the farm; and Dr Belilovsky, a Jewish gynaecologist from Kiev who specialized in peacemaking whenever conflicts flared up among the farm's ill-assorted occupants.

Probably the one thing all these people had in common was their total ignorance of farming. The general, who was supposed to be responsible for the woodland, insisted on having a local farmhand aide called Pug whom he marched down to the woods every day, carrying a dark blue umbrella as well as an axe 'at the slope.' Uncle Kolya also loved to take all of us on route marches down to the seaside. On one such occasion the family dog – a retriever called Jack – mistook a lady's leg dangling from a deck-chair for a lamppost, with embarrassing results. The general rose to the occasion with the only two English phrases that came readily to mind. 'Jack good dog!' he reprimanded the culprit, and 'I loff you,' he apologized to the lady.

The colonel was put in charge of farm machinery, including a huge tractor which was his pride and joy. Never had such a large tractor been used on so few acres of arable land. Since the colonel's training as an infantry officer did not include tractor driving, he frequently landed in a ditch from which both he and his vehicle had to be extricated. Villagers who were summoned to assist in these rescue missions claimed that they usually ended up putting back in circulation some local maiden along with the tractor and its driver.

The judge assumed responsibility for the herd of approximately thirty cows, even though there was no evidence of empathy between him and the animals. I remember him being sent sprawling by a cow he was trying to milk, and he was convinced the wicked animals were deliberately kicking over the pail whenever he tried to milk them. On one occasion he enlisted the help of the general and the colonel to call for a new cow at the railway station. Presumably bewildered by its strange escort, the animal turned into the village street and followed a woman through an open door into the parlour of her house, with the three Russians in hot pursuit. It cost father five pounds to undo the damage.

Mother, who had never even learned how to do her own hair before the revolution, was cast in the role of both cook and housekeeper. Unfortunately, the cooking lessons she had taken at the Cordon Bleu during our brief stay in Paris were not exactly designed to cope with the gigantic appetites of five growing boys or the dwindling resources of seven adults. On one occasion when a main course of 'marrons glacés,' one of mother's Parisian specialties, turned out as hard as bullets, the general decided to launch a revolution, and it took all of Dr Belilovsky's diplomatic talents to restore peace and order. Once in a while, when her patience was tried past the breaking point, mother would retire to her bath muttering to herself and taking along a variety of pills and perfumes plus either a bottle of port or a cup of tea. But most of the time she coped remarkably well, which was more than could be said for the rest of the household.

For me, the comic opera aspects of life on the farm were eclipsed by the sheer joy of being with my family, close to nature, and away from Peggy. Father, who was trying to run a dairy, personally delivered the milk to his customers in his brand new Renault car, and even though it meant getting up at five in the morning, I loved going with him. These milk rounds provided me with my first opportunity to talk to him for any length of time and find out what sort of person my father was. He certainly bore no resemblance to the stereotype of the effete, self-indulgent Russian aristocrat. Very much under the influence of Leo Tolstoy, he had an almost mystical faith in the common man and in the cleansing power of hard work. A job well done was to him the ultimate achievement. His tastes were puritanical, and though he had taken up smoking during the revolution, alcohol and cards were taboo in our house (mother's port was 'medicinal' and therefore exempted from the prohibition). He read widely, but only for information, never for pleasure. I still remember the apparent satisfaction with which he finished a book and said as he put it down: 'Now that's done.'

Unlike many White Russian refugees, father refused to live out of a suitcase or to indulge in dreams of an imminent restoration of the tsarist regime. Though he continued to raise money for the Russian Red Cross he made it clear that, as far as he was concerned, the past was over and done with. Many of his friends and relations interpreted this attitude as yet another manifestation of an excessive liberalism which, they claimed, had paved the way for the revolution. Why, they wondered, had father been released by the Bolsheviks after his arrest even though all the other prisoners were shot? And why had he refused General Denikin's offer of a cabinet post should the White Russians succeed in forming a government?

Their suspicions were reinforced by the supposedly scandalous behaviour of my father's cousin Alexis, who had spent the war years in Paris as military attaché and representative of the Russian imperial army at Allied headquarters. He had at his disposal large sums of money intended to pay for armament purchases, and after the revolution the White Army generals assumed that he would turn these funds over to them. But he refused because, he said, the money belonged to the Russian people. The Soviets were of course delighted, and eventually my 'Red Uncle' accepted an invitation from General Tukhachevsky to return to Russia. When Tukhachevsky was later shot during the Stalinist purge of the armed forces, we assumed that uncle Alexis had met his fate along with his newfound comrades. Much to our surprise he surfaced during World War II as a major general in the Soviet army and inspector general of staff colleges. Apparently part of his job was to bolster the sagging morale of the Soviet officer corps during the initial Nazi onslaught by reviving some of the traditions that had been the pride of the pre-revolutionary guards regiments. I understand he was responsible for introducing the Bolsheviks to such trappings of military life as dress uniforms with fancy epaulettes.

Most of the White Russian community in England and continental Europe was pretty reactionary, and in the eyes of its members my Red Uncle's treachery tinged all the Ignatieffs with a pinkish hue. Years later, when I travelled in the Balkans, I was welcomed in the Bulgarian city of Turnovo as the grandson of the country's liberator – until the local Russian exiles asked the mayor whether he was aware of the fact that the Ignatieffs were notorious Communists, and that I might well be a Soviet spy. Later during the same trip, while having dinner in Vienna in a Russian restaurant, I asked the band leader whether he could play the military march of the Preobrazhensky Guards. He asked what was the reason for my request, and when I explained that the guards had been both my father's and my uncle's regiment, he drew himself up and said, 'There was a time when the Ignatieffs commanded respect among Russian soldiers; they don't any more.'

Needless to say, father had no contact with his renegade cousin and no sympathy for his views. In fact he told me during one of our milk runs that the main reason why he had subjected us to Peggy Meadowcroft's brand of forcible anglicization was to decontaminate us of any Marxist notions we might have picked up during our exposure to the civil war in Kislovodsk. He admitted that I was too young to have caught the bug, but apparently Nick, who was sixteen at the time we left Russia, felt that the Bolsheviks were not that wrong when they claimed the aristocracy had been exploiting the Russian people. 'I wasn't going to have a revolutionary in the family,' father said. As it turned out, the most effective act of rebellion was committed by Alex, who decided he wouldn't put up with Peggy's tyranny any longer and ran away. Once again Dr Belilovsky came to the rescue by warning mother that she would lose all her children unless she got rid of 'that woman.' So the rest of us were sent to boarding school and Peggy departed, presumably to torment other children.

St Paul's was typical of England's so-called public school system in that its overriding objective was the pursuit of excellence. It cultivated students who stood out intellectually or athletically, preferably both, because they had the minds and the physical fibre that leaders of empires are made of. It was not a congenial environment for a boy who didn't speak English very well, whose attempts to play games were less than successful, and whose scholarship left a good deal to be desired. I was considered an oddball and a foreigner, and I didn't like it. The one redeeming feature about St Paul's, as far as I was concerned, was my friendship with Isaiah Berlin. Isaiah's English was more heavily accented than mine and he was a Jewish immigrant from Riga, so you might think he was even more of a misfit than I; but he was intellectually brilliant and that made him acceptable. Though he was a year or two older than I was, he obviously liked me, and I looked up to him as though he were some sort of god. Years later when I arrived in Oxford as a Rhodes scholar, Isaiah had just been elected a Fellow of All Souls and was generally acknowledged as outstanding among the university's up-and-coming philosophers. I felt truly privileged when he accepted me as his student, and I am proud to consider myself his friend to this day.

Apart from Isaiah, what I liked best about St Paul's was the opportunity to escape on Sundays to the London flat of aunt Mara, my favourite among the odd assortment of Russian relatives who had made their way to England. She was the wife of Prince Mestchersky, my mother's decidedly eccentric elder brother known to us as uncle Sasha. He didn't like children, probably because they weren't green, the one colour that he considered infinitely superior to all others. Back home on the family estate he had indulged this passion by growing green orchids. In England he switched to eating pea soup and wearing green suits, preferably made of billiard cloth. At one time the Mestcherskys had been fabulously wealthy, and much of their fortune had been abroad, invested among other things in a house in Montreal. But they were fierce patriots, and when World War I broke out, they repatriated all this money to Russia. During the revolution the Bolsheviks burned their estate, both uncle Sasha and aunt Mara went to jail, and in the end they were lucky to escape with little more than their lives. Aunt Mara lavished her maternal instincts on me by letting me feast every Sunday on vast quantities of borsch, cucumbers, and black bread.

Years later, after uncle Sasha had died and aunt Mara had nothing to live on except her old age pension and what little help my wife and I were able to give her, Alison gave her a cheque as a birthday present and urged her to buy something she really wanted. Mara took a taxi to a famous tea shop on Brompton Road and ordered a pot of Princess Mestchersky tea – a mixture which had been specially made for her at a time when she could afford that kind of luxury.

During the four years I spent at St Paul's School, it became painfully obvious that the family farm was losing money and that something would have to be done to salvage whatever was left of the Ignatieff nest-egg. Father could not bear the thought of depriving his lame duck entourage of the only home they had known since they left Russia. But while he was away raising money for the Red Cross my brother Jim, who had graduated from an agricultural college, persuaded mother that the farm could never produce enough revenue to support so many dependants. They agreed that the only sensible solution was to sell the farm, and father was presented more or less with a *fait accompli*.

The family was on the move again. Nick was already in Canada working as a hydro engineer, and Jim went off to the prairies as a harvester. Alex, a mining engineer, chose to try his luck in Africa, and father decided to continue his Red Cross work in Geneva and Paris. In September 1928 mother set out with Leonid and myself to join my two brothers in Canada.

FOUR

The Canadianization of the Ignatieffs

Jim was there to meet us when the Canadian Pacific liner *Montrose* docked in Montreal. He took one horrified look at my bowler hat – an integral part of my Sunday outfit at St Paul's – grabbed it, and sent it flying into the waters of the St Lawrence. 'That's one thing you won't need here,' he remarked. The sight of that silly hat floating down the river seemed to me a good omen, the first step in my emancipation from the convention-ridden life I had left behind in Europe.

For a while it seemed as though the first step would also be the last, at least for some time to come. It was characteristic of my parents' faith in education that, even though we had barely enough money for basic necessities, mother managed to squeeze enough out of the household budget to send me to the most expensive school in Montreal. She figured that Lower Canada College was similar to the school I had attended in England and that I would therefore have no trouble adapting to it. She was right on the first count, dead wrong on the second.

The school was staffed mostly by Englishmen, some of whom bore an uncanny resemblance to my teachers at St Paul's. The headmaster, known to us as 'The Boss,' was a tall, wiry gentleman whose main ambition apparently was to produce in Canada the closest possible facsimile of an English 'public' school. He came pretty close, though there was one important difference between the two systems. At St Paul's you were somebody if you excelled intellectually or scholastically. At Lower Canada College what seemed to matter most was being rich or being good at games. I was neither, as my schoolmates were quick to discover.

This bastion of Montreal's English-speaking establishment was light-years removed from the home life I led with my mother and my brother Leonid. The only income we had was the interest on the proceeds of the sale of the family farm, which came to a little over one hundred dollars a month. That wasn't much even in 1928, but mother was at her most resourceful when it came to making ends meet. She managed to rent an apartment for forty-five dollars a month in a decidedly unfashionable part of Notre-Dame-de-Grâce, where we found ourselves battling bed bugs for the first time since our escape from the Bolshevik revolution. Undaunted, mother walked five miles or so every day to the Bonsecours market and back again, to buy fresh fruit and vegetables at the cheapest possible price. Sometimes she stopped along the way at second-hand shops whose Jewish proprietors had emigrated from Russia and knew what father had done for the Jews when he was minister of education. They would invite her to join them for a cup of tea and a talk about old times, and they'd tell her where there were special bargains to be had.

I went to see one of these families years later, after mother had died, to thank them for being kind to her. It was shortly after my marriage, and the Department of External Affairs had presented me with a wedding present in the form of a cheque for twenty-five dollars. What, I asked mother's friends, could I buy with that money? They produced a beautiful carving set and insisted that I take it, even though I suspected that it was worth much more than the cheque. It is one of the few possessions I really treasure; it has travelled with me all over the world.

Somehow we made it through that first Canadian winter, and when spring came I went to the Canadian Pacific Railway to see what the chances were of getting a summer job out west. Colonel Dennis, an official of the colonization branch, agreed to let me have a railway pass as far as Winnipeg, where I was to see a Mr McLeod of the CPR's western engineering branch. Mother wasn't at all keen to let me go, which is hardly surprising since I wasn't even sixteen years old. When she finally agreed, she pressed twenty-five dollars into my hand and warned me in rather mysterious terms to steer clear of 'loose women' unless I wanted my nose to fall off. While her lecture left me decidedly baffled, it did nothing to dampen my enthusiasm for the adventure that lay ahead.

In the tourist coach of the CPR transcontinental, I promptly made friends with a farmer from Swift Current who was returning home after his first visit to the nation's capital. When the train deposited us in Winnipeg, we set out together in search of a cheap hotel. We found one near the station, only to discover that it was an establishment used by railway crews for a 'quickie' between trains. The patrons were so annoyed to find one of the rooms occupied by two 'queers' that they tried to break down the door; we only managed to retain possession by barricading ourselves inside the room. However, mother would have been relieved to now that, far from trying to corrupt me, my farmer friend read me to sleep with the help of a Gideon bible.

When I went to see Mr McLeod, he told me that the only job he had to offer was that of an axeman on the Kootenay Lake construction site in British Columbia, more than a thousand miles further west. My twenty-five dollars had already been depleted by the price of a berth, two days' food, and my hotel bill. However, he gave me another railway pass to Kootenay Landing and I figured that, if I sat up all night in a day coach, I could make it. I did, but only just. By the time I reached Medicine Hat I was down to three dollars, part of which I used to buy a loaf of bread and a chocolate bar. This saw me through to Kootenay Landing, where I found I had to pay for my fare to the Procter work site. I arrived without a cent in my pocket.

The crew that I was about to join was doing the survey for a railway which was to link the Crow's Nest Pass line with the Kettle Valley railway to Vancouver. The purpose was to provide land transportation for the lead and zinc concentrates which, up till then, had had to be ferried in barges across Kootenay Lake on their way to the Trail smelter. This part of the railroad had not been built earlier because the terrain was too difficult and construction costs were too high. But recently the demand for ore concentrates at the Trail smelter had increased to the point where it was decided to build the railway after all.

The survey party consisted of a resident engineer, who was the boss, an instrument man, a rodman, a chainman, and one or two axemen. Axemen, as I was about to discover, were expected to fell trees, chop them up, and make cedar stakes to mark the right of way for the roadbed. This was not an easy terrain for my initiation into railroad construction. Not only did I have to learn how to handle an axe – a skill to which I had never been exposed before – I had to do it while dodging rock slides, clambering over steep cliffs, and avoiding contact with the icy waters of the lake. My teammates didn't quite know what to make of this greenhorn with a Russian name and an upper-class English accent. They associated the accent with British remittance men who usually got jobs with the police and were therefore by definition suspect; and the only Russians they knew were the Doukhobor Sons of Freedom whose nudist parades were already notorious. They christened me The Douk and treated me, at least at first, with considerable reserve.

My living quarters consisted of an abandoned shack where two of us shared a broken bed. One night after I had fallen asleep, the man who shared my bed returned with a group of friends from the local beer parlour and decided it would be fun to 'throw the Douk in the drink.' I woke up in the icy water of the mountain creek which ran past our shack. What the other axemen did not know was that the Douk had had boxing lessons in England, and had taken to this sport a good deal better than to the more genteel games taught at boarding school. That fight marked the end of my initiation; nobody ever tried to play a similar trick on me again. My fighting skills, however, were tested repeatedly that summer. The heat, the pressure of work, and a natural tendency to lose my temper landed me in a number of skirmishes, some of them more violent than others.

A major break came my way when I was allowed 'out on the line' under the direction of a seasoned CPR engineer. He taught me how to handle a single-headed axe as well as a 'methodist' one, which, he claimed, owed its name to being double-faced. He taught me how not to swing when in the bush, how to keep my legs out of the way, and how to choose the best cedar logs to split into smooth-panelled stakes. He even taught me how to row. When after ten days I rejoined the rest of the survey party, I still had to work hard to keep up, but at least I could hold my own – most of the time. There were occasions when the axe missed its mark, and it was just as well we had a medical student from McGill on the party to bind up my wounds.

Before that summer was over, I had learned quite a few things other than swinging an axe and filling the perpetual demand for stakes. My vocabulary was enriched by a potent combination of blasphemy and sex. I also learned how to make a quick dash for the bush whenever the police raided the beer parlour in search of minors like myself; and I discovered the delicious fruit grown in the nearby Okanagan Valley. One day a farmer caught me red-handed in a tree picking cherries. 'Why didn't you come and ask me?' he said. 'I would have given you all the cherries you wanted.' I was so conscience-stricken that I bought a crate for the huge sum of three dollars and sent it home to mother in Montreal. She must have been surprised to be charged ten dollars for a crate of cherries which arrived express collect all the way from Nelson, BC.

I had some close calls. Once I nearly drowned when I lost my footing climbing down a trestle bridge over the lake, and an axe fight with an Irishman as hot-tempered as myself might well have killed either one of us. We were both fired for this misdeed, and promptly rehired since there was no one around to take our place on the crew. But the most frightening experience of all was my encounter with forest fires. A tell-tale haze and the smell of smoke had been hanging over Kootenay Lake for days. Then one evening, fanned by sharp gusts of wind, the flames spread over miles of mountainside in a matter of minutes and turned the shore across the lake into a sheet of fire. I hadn't seen anything so terrifying since the Russian revolution. We formed a bucket brigade and spent all night pouring water on our tents, shacks, and piles of lumber to protect them from the sparks which the wind carried across the lake. In the morning, all we could see on the other side of the lake was complete devastation. The fires continued to burn out of control for weeks, but the wind had changed and our camp was spared.

In spite of these experiences, or perhaps because of them, that summer in the Kootenays marked the beginning of my lifelong love affair with the west. The beauty of the lake and the surround-

ing Rockies, the crystal clear water, the taste of the most delicious
salmon trout I have ever eaten, and the generosity of the people all
made me feel that this was the Canada I had been looking for, the
country my brother Nick was so enthusiastic about.

Above all, I loved the experience of proving myself, of being
accepted as one of the boys by teammates who couldn't care less
who I was or where I came from. Before I left, the resident engineer,
an Englishman by the name of Henderson who spent his evenings
going through the *Encyclopaedia Britannica*, came across my grandfather's name. At breakfast the following morning, he asked me
whether I was related to the Count Ignatieff who had been a
Russian diplomat. My mind was on griddle cakes and maple syrup
rather than a grandfather I had never known, but I couldn't very
well deny my ancestry. Major Henderson was clearly impressed,
while my companions began joking about the 'count of no account.'
As for me, my reaction was complete indifference. Almost to my
own surprise, I realized that I was emancipated beyond the point
where I needed the prop of being a count. The promotion I had
earned that summer, from axeman to rodman, had done more for
my self-esteem than any number of inherited titles.

On my way back to Montreal, I arranged a meeting in Calgary
with Nick, who was working as an engineer with the Calgary
Power Company. We agreed that, as soon as he could find a job
with Ontario Hydro, I would join him in Toronto and prepare to
become a civil engineer. Mother wasn't at all keen on our scheme
and tried to persuade me to stay at Lower Canada College for
another year, but the 1929 stock market crash came to my rescue.
It turned out that mother had been trying to stretch our modest
resources by buying stocks on margin. When the market collapsed,
it decimated her capital and income to the point where she could no
longer afford to send me to a private school.

Though the great depression made our financial situation more
precarious than ever, it did serve as a catalyst in reuniting most of
the Ignatieffs by forcing us to seek shelter under one roof. Father
finally gave up trying to raise money in Europe for Russian refugees
and joined the rest of the family in Canada. Nick and I had found an
old farmhouse in Thornhill on the northern outskirts of Toronto,

and there father spent the depression years growing vegetables while mother resumed her activities as cook-housekeeper for the clan. Jim also came to Toronto after losing his Peace River homestead to a hailstorm, and got a job as a Fellow in the Department of Biochemistry while working for his doctorate at the University of Toronto; his modest earnings kept the family going through the worst period of the depression, after Nick had been laid off by Ontario Hydro. Leonid joined us after completing his law studies at McGill and decided to switch to teaching languages and history. Only Alex, who had returned to England from Africa and was working as a mining engineer, decided to remain behind in England, though he too joined us eventually after the war.

Meanwhile my own attempts to become an engineer foundered on my inability to master the mathematics and physics courses at Central Technical School in Toronto. Without these prerequisites engineering was out of the question, which was probably just as well since my interest became increasingly focused on the causes of the depression and unemployment. I therefore transferred to Jarvis Collegiate and, after graduation, enrolled as a student of political economy at the University of Toronto. This turned out to be a particularly fortunate choice. I was exposed to the innovative ideas and influence of Harold Innis and Donald Creighton, then the rising stars of Canadian economic and political history. From them I gained an insight into both the unity and the diversity of the country, the need to balance its cohesive forces against its economic regionalism and the cultural duality of the founding races. To me these were new concepts, but they tied in remarkably well with my own experiences in western Canada and in Montreal. I had observed at Lower Canada College the isolation of the English-speaking establishment from its French environment; and I had seen in the west what Innis called 'the application of mature techniques to virgin natural resources.'

Yet the depression provided plenty of evidence that Canada was not really an inexhaustible source of wealth just waiting to be harvested by modern technology. Much though I admired Innis, I couldn't reconcile some of his ideas with the appalling unemployment, poverty, and unequal distribution of wealth that I saw all around me. To discuss these problems I turned to Nick, who had himself tasted unemployment and had spent a few months touring Canada with a sixty-three-pound pack on his back, hitching rides, getting to know the country better than most home-grown Canadians ever have, while making a living as a journalist and lecturer. During this time he had developed definite ideas about the need to use the agricultural potential of the north as a counterweight to the outflow of resources from the south, and about the role of governments in helping immigrants adapt to a vast and alien land. He wrote and spoke about these issues so eloquently that Principal William Grant offered him a teaching position at Upper Canada College. This was a fortunate turn of events for at least two reasons: it provided Nick with an income with which he was able to help support the rest of the family; and it led to my first meeting with Alison, the principal's youngest daughter and my future wife.

Nick's ideas and the devastating effects of the depression also awakened my curiosity in constitutional questions. I felt I had to know the responsibilities of various levels of government before I could draw any conclusions about ways to alleviate economic problems. Strangely enough, Canada's constitution was not part of the political science curriculum at the University of Toronto, so I left my summer job in a hotel kitchen as soon as I had made enough money to see me through the next term at university and proceeded to study on my own during six glorious weeks that I spent with Nick on a small island in Georgian Bay. This idyllic setting for reading, talking, and thinking was apparently just what I needed. When I later wrote the examination, I was awarded the Maurice Cody scholarship, one of the highest honours the university had to bestow on undergraduates.

I was now in my third year of university and happier than I'd ever been before. Not only was I finally hitting my stride academically, I was also participating in every conceivable facet of life at Trinity College, where I was registered as a non-resident student. Unlike the schools I had attended in England and Montreal, Trinity never made me feel like an outsider. From the day I enrolled I found myself involved in debating, dramatics, and even campus politics, all of which provided me with much pleasure as well as sorely needed self-confidence. For the first time in my life, I felt part of a community where I truly belonged.

But graduation was just around the corner and there were career decisions to be made. I was offered a teaching position at Trinity College School, which I considered an honour as well as a stroke of good luck, given the scarcity of available jobs in the mid-thirties. I was all set to accept but decided to discuss the offer first with Burgon Bickersteth, the popular warden of Hart House whom I had got to know when I represented Trinity on the Board of Stewards. At the time he was one of the few people on the campus to whom students could turn for this kind of advice. Much to my surprise, he took a dim view of my teaching plans. What he said to me in effect was: 'Why should you inflict your ignorance on these unsuspecting children? All you'll have is a BA, which doesn't amount to much; go to Oxford and get yourself some real education before you try to educate others.'

I protested that I had no money to go to Oxford or anywhere else, at which point he suggested that I apply for a Rhodes scholarship. The thought had frankly never crossed my mind. For one thing, I was not yet a Canadian citizen and therefore not a British subject, as required by Cecil Rhodes' will. Indeed no Canadian student born outside the country had ever won the coveted scholarship. To make matters worse, I was competing with such outstanding scholars as Claude Bissell and Saul Rae, and I didn't know any of the members of the selection committee other than the Reverend John Lowe, who taught religious knowledge at Trinity at the time. He later became vice-chancellor of Oxford, while 'Roly' Michener, secretary of the Rhodes Trust for Canada, rose to become Speaker of the House of Commons, high commissioner to India, and governor general.

My prospects of impressing people of this calibre seemed dim, to say the least; but Bickersteth had rekindled my imagination and there seemed no harm in trying. When I won, nobody was more surprised than my parents – surprised and upset. As they saw it, going to Oxford would mean turning my back on the family's adoptive country in order to return to an environment where I had obviously been unhappy. Father had just become a Canadian citizen, even though he had not been in the country long enough to qualify for citizenship. But this technical difficulty was overcome thanks to Sir William Mulock, a neighbour with whom father loved to discuss the world's problems. Shortly before the 1935 federal election which returned the Liberals to power, Mulock suggested to his friend Mackenzie King that he might be able to help the Ignatieffs become Canadian citizens, and King promised to see what could be done. He kept his promise and so, by Order-in-Council dated 20 March 1936, father became a Canadian. The rest of us had to wait a few more months, but by the time I sailed for England, I too had my Canadian passport.

Though I had some qualms of my own about going back to England, I could not conceive of turning down the opportunity which was being handed to me and letting down the people who had expressed their confidence in me. As it turned out, that decision was a turning point in my life. A Rhodes scholarship in those days was an important stepping stone for admission to External Affairs. Without it, I doubt whether I would ever have become a diplomat.

Any concerns I had as to my compatibility with the English system of education proved to be completely unfounded. Unlike boarding school, with its pressures to conform to predetermined standards, Oxford encouraged individuality and elevated eccentricity to a virtue. I still remember the essay I brought to my first Oxford tutorial. After listening to me with closed eyes, the tutor remarked somewhat coldly, 'You must give me credit for having read the texts which I recommended to you in my bibliography; what I want to know is what *you* think.'

There were times when I doubted my ability to rise to the high standards of intellectual originality that were being set at Oxford by Isaiah Berlin in philosophy, Richard Crossman in political science, Harold Wilson in economics, and Richard Pares in history. Still, I couldn't have been too dismal a failure. Years later, when I met one of my former tutors in Washington, DC, he didn't seem at all anxious to acknowledge our previous acquaintance. However, he phoned me later to say that he had looked me up in a little book where he recorded the academic standing of his former students.

'Your results are quite creditable,' he concluded. 'You may come and see me.'

One thing Oxford did have in common with boarding school was the insistence that every student should be a 'sport.' I tried to resist these pressures but, after a particularly wet fall and several colds which turned to bronchitis, I enquired about the chances of having some heat in my rooms at New College. I was told very firmly that such a concession would require a medical certificate, so off I went to see a doctor. He asked me what I was doing to keep fit, and, having established that I wasn't climbing steeples, boxing, playing cricket, or engaging in any other athletic activities, he suggested that I'd better 'go down to the river.' I followed his advice, and though I found rowing on the Isis quite different from my previous exposure to the sport on Kootenay Lake, I qualified for a college 'eight' and, in the process, made a number of new friends. It's difficult to share a boat day after day in the rain with seven other people without exchanging a few words, which was more than strangers were expected to do at Oxford under normal circumstances.

My stay at Oxford also provided me with an opportunity to re-establish contact with my Russian friends and relatives. On my arrival in England I was met by my former nanny, Manya, who proceeded to introduce me to her English friends as a count and her foster-son. She also made sure that my Oxford diet was supplemented with frequent packages of wholesome Russian delicacies, including vodka and boiled onions, which she considered much more effective antidotes to colds than rowing.

Even more disconcerting was my reunion in Paris with assorted aunts, uncles, and cousins. Aunt Sonia Wassilchikov, who had lived with us on the farm in Sussex, was now helping her sister-in-law, Princess Vera Mestchersky, run a finishing school. Aunt Vera insisted that I must tell her charges about life in Canada. 'Is it true,' she asked by way of introduction, 'that bears roam the streets of Ottawa?' Seated before a bevy of girls in what must have been at one time the ballroom of an aristocratic residence, I was appalled by this display of ignorance. As I leaned forward to set the record straight, the delicate Louis Quinze chair on which I was sitting shot out from under me and I landed flat on my back, to the obvious amusement of the girls. As I lay on the floor, my predicament was not improved when my uncle Peter tried to break the awkward silence by enquiring whether I had been to Les Invalides. I spent the rest of my stay in Paris trooping around with aunt Sonia, meeting more relatives and becoming increasingly convinced that I was too much of a Canadian to be even temporarily recycled into the White Russian milieu.

My years in Oxford coincided with the Spanish civil war, the growing militarization of the Axis powers, and the apparent unwillingness of the western democracies either to defend themselves or to join forces under the banner of collective security. I remember a meeting of Canadian students organized by Mike Pearson in the London residence of Vincent Massey, the Canadian high commissioner. There must have been fifty or sixty of us, and the question we had come to discuss was: what should be the attitude of Canada in case of war? The prevailing view was that Canada should mind her own business, that Neville Chamberlain's appeasement policy had got the world into a mess, and that it wasn't up to us to pull the chestnuts out of the fire. That wasn't Pearson's view any more than it was mine. We argued that Canada had an obligation under the League of Nations to resist aggression; but ours was decidedly a minority opinion.

To make sure that I wasn't misinterpreting what to me were the portents of another world war, I travelled as much as I could in Germany and Italy, and I was appalled at the sight of hundreds of thousands of storm troopers parading in front of the Führer at Nürnberg. I also spent more than six months in the Balkans doing research into the origins of World War I and, in the process, learning more about the military and diplomatic expoits of my grandfather, about his attempts to promote the independence of Bulgaria and Herzegovina, about the reasons why Turkish domination in that part of the world had been superseded by the German and Austro-Hungarian empires, about the likelihood of the Balkans becoming once again the spark-plug for a global conflagration. I was welcomed wherever I went as the grandson of the author of the Treaty of San

Stefano; yet the ubiquitous evidence of German infiltration made me feel apprehensive and isolated.

My stay in Bulgaria came to an abrupt end when I was informed by the British legation in Sofia that war was imminent and that, with my name, I would be well advised to leave the country as quickly as possible. I returned to England the day before the outbreak of World War II.

FIVE

Diplomatic apprenticeship

⇗⇝⇝⇝⇝⇝⇝⇝⇝⇝⇝⇝⇝⇝⇝⇝⇝⇝⇝⇝⇝⇝⇝⇝⇝⇝⇝

I was in London at my brother Alex's house on 3 September 1939 when the wailing sirens announced the city's first air raid. In accordance with instructions we had heard on the radio, we grabbed our steel helmets and gas masks and dived under the kitchen table, which happened to be the only available shelter. We looked and felt so ridiculous – Alex, his wife, his daughter, two other visiting Canadians, and myself – all with our bottoms sticking out from under that table, that we decided to take our chances and came out long before the 'All Clear' sounded. As it turned out, it was a false alarm.

Along with many other Canadian students in London, I went to Canada House to see what I should do about enlisting in the Canadian armed forces. Our request seemed to baffle Corporal McLeod of the RCMP, who had been assigned to deal with the flood of Canadians in search of information and direct them to whatever office was most likely to help them. Eventually we found our way next door to the Sun Life Building, where a nucleus of a Canadian military headquarters was beginning to take shape. The advice we got was to go back to Canada, at our own expense, and enlist there.

I had neither the money nor the desire to cross the Atlantic, particularly after some of my homeward-bound friends went down with the *Athenia* when she was torpedoed during the first week of the war. So I decided to try my luck with the British army instead. 'Ignatieff,' said the recruiting sergeant suspiciously as he eyed my application form, 'what sort of name is that?' 'Russian,' I replied, bracing myself for some well-chosen expletives; the Soviet Union had only just signed a treaty of friendship with Germany, and Russians were not exactly popular in Britain at the time. Much to my surprise, that wasn't the way the recruiting sergeant felt about my native country. He proceeded to tell me that he had served with the British forces which supported the White Army at Murmansk towards the end of World War I. 'Wonderful fishing at Murmansk,' he recalled nostalgically. 'Throw a Mill's bomb [grenade] upstream and you could pick up the fish with your hand, you could.' A firm thump on the chest and I was pronounced fit for service in His Majesty's Forces.

Having been a member of the cadet corps at Lower Canada College in Montreal and later at the Univesity of Toronto, I was convinced that I was destined to serve the Allied cause as an infantry soldier. But a tribunal of senior representatives of the three armed forces decided otherwise. A recruit who spoke Russian, French, and Bulgarian, they decreed, was clearly destined to become an officer in the Intelligence Corps. I would have had no quarrel with that decision had I been able to obtain the basic training I needed in order to be commissioned. But the War Office informed me that they were too busy providing the British Expeditionary Force with infantry training to be bothered with the likes of me. I was given a choice of training as a cavalry officer or waiting until the BEF had left for France. Since I considered intelligence on horseback somewhat obsolete, not to say conspicuous, I elected to wait.

I spent the next few weeks marching through various parts of London, on the assumption that this would toughen my feet for the training that lay ahead. During one of these mock forays I ran into Fitzroy Maclean, a Foreign Office man whom I had met during my student days at Oxford. Maclean, who was to become famous for his exploits with Tito's partisans in the mountains of Yugoslavia, asked me whether I would be interested in joining an intelligence unit which studied the implications of the Nazi-Soviet Pact. This chance meeting led to an interview with a Major Zambra, who wanted to know whether I was willing to die for the Allied cause. When I replied that anything would be better than dying of boredom while waiting for my basic training, I was told to report to

Department EH at Woburn Abbey, the country home of the duke of Bedford.

Department EH (for Electra House) turned out to be the cover name for a collection of intelligence activities carried out by a weird assortment of military personnel of various nationalities, plus a sprinkling of journalists, broadcasters, academics, and show business people. The department was under the direction of Sir Campbell Stuart, a Canadian who made a name for himself during the final days of World War I by advising the British to spread Allied propaganda among the retreating German soldiers. This advice did contribute to the demoralization of the enemy, and, like many of his contemporaries, Sir Campbell figured that anything that worked in 1918 was bound to work equally well in 1939. One EH contingent was therefore busy composing the text of pamphlets which the RAF had to drop over Germany, no doubt to the amusement of the recipients.

My own assignment was more interesting, though less dangerous than I had been led to believe. I suspect I may have been recruited so I could eventually be parachuted into Bulgaria, the same way Fitzroy Maclean was dropped into Yugoslavia. But for the time being my work consisted of reading east European newspapers and any other documents we could get hold of and analysing them for hints as to the implementation of the Nazi-Soviet pact of 'friendship and non-aggression' signed by the two governments on 23 August 1939. After the war, when the full text of this infamous treaty was found in Germany, it turned out that its secret part provided not only for the partition of Poland, but also for the division of eastern Europe into spheres of influence which would give the Soviets access to the Mediterranean. It occurred to me that the Russians were being promised exactly what my grandfather had tried to get from the Turks at the time of the Treaty of San Stafano, and what the tsar would presumably have claimed as his share of the booty at the end of World War I had he lived to participate in the Allied victory. Imperialism is strangely impervious to the ideology of the government in power.

Part of my job was to piece together whatever information I could find as to shipments of raw materials, particularly oil, from the Soviet Union to Germany, and the extent to which these shipments were meeting the demand. There was evidence even at that early stage of the war that tension was building up between the partners of the alliance. I came across frequent demands for larger quantities of supplies and German allegations that the Soviets were not living up to their side of the bargain.

Life at Woburn Abbey was interesting in more ways than one. Though I never met the current owner of this beautiful estate, I soon reached the conclusion that the duke of Bedford was just as eccentric a gentleman as some of my own relatives. My uncle Sasha's addiction to green orchids had its counterpart in the duke's passion for all kinds of rare birds, which were wandering all over the grounds. In the stables, which had been converted into our living quarters, a notice proclaimed that other ranks were prohibited from molesting the black swans. I never did find out what molesting black swans involved, or why the prohibition did not apply to officers; but I was sure I wasn't interested in molesting swans of whatever colour, even if I had not been told that the duke kept a shotgun with telescopic sights handy to enforce his edict.

One night, however, when I was returning in the dark to my quarters, I ran into a creature that let out a dreadful squawk, and when I grabbed at the unknown presence, something soft and downy came away in my hands. Instinctively I turned and ran, with the irate bird in hot pursuit. Back at the stables I was informed by a colleague that I was clutching in my hand the rear feathers of a rhea, a three-toed ostrich native to South America.

Once in a while I went to London to attend meetings, and during one such visit I decided to drop in at Canada House to see Mike Pearson. During my stay in London in the fall of 1939, while I was waiting for the basic training I never got, Pearson had told me that there was to be an open competition for a position as third secretary in Canada's foreign service. He urged me to write the examination, even though I pointed out to him that I had joined the British army and was in no position to accept a civilian appointment. 'It might come in handy after the war,' he replied, possibly on the assumption that the war wasn't going to last long. So I wrote the examination and promptly forgot about it.

When I saw Pearson again in the spring of 1940, he informed me that I had stood first among those candidates who wrote the examination in London. Canada House, he said, was desperately understaffed: would I be interested in helping them out? I said I would, provided the Canadian government could persuade the War Office to release me from the British army. In the back of my mind was the thought that a stint at Canada House might serve as an ideal stepping-stone to enlistment in the Canadian armed forces, which was still my ultimate objective. I reported for duty on 15 June 1940, just as the German forces were closing in on Paris. Two days later, the French sued for an armistice.

I couldn't have joined the foreign service at a more eventful time. The Battle of Britain began on 10 July with the first of many daylight raids on docks, shipping, airfields, and centres of communication. Then in September the enemy bombers switched their attacks to England's major cities, mainly London. Some fifty thousand civilians were killed or injured by these raids before the end of 1940. Throughout this traumatic year and the year after, until the Japanese attack on Pearl Harbour in December 1941 and America's entry into the war, Canada was Britain's principal ally. Canadian forces under General McNaughton built and manned the defences in the south of England. Canadian military headquarters had been set up in London. Back home, Canada's production of munitions and war materials was being co-ordinated with that of the United States, in accordance with the Hyde Park Agreement signed by Franklin Roosevelt and Mackenzie King. The Commonwealth Air Training Plan was getting under way.

This was no time for a fledgling third secretary to undergo formal training in diplomacy. My apprenticeship consisted of observing and trying to absorb some of the expertise of the three remarkable men who were my superiors at Canada House: Vincent Massey, the high commissioner – a strict disciplinarian and stickler for protocol, concerned above all else with quality, beauty, and form; Mike Pearson, the official secretary, whose pragmatic style of diplomacy and ability to inspire confidence in people of all nationalities would eventually earn him the Nobel Prize; and Hume Wrong, counsellor for economic affairs, the brilliant intellectual with a rare capacity for objective analysis. Another member of the professional staff was Charles Ritchie, Vincent Massey's urbane personal secretary, soon to become my friend, whose powers of observation and sense of humour have found fitting expression in his recently published diaries. It would have been difficult to find four men who were more different in personality or outlook on life. Yet their talents seemed to complement each other, and give or take occasional differences of opinion, they worked as a remarkably effective team.

One of my first assignments was to prepare a plan for repatriating hundreds of Canadian civilians, mostly women and children, who were either living in Britain or stranded after escaping from enemy-occupied Europe. I had to assemble them in places such as the old Scala Theatre in Bloomsbury, find ships which were headed empty across the Atlantic to pick up Canadian troops, issue food vouchers to be used during the journey, arrange land transportation to the embarkation point, and entertain the children while they were waiting to leave. Apart from an occasional word of encouragement I received no guidance from Mike Pearson, who was my immediate superior. Having issued his instructions he clearly expected me to find the means for carrying them out. Only months later, when I was promoted from 'temporary senior clerk' to 'temporary junior secretary' did I discover that Pearson had written a letter to Ottawa commending me for my work.

Another of my varied responsibilities was the paperwork connected with the transport of prisoners of war and so-called enemy aliens from Britain to Canada. After the fall of France, when a German invasion seemed imminent, the British government panicked and interned all German and Austrian nationals on the assumption that they might be fifth columnists. There was no attempt to differentiate between nazi sympathisers and people who were refugees from political or racial persecution in Germany. As it turned out, many of the latter were outstanding intellectuals and artists, such as the future Father Gregory Baum, the musician Helmut Blume, and the scientist Joseph Kates, who later made important contributions to Canadian life. But at Canada House we had no access to these people and no reason to believe that they were anything but potential spies. All we got from the British were documents, and since our government had agreed to keep these supposedly dangerous individuals interned in Canada for the duration, we went ahead and made the arrangements.

It is now common knowledge that the whole affair was a major blunder, totally inconsistent with the British sense of justice and fair play. People who had come to Britain in search of refuge were being subjected to further persecution. What is not generally known is that one of the senior officers involved in this operation, Colonel Coates, actually robbed the refugees of their belongings. I first realized that something was radically wrong when I was asked by the Swiss embassy, which was handling German interests in wartime, whether we had received the money transferred by the German government for payment to German prisoners of war. The Swiss had handed the funds over to the British War Office, which was supposed to pass them on to us, since the prisoners were in Canadian custody. I said we had received nothing and promptly reported my suspicions to Ottawa. An investigation was launched and it turned out that Coates had misappropriated not only the pay of the German prisoners of war but also valuables which the anti-Nazi refugees had been ordered to hand over for 'safe keeping.' At this point Britain's judicial system did swing into action. Coates was tried at the Old Bailey, convicted, and sentenced to several years in jail. His commanding officer committed suicide.

Life at Canada House was hectic during those months of unremitting air raids. Once it became clear that we couldn't possibly get our work done if we trooped down to the shelter every time there was an alert, we decided to take turns watching from the roof for the warning flag on the roof of the Air Ministry. When that flag was raised, we knew that enemy bombers had penetrated the air defences of London and that it was time to make a beeline for the basement shelter. Fire-watching, however, called for more specialized training. In order to qualify I had to pass a test in putting out incendiary bombs as well as dragging volunteer fire victims from a smoke-filled room. Instead of using artificial respiration, we revived the volunteers from their ordeal with a shot of whisky.

Early in 1941 Mackenzie King, who was secretary of state for external affairs as well as prime minister, decided that the talents of Mike Pearson and Hume Wrong were more urgently needed in Ottawa than in London. Their transfer caused a major reorganization at Canada House and, incidentally, a substantial increase in my workload. Since Charles Ritchie fell heir to Pearson's political duties, I succeeded Ritchie as Massey's personal secretary while continuing to provide assistance to stranded Canadians, handle work related to internees and prisoners of war, code and decode telegraph messages, and, of course, attend to my air raid and fire-watching duties.

Of all these responsibilities, the one which I found the most demanding by far was the drafting of Massey's correspondence and speeches. In the midst of round-the-clock air raids and disastrous losses at sea, at a time when the survival of Britain was in serious doubt and negotiations were under way for the possible transfer of the government to Canada, Mr Massey insisted on absolute perfection of style and tone in all his utterances. Letters would be returned to me five or six times for rewrites, to the extent that it seemed to me that he polished his speeches until they glistened like his shoes. Even banalities ended up sounding like words of wisdom. There were times when this relentless pursuit of the right word or nuance almost drove me to distraction. Here we were with bombs falling all around us, and I was working on my umpteenth draft of a letter to lord such-and-such, thanking him for a gift of antlers he had seen fit to bestow on the high commissioner.

Yet, as time went on I learned to appreciate the tough apprenticeship to which I was being subjected. Nobody could have been better qualified than Vincent Massey to introduce me to the formal and ceremonial aspects of diplomacy. From him I learned that protocol is really a language, a set of rules and conventions which enable people of different nationalities, social backgrounds, and political persuasions to feel comfortable with each other, to avoid embarrassing situations, even to enjoy each other's company. He was a perfectionist, a stickler for detail who would spare no effort in planning every aspect of social functions, down to making absolutely sure that people had compatible neighbours at the dinner table. Punctuality with him was almost a fetish. Nobody working for Massey was in danger of developing sloppy habits, no matter how incongruous our activities might seem in the context of an all-out war. Hume Wrong didn't like Vincent Massey any more than Massey liked Wrong; but Hume used to say that every new recruit to External Affairs should spend at least a year being trained by the Masseys – both Vincent and his wife, Alice – in the fundamentals of diplomatic procedure and protocol.

My own relations with Massey were consistently cordial. He was a demanding and occasionally exasperating boss, but I admired the work he was doing and the way he and his wife represented Canada among their many British friends. Like other members of the Canada House staff, I was treated by the Masseys as a member of the family and invited occasionally to dinner 'just for ourselves,' or 'JO' as we called it. These informal gatherings provided me with an opportunity to observe a different side of Vincent Massey's personality: his quick intellect, his sense of fun, his acting talent, his palpably affectionate relationship with his wife. As far as I was concerned, a particularly enjoyable aspect of these JO evenings was the opportunity to renew my acquaintance with Mrs Massey's favourite niece, Alison Grant, whom I had met years earlier when her father was principal of Upper Canada College and my brother Nick was an English teacher on his staff. Like myself, Alison happened to be in England when war broke out, and she too volunteered for service in British intelligence. She was assigned to MI-5 at the War Office, and we saw little of each other before I came to work at Canada House, but during the months that followed, I became increasingly convinced that she was the girl I wanted to marry.

The one aspect of Massey's personality which I could never come to terms with was his snobbishness and his extraordinary admiration of the British upper classes. Having myself attended an English public school and reacted against its intolerance, its élitism, its basic assumption that the British were born to be empire builders, I could neither understand nor condone Massey's belief that Britain's aristocracy personified the most admirable features of western civilization. I remember accompanying him to Newcastle-on-Tyne for the launching of one of the Tribal class destroyers. Massey was invited to lunch by Sir Eustace Percy, the vice-chancellor of the university, and when I was introduced to Sir Eustace he asked whether I was by any chance related to Count Paul Ignatieff. I said 'Yes, he is my father,' upon which Sir Eustace said he had been minister of education in Lloyd George's cabinet when father came to England, that he was a great admirer of the educational reforms father introduced in Russia, and that I simply had to stay for lunch along with Vincent.

I could see this did not suit Mr Massey at all, but there wasn't much either of us could do about it. During lunch Massey started holding forth on his favourite subject – the virtues of the British and how they were the only people in the world who knew how to rule others justly and effectively. Sir Eustace looked at him quizzically. 'And in what respect, Vincent,' he said, 'do you consider that ideology different from the one we are fighting?' Mr Massey was clearly taken aback, though I am sure his faith in Britain's God-given talent to excel above all other nations remained unshaken.

Not that I was insensitive to the tremendous bravery and quiet determination of the British during those dark days of the war. The stoic courage of the people, their spirit of comradeship, their sense of humour and remarkable gift of understatement inspired awe and admiration in all observers, myself included. But that is not the same thing as putting on a pedestal those who, because they were born to titles and wealth, consider themselves superior to other humans. Father had brought us up to believe, in the tradition of Peter the Great, that privilege was nobody's birthright, that pre-ferment had to be earned by service to the country. By modern standards I'd say he went too far in subordinating individual rights to those of the state. But even so, his philosophy seemed to me vastly preferable to the British system, where an aristocratic pedigree, attendance at certain schools, and membership in select clubs were considered prime qualifications for leadership. The fallacy of such assumptions should have been evident even in 1940, considering that it was Chamberlain and his upper-class colleagues whose incompetence brought Britain to the verge of disaster. Nevertheless, British authorities went on placing unquestioning faith in traitors such as Philby, Maclean, and Blunt whose impeccable family and school credentials provided a perfect camouflage for their subversive activities.

On 21 June 1941, Hitler launched his attack on the Soviet Union and, for the first time in almost a year, the immediate threat of an enemy invasion of Britain was lifted. However, the news from the eastern front was grim. In spite of repeated warnings from Churchill, the Soviet forces were completely unprepared for war, and German tanks rolled apparently unchecked across the plains of Russia. At this point I was invited by the Royal Institute of International Affairs to speak at a meeting which had been planned to discuss the Soviet Union's attitude towards the war. The featured speaker was to have been Ivan Maisky, Soviet ambassador to Britain. But in view of the reverses suffered by the Soviet army, he decided to beg off, and I suspect he may have suggested that I be invited to take his place. We had met several times when he was a guest at Canada House – he was a highly intelligent, cultivated man who had many friends among the Masseys' social circle. I remember telling him what he undoubtedly knew, that though I was born in Russia and spoke the language I was a refugee from communism and therefore did not share his political persuasion. He asked me how old I was at the time I left Russia and when I told him, he shrugged: 'You were too young to know any better.'

In my speech at Chatham House, I told the audience that while I was not a military expert, I was proud to be a descendant of Marshal Kutuzov who commanded the Russian forces in the war against Napoleon in 1812, and I felt I could draw an analogy between that invasion of Russia and the one currently under way. I went on to predict that, unless the Germans scored a decisive victory before the onset of winter, their armour would get bogged down in snow and ice, the Russian people would unite to fight the invader, and Hitler's army would suffer the same fate as Napoleon's. It took four years and millions of human lives to do it, but eventually my forecast proved correct.

A less dramatic event but one which occupied much of our attention at Canada House in 1941 was Mackenzie King's visit to Britain. The visit did not start off on a propitious note. As the high commissioner's private secretary I had made arrangements for an honour guard to be at the Prestwick airport and had promised the commanding officer that I would signal the approach of the prime minister so that his men could present arms. What I did not realize was that Mr King would emerge not from a door but from the bomb-bay of the converted Liberator in which he had crossed the Atlantic. Not a rifle moved as the prime minister carefully lowered himself to the ground and retreated from the aircraft, presenting his backside to the honour guard.

Next to disembark was General Georges Vanier, at the time Mackenzie King's military adviser. He had lost a leg in World War I, and though he managed remarkably well with an artificial leg, he always carried a spare in case of trouble. 'Would you mind finding my spare leg?' he said to me as he left the plane. He was followed by Norman Robertson, the under-secretary of state for external affairs. When I asked Norman where I might find the general's leg, he replied that I was shouting into his deaf ear and he couldn't tell what I was saying. Jack Pickersgill, the prime minister's executive assistant and the fourth member of the official party, turned out to be deaf in the other ear and couldn't hear me either. It occurred to me that this strange delegation was not likely to add anything other than confusion to an already confused war effort.

Apart from Mackenzie King's private talks with Winston Churchill, the most important part of the visit was the speech the Canadian prime minister was to deliver at Mansion House on 4 September. King's ghost writer, Leonard Brockington, was sending over from Ottawa reams of patriotic prose about Canadian soldiers marching into battle 'shoulder to shoulder' with their British comrades. What he obviously did not realize or understand was that King and Churchill had already decided that the most important contributions Canada could make to the war effort at that particular time were of a political and economic rather than military nature. Helping to bring the United States into the war, producing equipment and supplies, and training air crews for the Battle of Britain all rated higher priorities with Churchill than providing regiments of foot soldiers. It was part of my job to take Brockington's drafts over to the Dorchester Hotel where Mackenzie King's staff were working on the Mansion House speech. 'The trouble with Brockington,' the prime minister commented at one point, 'is that he thinks all my utterances must be immortal; actually it's much more important that they be appropriate.'

Striking the appropriate note, King decided, meant expressing his faith in Britain's ability to achieve supremacy in the air. He wanted to quote a verse he had seen recently which expressed that very sentiment, and the day before he was to deliver his speech he instructed me to track down the mystery poem. Without any clue where I should look, I decided to try the London *Spectator* on the assumption that it was the kind of publication the prime minister might find time to scan in the midst of his busy schedule. I found it, of all places, in an advertisement for Gold Flake cigarettes. The verse, to the effect that 'Britain long mistress of the sea' would soon extend that mastery to the air, came from Thomas Gray, the author of the famous 'Elegy in a Country Churchyard.'

The speech was a success, which was more than could be said for the prime minister's visit to the Canadian forces in Britain. After more than a year of training and boredom, the troops' morale was wearing thin, and their patience was strained even further while waiting in the rain for a prime minister who chose to be late. When he finally arrived he was greeted with a mixture of boos and faint applause – an incident which received widespread publicity back home. King himself shrugged the experience off as an occupational hazard: 'As a politician I am quite used to being booed,' he told me.

During his entire stay in Britain, the prime minister paid only one brief visit to Canada House, and it was obvious even to a junior secretary like myself that he didn't want to see any more of Vincent Massey than was absolutely necessary. Though the two of them had been friends and Massey still called him Rex – a privilege accorded to very few individuals – King had apparently reached the conclusion, as he confided to his diary, that Massey was too anglicized, too preoccupied with cultivating high society to be a fitting representative of his country.

No doubt his suspicions would have been reinforced had he been a witness, a few months later, to the meticulous planning that went into the forthcoming Westminster Abbey service commemorating the seventy-fifth anniversary of Confederation on 1 July

1942. The king and queen had been invited, the archbishop of Canterbury was to preach the sermon, the colours of the three services were to be carried in procession to be blessed at the altar. The guest list caused Mr Massey as many sleepless nights as the bombing of London. Should he invite R.B. Bennett, who was living in retirement in England? After much soul-searching he decided that he could not welcome as his guest a man who had replaced him with a high commissioner of his own choosing when he became prime minister way back in the 1930s.

What with these agonizing decisions, the organizers didn't notice until the last moment that they had failed to invite Winston Churchill, and I was sent to 10 Downing Street to see what could be done to repair the damage. Knowing that the British prime minister was too busy running the war to spare time for high commissioners, let alone their underlings, I decided to try my luck with Mrs Churchill. I explained to her that we had intentionally not sent an invitation to her husband because we knew how difficult it was for someone carrying his heavy burden to commit himself ahead of time to attendance at this type of function. Nevertheless, we very much hoped he might come. Mrs Churchill said she understood perfectly and that, as a matter of fact, her husband would have to be in the House of Commons at that particular time. 'But if you'll take me,' she added with a smile, 'I would be glad to come.' My colleagues at Canada House were decidedly impressed when they saw me walk up the main aisle of the abbey with Mrs Churchill on my arm.

Less than two months later the Canadian forces overseas at last did go into action, and suffered unconscionable losses. The raid on Dieppe was described as a 'reconnaissance in force,' intended to test the German defences on the Channel coast; instead it turned into a blood-bath. Mr and Mrs Massey knew nothing about the heavy casualties when they left London on 21 August 1942 to welcome the troops back from Dieppe. As we approached the south coast we were stopped by a dispatch rider who told us there had been a change of plan and that we were to go to a hospital instead. Even then we were totally unprepared for the sight which awaited us. The hospital was overflowing with the dead, the dying, and the wounded waiting to be tended. The landing craft were still arriving from France, and each one brought more casualties.

This was where that remarkable woman, Alice Massey, was at her best. I was full of admiration as I watched her talking individually to the men, finding words of comfort for those in pain, reassuring the ones going into surgery, promising to write to their wives and parents. She even knew what to say to an obviously frightened German boy – he couldn't have been more than eighteen – lying there on a stretcher among the wounded. She told him, in German, that her own son had been wounded in action and was a prisoner of war in Germany. 'Don't be afraid,' she assured him, 'you'll be treated well in Britain just as I know that my son Lionel is being treated well by your people.' You could see the relief and gratitude on his face.

It would be hard to exaggerate the humanizing influence that Mrs Massey had on the life of Canadians in wartime Britain. She organized clubs for soldiers, she cooked meals and served them, she wrote to the families of members of Canada's armed forces who were killed or missing. She always seemed to know the right thing to do or say to make people feel better. I didn't realize until I returned to Canada that she wrote frequently to my mother to tell her that I was well and that my work was appreciated.

Alice Massey's talents as a hostess also smoothed the way for some of her husband's more sensitive diplomatic initiatives. The time the Masseys invited General de Gaulle to lunch is a case in point. It was in 1941, when our transatlantic convoys had suffered particularly heavy losses, and the question arose what could be done to stop German submarines from refuelling at Saint Pierre and Miquelon, the French islands in the Gulf of St Lawrence that were administered by the puppet Vichy regime. If somehow we could deny the enemy U-boats this facility, we would sharply curtail their ability to operate thousands of miles away from their home ports.

The Canadian government reached the conclusion that it had the choice between two unpalatable alternatives: either have Canadian forces occupy Saint Pierre and Miquelon, which would arouse adverse reaction in Quebec, or arrange for the Free French to do it and risk the displeasure of the Americans, who didn't like de Gaulle and considered the Free French no more than a splinter group. On balance, Mackenzie King decided that the latter was politically more acceptable, and he instructed Massey to put out feelers with de Gaulle in London.

I met the general in front of the Dorchester Hotel when he arrived in his car and conducted him to the Masseys' suite. De Gaulle had just returned from his unsuccessful meeting with Churchill and Roosevelt in Casablanca, where he had failed to obtain any recognition for his Free French forces, and he was obviously in a black mood. The luncheon started out as an embarrassingly stiff affair, punctuated by long silences from the general. Undaunted, Mrs Massey turned to him and said, in French: 'I understand you have recently paid a visit to the seaside; tell me, what was it like?' The question obviously amused him, 'Ce n'était pas pour le plaisir, madame, je vous assure,' he replied, suddenly breaking into a grin. It was as though she had dispelled the dark clouds, and the conversation flowed smoothly from then on. Further meetings were arranged, and in due course Admiral Muselier and his Free French forces embarked on their bloodless conquest of the two islands.

Being private secretary to Vincent Massey did at times involve me in some strange encounters. For instance, he had a crazy relative, a wealthy woman who decided for no apparent reason to spend the war at Claridges in London. One day she swept into my office insisting that I tell the hotel management to stop electrocuting her. 'I keep rising and falling in bed,' she explained. So I phoned the manager at Claridges, whom I knew because one of my duties was to make reservations for visiting dignitaries, and suggested that he stop electrocuting the high commissioner's cousin. He pointed out that she was crazy, which was no news to me, and that might have been the end of the incident if it had not occurred to her to ask my name. When I introduced myself as George Ignatieff, she exploded 'That's the whole trouble, the world is in the hands of foreigners,' and rushed into Massey's office demanding to know why he employed a foreigner as his private secretary. A few weeks later she was back, complaining that the hotel was swindling her, so I dutifully phoned Claridges and told them the swindling had to stop. 'What's your name?' she asked. I said 'Smith.' She was obviously pleased: 'Last time I was here there was a foreigner.'

As the Commonwealth Air Training Plan began turning out vast numbers of airmen for the defence of the British Isles, as Canadian ships fought to keep the sea lanes open and Canadian troops and supplies poured across the Atlantic, Canada's contribution to the Allied war effort became increasingly apparent. With a population less than that of New York State, Canada had become the fourth most important partner in the anti-Axis alliance. Individuals such as Beaverbrook as Britain's minister of aircraft production and C.D. Howe as Canada's minister of munitions and supply ranked with the generals as architects of victory. I'll always remember Howe and E.P. Taylor, one of the dollar-a-year businessmen recruited by Howe for his organization, arriving in Britain for one of their conferences with Beaverbrook and Churchill. They had started their journey on the *Western Prince*, which was torpedoed in mid-Atlantic, but seemed none the worse for the experience. Howe commented on the way people in that kind of predicament instinctively protect their most valued possessions. There had been some nuns aboard the *Western Prince* and he noticed how tightly they held their skirts around their legs as they boarded the lifeboat.

Unlike the Americans, who never quite overcame their public relations problems, Canadians were made to feel welcome in Britain – so much so that the hospitality extended to them occasionally went beyond the call of duty. I particularly remember a letter from a British housewife who explained that, because a Canadian soldier had spent his leave in her house, both she and her daughter were pregnant. To compound the felony, the visitor had taken off with her daughter's bicycle. 'She needs same to go to work,' the letter concluded without apparent rancour. 'Please have it returned.' We did.

Though I welcomed these occasional bits of comic relief in an otherwise exacting and exhausting job, I remained convinced that my place was in the army rather than behind a desk at Canada House. After the Dieppe raid, both Charles Ritchie and I spoke to Vincent Massey and asked to be released so we could join our contemporaries in the armed forces. He was non-committal but promised to look into it. Some time later we both got letters from the prime minister to the effect that we were serving our country more effectively at Canada House than by being at the front, and that we were therefore to remain at our posts in London.

Meanwhile the war had finally begun to turn in our favour. The German surrender at Stalingrad, the British victory at Alamein, and the Allied conquest of North Africa all led up to the landing in Sicily in July 1943. A crisis of sorts developed when Mackenzie King discovered that the draft communiqué which was to be issued the day of the landing made no reference to the participation of Canadian forces. He instructed Canada House to make representations at the highest level to have the omission corrected, but when Vincent Massey tried to reach Churchill, he was told that the British prime minister was in conference and could not be disturbed. As a result I was dispatched to 10 Downing Street with instructions to get hold of the highest placed person possible and make sure the Canadian division received appropriate mention.

I dutifully sent word to General Ismay, military secretary to the war cabinet and chief staff officer to Mr Churchill, that I had a message from the prime minister of Canada. Ismay looked unshaven, crumpled, and desperately tired as he listened to me deliver my little speech. 'The Prime Minister of Canada attaches the utmost importance to this change so that the communiqué should accord with the facts,' I concluded, probably sounding insufferably pompous. 'No doubt he does,' replied the general. 'But I'll have you know that we have been in that conference room for forty-eight hours, planning every aspect of this landing from the state of the tides to the rations, and here you come at the last moment with a demand to change the wording of the communiqué.' He paused for an instant, then added: 'All I can say is that this war is becoming too complicated to wage.'

Not only was the war becoming increasingly complicated; so were the plans for the impending peace, and the kind of world order that would emerge from it. To help plan the part Canada should play in the post-war world, I was recalled to Ottawa in March 1944. I left London with some overwhelming impressions imbedded in my mind. One was the conviction that, since modern warfare does not distinguish between civilian and military targets, civilians should have more say in decisions concerning national defence. In a sense it could be argued that the war was won just as much in the streets of London and Coventry and dozens of other cities as it was in the air and at sea and on the beaches of Normandy. It therefore seemed to me self-evident that civilians should participate in decisions which might lead up to war or, preferably, prevent a war from happening.

For my own part, living through the blitz reinforced in me the horror of war that I first felt as a child in Russia. I remember being on duty at Canada House one Sunday morning after the *Luftwaffe* had concentrated its attacks on Whitehall. Pearson was still official secretary, and together we watched the charred remains of civil service files fluttering in the wind as the fires were burning out of control all around us. Pearson said something to the effect that civilization could not stand much more of this kind of destruction and that we would have to try to stop it. I knew what he meant: it wasn't a case of giving in to the Germans, but rather working for peace in the future. This was about the only time I heard Pearson express personal feelings; he was not a communicative man. But he was dedicated to peace, as I was and still am. In spite of innumerable disillusionments, I remain convinced that that is the direction in which we have to go, because the alternatives are so appalling.

SIX

Junior planner

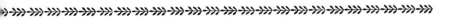

'What is agreed upon before the end of the war is likely to determine the course of history for many years to come,' Hume Wrong told the cabinet war committee in March 1944. As associate undersecretary of state for external affairs, Wrong was convinced that the time had come to establish a formal post-war planning mechanism similar to the one that had been in existence in Britain for some time. It was not, he told the cabinet, a case of Canadians deluding themselves that they could determine the major directions in which the world was going to move; but Canada could and should study the major issues and analyse the plans that were being developed by the great powers 'so that we can comment on them from the Canadian point of view.'

The need for more systematic post-hostilities planning had been becoming increasingly apparent during the previous year. As early as December 1942 External Affairs had been advised by Britain's secretary of state for dominion affairs that the British government was studying 'problems which will arise as the war draws to a close and in the immediate postwar period.' Two ·further telegrams addressed to External Affairs in June 1943 informed the Canadian government that the United Kingdom was ready to discuss problems connected with the end of hostilities with the governments of the United States and the USSR. One of the telegrams asked specifically whether Canada was prepared to participate in the proposed United Nations Commission for Europe.

Two or three years earlier, the answer would almost certainly have been 'no.' Mackenzie King was notoriously allergic to international commitments, and he had little faith in either the League of Nations (he called it the League of Notions) or any organization that might eventually take its place. But he was also highly sensitive to public opinion, particularly with an election looming on the post-war horizon and public opinion had undergone a noticeable shift in the early forties. John Holmes, at that time executive assistant to the under-secretary of state, Norman Robertson, reported in a study of views expressed in the press and in Parliament that pre-war isolationism and reluctance to become involved in European affairs had given way to a widespread conviction 'that Canada has special interests which she cannot afford to have neglected in war or peace councils.' External Affairs officials made sure that Holmes' study found its way to the prime minister's desk.

In point of fact, Canada's vote did not count for much in the councils of war. Ever since Pearl Harbor there had been a tacit agreement that major military decisions should be taken by those members of the alliance whose forces far outnumbered all others on the battlefield. But once the shooting stopped and the job of rebuilding began, Canada, by virtue of her economic strength and acknowledged role as the 'arsenal of democracy,' was obviously going to be involved at least as much as Britain, probably more. As the government said in its reply to the London telegrams, Canada expected a membership on the United Nations Commission not only because of the country's military contribution to the victory in Europe, but also because of the extent to which Canadians were going to participate in the commission's relief and rehabilitation responsibilities.

In other words, there was to be no taxation without representation. This was the so-called functional principle which, incidentally, has governed Canada's participation in international organizations ever since: that if we were to make a major contribution in any given area, we would have to be part of whatever decision-making body was set up for that area.

Canada's commitment to the political, social, and economic order in post-war Europe and the growing realization that victory was finally in sight underlined the need for concerted planning. By the time I arrived in Ottawa in March 1944, Wrong had persuaded the government to approve a two-tiered planning structure with a clearly defined mandate and objectives. On the upper level was the post-hostilities advisory committee, which consisted of the secretary of the cabinet (Arnold Heeney), the under-secretary of state for external affairs (Norman Robertson), the three chiefs of staff, and the deputy minister of finance (Clifford Clark). Other senior officials such as Graham Towers, the governor of the Bank of Canada, or his deputy, Louis Rasminsky, frequently attended the committee sessions.

The function of this high-powered group was to present the war cabinet with policy recommendations based on studies undertaken by the planning committee under its chairman, Hume Wrong. John Holmes was the planning committee's secretary, and I was assistant secretary until the fall of 1944, when John was transferred to London and I took his place.

Most of our work consisted of drafting commentaries on proposals that came to us from London or Washington. Essentially our role was to make sure that the British and Americans knew where Canada stood on the issues they were discussing and the extent to which we were willing to participate in any decisions the major allies might arrive at. As chairman of the so-called junior drafting committee, I was supposed to iron out any interdepartmental or inter-service differences before submitting our proposals to the planning committee. There they invariably underwent extensive revisions before proceeding for approval to the advisory committee and finally to cabinet.

Some of the issues were relatively simple. On the subject of post-war defence arrangements, for instance, it was obvious that, in future, our security was going to be much more intertwined with that of the United States than with Britain's. This was in line with the Ogdensburg agreement and Franklin Roosevelt's pledge to Mackenzie King that the United States would not stand idly by if there were a threat to the security of Canada. So the recommendation to establish the permanent joint board on defence went through quite easily, though the Canadian government may have interpreted its purpose and implications differently from the Americans.

On the other hand, a study of Commonwealth defence plans produced fireworks even within our junior drafting group. The study was prompted by a message from Lord Cranborne, Britain's dominion secretary, requesting clarification of Canada's stand. For instance, would Canada consider herself at war whenever Britain was at war? The only guideline we had was a cryptic note from the prime minister to 'go back to 1939.' What did he mean? Lt Colonel Hogg, the army spokesman in our group, interpreted King's directive as a reaffirmation of unconditional loyalty to Britain. Any time the mother country was at war, Canada would fight by her side.

I disagreed. To my mind, the prime minister was reminding us that, in September 1939, he had deliberately waited several days after Britain's declaration of war before announcing Canada's decision to fight, subject to parliamentary approval. Indeed we discovered that, through some oversight, Canada never did declare war on Bulgaria, one of Germany's reluctant allies. As I understood it, 'Go back to 1939,' meant that no one other than Canadians themselves could decide whether or not the country was at war.

Hogg protested that, because many Canadian regiments were affiliated with their British counterparts, it followed that every self-respecting Canadian officer would have his sword out of its scabbard the moment his king was at war. As someone who wasn't British, he added, I presumably couldn't understand such feelings of loyalty. I replied that I understood perfectly, all the more so since my brother was overseas with the Calgary Highlanders, a regiment affiliated with the British army's Argyle and Sutherland Highlanders. But that surely was not the point. Our job was to try to interpret the wishes of the prime minister rather than follow our personal inclinations.

I might have added that he was one of only two Canadians I ever encountered in the course of my public service career who ever implied that I was a foreigner. The other, curiously enough, was Greg Clark, the well-known journalist who came to Britain to report on Canada's war effort while I was still at Canada House. As

Vincent Massey's secretary I was assigned to entertain him and a group of other visiting newspapermen. 'George,' Clark said to me at one point, 'you'll never be a Canadian until you're six feet under good Canadian soil.' I have no idea what he meant, unless he was referring to my English accent. But I do know that, having been for many months exposed to the German blitz while Clark was safe in Toronto, and having done my best to serve Canada under rather difficult circumstances, I found the remark gratuitous and offensive.

As for joint Commonwealth defence, Lord Cranborne's question remained unanswered until after the war and the change of government in Britain. During King's post-war visit to England and his conversations with Prime Minister Attlee, he accepted a proposal which fell far short of any commitment to join Britain in any future conflict. Essentially, it was an undertaking to station Canadian defence staff representatives in a liaison capacity in London. According to King's published diary, he told Attlee that this arrangement would be similar to the one we had with the United States which, in peace-time, would amount to little more than 'some joint arrangement for the defence of our coasts.' Whatever talents he may have had as a prophet, they apparently failed him in this particular instance.

My work on the post-hostilities planning committee brought me into close contact with Hume Wrong, who to my way of thinking represented everything that was most admirable about Canada's foreign service. His experience, first at our embassy in Washington, then as Canada's permanent representative to the League of Nations in Geneva, and finally as officer in charge of wartime economic problems at Canada House in London, added up to an ideal background for post-hostilities planning. But more than his formal qualifications, it was his capacity for dispassionate, objective analysis that I found so impressive. Like his desk, his clear, methodical mind was totally devoid of clutter. He knew exactly how to strip an issue of non-essentials until its gist emerged with compelling clarity.

Wrong's intellectual approach to problem solving was quite different from Pearson's pragmatic, often intuitive style, and though their friendship dated back to their undergraduate years at university and service in World War I, they didn't always see eye to eye. A few years later, when Wrong was ambassador in Washington and I was once again on his staff, I found him one day at his desk scratching the back of his head – a sure sign of exasperation. It turned out he had just had a long-distance conversation with Pearson, by then our secretary of state for external affairs. 'The trouble with Mike,' Wrong exploded, 'is that you never know what principle he is acting on.' Pearson, he explained, was like a Houdini: tie him up in knots, drop him in the middle of an international mess, and he'll not only get himself out of it but transform frustration into a triumph. 'But ask him how or why he did what he did – and he can't tell you.'

Working for Wrong was an exciting, exacting but, rewarding experience. The text of any document with which he was associated had to be clear, logical, free of any superfluous verbiage or trace of bias. As he frequently reminded subordinates, foreign service officers were paid to think, not to feel. Shortcomings quickly fell victim to his blue pencil and piercing marginal comments. On the other hand, a draft which met with approval was pronounced 'workman-like' – the highest compliment in Wrong's vocabulary.

Like his maternal grandfather, Edward Blake, Wrong had the reputation of being an aloof intellectual, and there were times when he seemed determined to live up to that image. I was in his office one day when a member of the parliamentary press gallery phoned to ask for his comment on a subject Wrong was not prepared to discuss. 'The answer is no,' he snapped and hung up. Fortunately he reserved this disdainful manner for his superiors (including the prime minister) and people he neither knew nor cared about. With his subordinates he was invariably fair, helpful, and patient. As I discovered following the death of my parents, the aloof mask also concealed a man of rare warmth and generosity.

I was called to mother's bedside in the Eastern Townships in 1944, shortly after my return from England. She was obviously suffering from malnutrition, brought on by her obsessive fear of cancer and the notion that a starvation diet would bolster her resistance to the disease which had killed her mother and her sister. As a result she was so weak that she was unable to fight a severe throat infection she had developed.

Though she clearly knew she was dying, she retained both her spirit and her sense of humour. We spent most of the last night talking, and in the morning she asked me to bring her something to drink. When I suggested tea, she indicated that a glass of port would be much more acceptable. Deeply grieved by her death, father lived on for less than a year before he suffered a fatal heart attack. Up to the end, he was keenly interested in world affairs. Just before he died he expressed the hope that the Allies would have the wisdom and foresight to leave Japan's emperor on his throne rather than putting him on trial as a war criminal.

To the chants of the requiem mass of the Russian Orthodox church, my father was buried beside his wife in the Presbyterian cemetery of St Andrew's Church at Mount Pleasant in Upper Melbourne, on a site overlooking the magnificent Eastern Township landscape they loved so well. The grey granite slab with the Orthodox cross which marks their grave stands out clearly among the surrounding white marble monuments of their Scottish neighbours.

Coming as it did so soon after my return to Canada, at a time when I was exhausted from my work in wartime London and trying to adapt to an equally demanding job in Ottawa, the death of both my parents had a shattering effect on me. Through all the years since we left St Petersburg, through all the dramatic changes in our lives, they had remained the focus of the family – a link with the past, a source of comfort for the present and advice for the future. I guess I must have come very close to a nervous breakdown.

This is when I came to know a side of Wrong's personality which remained hidden most of the time behind the cold intellectual facade. We were so shorthanded at work there could be no question of compassionate leave. But Hume and his wife, Joyce, insisted that I move in with them, and their friendship, comfort, and advice saw me through one of the most severe crises in my life. I had been appointed executor of my parents' estate, a job I wouldn't find easy at the best of times; given the condition I was in plus the unorthodox nature of my mother's bookkeeping, I couldn't make head or tail of the figures. 'George, you're hopeless,' Hume said as he watched me struggling with my task. 'Give it to me and I'll work it out for you.' Painstakingly he went through every scrap of paper and put together a statement of my parents' assets which, incidentally, turned out to be more substantial than I had been led to believe. He also advised me how to liquidate the estate and divide the proceeds among the five surviving brothers.

Eventually I began to resume the social life of a junior foreign service officer. A dilemma arose one night when I remembered that I was supposed to attend a formal dinner at the French embassy, only to realize that I had no idea where to find my dinner jacket. 'Take mine,' Hume said with characteristic generosity. I went upstairs and put on the first dinner clothes I could lay my hands on. They felt a bit tight, and when the Wrongs saw me they almost collapsed laughing. Apparently I was wearing the finery of their teenaged son, Dennis, and Joyce assured me I looked just like a busboy.

It was too late to change and I hurried off to the party, where I found myself sitting beside Mademoiselle de Hautecloque, one of the French ambassador's many daughters. After five years in wartime London I was not accustomed to five-course gourmet meals, and by the time we finished the entrée, I heard an ominous tearing sound coming from the back of my pants. I tried to compensate by releasing the pressure in front and managed to finish the meal without mishap. After dinner, Madame de Hautecloque suggested that I take her daughter to the ballroom for a waltz. I had learned to waltz during my student days in Vienna, and under normal circumstances I would have been delighted to display what I considered to be one of my few social accomplishments. But on this particular night, circumstances were far from normal. We had barely taken a few steps on the dance floor when the back seam of Dennis Wrong's trousers gave way and they fell to the floor. All I could do was pick up the pieces and make a dash for the exit.

Meanwhile events in Europe and the Pacific were moving rapidly towards a climax. The victory which for so many traumatic years had been an elusive goal was almost upon us, and the far away future suddenly loomed as the present. The United Nations concept, first mentioned by Roosevelt and Churchill in 1942 and subsequently fleshed out at conferences in Teheran, Quebec City, Yalta, and Dumbarton Oaks, was about to be translated into reality in San Francisco.

It was my responsibility, under the direction of Hume Wrong and with the assistance of some of my colleagues, to pull together and digest the mounds of paper produced during years of discussions and negotiations, analyse paragraph by paragraph the proposals that were to be placed before the founding members of the United Nations, and attempt to clarify the Canadian position. This monumental task had to be accomplished in a matter of days and, hard though we tried, we didn't finish until Mackenzie King and the other members of the Canadian delegation had boarded the train for San Francisco. I ran to the railway station and barely managed to push the suitcase that contained the fruits of our labours on the observation platform of the club car as the train moved out of the station. On the way back I met Arnold Heeney, who suggested I might have saved myself the trouble. He considered it highly unlikely that the prime minister had the time or the inclination to read all those laboriously produced commentaries.

Throughout the existence of the post-hostilities planning committee, Hume Wrong insisted that its members must not become ivory tower theoreticians divorced from the realities of the outside world. This is why none of us spent more than half our time on the planning committee and we continued to carry departmental responsibilities. I was in charge of the Commonwealth and United Nations desk, and when a large contingent of foreign service officers, headed by Norman Robertson and Hume Wrong, left to attend the San Francisco conference, I was appointed External Affairs duty officer.

Consequently I found myself handling all the communications that were coming through in connection with the end of hostilities in Europe. Most of the messages seemed to arrive in the middle of the night, and if they were important enough, I'd phone the finance minister, J.L. Ilsley, who was acting prime minister, get him out of bed, and take a taxi to his home to discuss what should be done. When General Montgomery accepted the German surrender on the western front, Ilsley assumed that the war in Europe was over and proceeded to broadcast an announcement to that effect. I tried to argue with him that, technically, such an announcement was premature, but he insisted on going ahead anyway. Canadians, he said, were entitled to know at the earliest possible moment that there would be no further casualties in Europe. We promptly received a stiff reprimand from Winston Churchill: VE Day, he informed us in no uncertain terms, would not take place until the surrender had been signed in Berlin by the Soviets as well as the western allies.

For me personally, the end of the war meant that I could look forward to an early reunion with Alison Grant, the girl I'd left behind in London. We had not seen each other for well over a year, though we had managed to keep up a regular correspondence with the help of John Holmes and Charles Ritchie, both of whom acted as our couriers and so overcame the delays normally encountered in wartime by transatlantic mail. Alison came back on a troopship, and as soon as I knew she had landed, I arranged to have myself invited for a week-end at Batterwood, the Masseys' home in Port Hope where they were enjoying a well-earned rest. I knew I had a staunch ally in Mrs Massey and I assumed, correctly as it turned out, that she would invite Alison for the same week-end.

I proposed in the rose garden, a truly romantic setting whose privacy was shattered only by Mrs Massey's voice pointedly announcing, 'I think I hear someone making a speech,' as she steered visitors to other parts of the beautiful grounds. The speech was successful and we celebrated our engagement over champagne with the Masseys and Alison's mother (Alice Massey's sister), Maud Grant. All our friends and colleagues seemed pleased with the news. 'You are to be congratulated,' said a typically tongue-in-cheek message from Mike Pearson. 'I don't know what to say to Alison.'

We were married in Montreal, in the United Church in deference to Alison's family and in the Russian Orthodox Cathedral for the sake of mine. The services seemed endless, particularly the Russian one with its full mass and singing by the cathedral choir. When it came to asking Alison whether she would have me for her husband, the bishop, who had learned what little English he knew from Ukrainians in western Canada, enquired: 'Do you take this boy for permanent – yes?' But he made up for his linguistic shortcomings at the end of the service when he mustered all the English at his command to pronounce the benediction. 'Now you are best friends,' he concluded. In retrospect, I can't think of a better prescription for a happy marriage.

Along with most Canadians, I was basking in the afterglow of the Allied victory in Europe and the formal birth of the United Nations organization at San Francisco when atomic bombs exploded over Hiroshima and Nagasaki. Incredible though it may seem today, all our post-hostilities planning had been done in total ignorance of the existence or potential impact of nuclear weapons. The Manhattan Project, as it was known in the United States, or Tube Alloys, as it was christened by the British at the Quebec City conference in 1943, was not revealed to junior planners like myself until the bombs were actually detonated over Japan.

The advent of the nuclear age revolutionized conventional thinking about war and peace. Instead of being the ultimate means for settling international disputes, war suddenly became unthinkable, a monstrous threat to the survival of mankind. In the words of Canada's General Burns, the real enemy was no longer any ideology or nation, but rather war itself.

The bomb had a profound effect on my career and on my philosophy of life. Because I was already secretary of the post-hostilities planning committee, I was also appointed secretary of the advisory committee on atomic energy, a cabinet subcommittee under C.D. Howe charged with preparing legislation on the control of uranium mining and drafting the various regulations which were to become part of the Atomic Energy Control Board's mandate. This appointment, in turn, launched me later that year in a new direction within Canada's foreign service. On a more personal level, the prospects of nuclear warfare reinforced the commitment to peace with which I had left London, and my determination to do whatever I could to prevent such horrors as the devastation of Hiroshima and Nagasaki from being repeated.

Even then, I had no illusions that maintaining the hard-won peace was going to be easy. As early as July 1944, the advisory committee on post-hostilities planning had based one of its reports

on the assumption that North America could count on being safe
from enemy attack for ten years following the end of the war, but
not necessarily beyond that. 'Even if tension were to become acute
between the USSR and the US,' the committee told the war cabinet,
'the problems of recovery and development in the USSR are so great
that the possibility of warfare between these two great powers
during the next decade is extremely remote.' Hardly reassuring
words with regard to two countries which were supposedly staunch
allies fighting a common enemy.

During the following months, as the triumphant Red Army advanced towards the heart of Europe, it became increasingly apparent that Soviet plans for the post-war world were vastly different
from those of the western allies. Any optimism I personally may
have felt was severely jolted by my correspondence with Arnold
Smith, an old friend from University of Toronto and Oxford days
who joined the foreign service in 1943 as third secretary at our
embassy in Moscow. As late as July 1944, Arnold assured me that
Russian leaders had no intention to 'socialise Poland or to interfere
at all drastically in internal Polish affairs.' All they did want, he
claimed, was secure borders and neighbours who did not harbour
hostile intentions towards the USSR.

As time went on, a note of doubt crept into Arnold's letters. He
admitted he might have underestimated the 'dangers of exclusive-
ness,' that is, the intention of Soviet leaders to impose governments
of their choice on Poland and other countries in eastern Europe.
Even so, I was not prepared for the passionate denunciation of
Soviet policies and practices which arrived in April 1945. He quoted
instances of 'hypocrisy and bland lying' in connection with both
Poland and Romania and described incidents which, in his words,
amounted 'at best to extremely sharp practices and at worst to
breaches of international agreements.' A month later, while the
United Nations was going through its birth pangs in San Francisco,
he went even further. 'How sure are you in your own mind,
George,' he asked in his last letter from Moscow, 'that a world
organization which includes the USSR is really a gain rather than a
liability for the long-run security of our civilization?' Coming as
they did from a man whose political leanings I knew to be liberal

and who had gone to Moscow wearing rose-coloured glasses, these letters had a profoundly disturbing effect on me.

Another potential threat to peace was emerging within the so-called third world, where dozens of former colonies were to be governed by the same revolutionaries who had fought successfully for their independence. The borders of these countries had been drawn in years past without regard to deep-rooted tribal loyalties and with no thought of eventual self-government. It did not require much imagination to foresee hostilities erupting between some of these newly created nations or the tug of war among the major powers for control of their political and economic destinies.

Finally, I was alarmed by the differences I could see developing in Canada between the military and civilian planners on the post-hostilities committee. To some extent, these differences were obscured so long as victory on the battlefield remained the over-riding common objective. But the closer we came to peace, the more obvious it became that the chiefs of staff and their subordinates considered national defence to be their exclusive domain.

In years to come, I became increasingly convinced that my alarm was fully justified.

SEVEN

At the UN
with McNaughton

》-》》

The most devastating threat facing the United Nations from the time of its creation has been and remains the possible outbreak of nuclear warfare. Was there a way of neutralizing that threat and making sure that this awesome source of energy was used exclusively for peaceful purposes? In the hope of arriving at a universally acceptable answer, the United Nations created as one of its first agencies the Atomic Energy Commission, consisting of members of the Security Council plus Canada. We were to have a seat on the commission whether or not we were on the Security Council, because of the part Canada had already played and would continue playing as a source of research and supplier of uranium.

When it came to appointing Canada's first representative to the Atomic Energy Commission, Mackenzie King enquired what kind of delegates the other member countries were choosing. He was told that some were sending diplomats, others scientists, and others politicians. 'I'll send McNaughton,' announced the prime minister. 'He's all three.' On the face of it, the validity of that statement was debatable. General A.L. McNaughton's scientific credentials were admittedly impressive; as a wartime commander, an engineer, and former president of the National Research Council, he knew more about the physics and potential impact of nuclear weapons than some of our scientific advisers. But his brief stint in politics, as minister of national defence in the King cabinet, had been marked by controversy and defeat at the polls. As for diplomacy, the general's forthright speech and decisive manner were not exactly consistent with the image of a smooth, discreet negotiator of compromise solutions. The fact that he proved an extremely effective ambassador is a tribute to his many other talents, and proof that diplomats are not necessarily all cast in the same mould.

Immediately after his appointment McNaughton was asked whom he would like to have along as his External Affairs adviser. 'Better send me someone who knows the background and who can help me on the diplomatic side,' he replied. It boiled down to a choice between Charles Ritchie and me, and to the best of my recollection, Hume Wrong suggested we toss a coin. I guess I lost. Alison and I had only been married a few weeks, and here I was being appointed to take on a supposedly temporary assignment, without any assurance how long I would be away. To take Alison along I would have had to pay her expenses, and on the twenty-five hundred dollars a year I was earning in those days, we wouldn't have lasted very long in New York.

McNaughton and I were not strangers. We had met repeatedly in London when I was secretary to Vincent Massey and he was commander of the First Canadian Army. In those days he was a frequent visitor at Canada House, and I in turn accompanied the high commissioner, the prime minister, and the minister of national defence during the latter's visits to Canadian army units. On a more painful note, I was entrusted with drafting the top secret and politically explosive correspondence between Massey and King which led up to the general's removal from the command of the Canadian forces. It was primarily the British who insisted that he be dismissed, supposedly because he was incompetent. I don't claim to be a military expert, so I have no way of judging the validity of those claims. Going by my own observation I would be prepared to concur that he may not have been a good judge of people, and that he surrounded himself with senior officers some of whom were indeed incompetent. Unlike his successor, he never fired anybody if he could possibly avoid it.

What I did not know at the time was that, according to McNaughton, British generals such as Montgomery, Brooke, and Paget insisted on his removal because he refused to have Canadian forces split up into divisional units and used as shock troops by the British.

He told me after we became friends in New York that he had fought, for instance, the plan to have two Canadian divisions assigned to the invasion of Sicily; he saw this as a repetition of the Canadians' experience in World War I when they were slotted piece-meal into British units and sent into battles where casualties were likely to be particularly heavy.

Another thing which is not generally known is that McNaughton never agreed to have Canadian troops committed to action until he had personally reconnoitred the terrain where they would be fight-ing. He went to Dunkirk, he went to Calais and Saint-Nazaire, he went to Norway when landings were being contemplated there. He was even all set to go to Murmansk at a time when there was a possibility that Canadian forces might be sent to help the Russians. This was something I personally admired.

The general was convinced that the conscription crisis would never have arisen had his views prevailed, that there would have been no need to plug the gaps left behind by our heavy casualties if the Canadian forces had remained united under their own com-mander, subject of course to overall Allied strategy and the com-mand of General Eisenhower. He also told me that he had been approached to run for Parliament on the Conservative ticket before he joined the Mackenzie King government as minister of national defence, and that his subsequent defeat in a by-election was due to what he called 'dark forces of reaction' which stopped at nothing, not even attacks on his wife's Roman Catholicism, in their deter-mination to humiliate him.

I asked him why he had never gone public with his own version of all these events. 'My papers are in the archives,' he replied. 'Let the facts speak for themselves.'

In June 1946 McNaughton asked me to fly to New York with him for the first meeting of the Atomic Energy Commission. The weather was so bad that all commercial flights had been grounded, but the general was determined to go, and so we took off in an Air Force DC-3. Over Albany we ran into an electrical storm with lightning crackling all around the wings of our aircraft. Suddenly we seemed to be falling through space. We had hit an air pocket, and the cases of official papers which a moment earlier had been lying on the floor of the aircraft hit the ceiling. My neck felt as though I were being hanged. Frankly scared, I looked over at the general. 'It seems to be a little bumpy,' he remarked calmly while trying to retrieve his spectacles which had fallen off.

The bumpy flight and McNaughton's unruffled reaction to it turned out to be a fitting prelude to the lengthy and frustrating debate into which we were plunged in New York. Bernard Baruch, the United States representative on the commission, proposed that all aspects of the production and use of atomic energy should be entrusted to an international atomic development authority. To this extent the Baruch Plan coincided with proposals put forward earlier by Dean Acheson, President Truman's secretary of state, and David Lilienthal, head of the Tennessee Valley Authority. These proposals envisaged an international control agency to which the United States would relinquish its nuclear monopoly, provided adequate safeguards could be worked out to prevent abuses of atomic energy. It was a generous and far-sighted concept, all the more so since the Americans had no idea how short-lived their nuclear monopoly was destined to be.

The trouble was that Baruch tried to embellish the Acheson-Lilenthal proposals by adding a clause to the effect that any breach of the agreement would trigger 'condign punishment,' and that this punishment would not be subject to a Security Council veto. As a result the Soviets could claim that the plan was unacceptable because it was contrary to the agreement they had hammered out with Roosevelt and Churchill at Yalta, to the effect that any one of the great powers could veto any Security Council resolution. Personally I am convinced they would never have accepted the degree of inspection which the Acheson-Lilienthal proposals envisaged; but the fact remains that Baruch had handed them a perfect alibi.

I had other reasons to believe that Baruch lacked the negotiating skills, the flexibility, and the vision which the situation clearly called for. We had met for the first time soon after my arrival in New York, when Baruch tried to call McNaughton but was told the general was away in Ottawa. However, the telephone operator at the Canadian mission informed him, 'Mr McNatieff' was available. 'What kind of name is that?' Baruch demanded to know when I answered the phone. I of course didn't know what the operator had said. 'Well, that's something you and I have in common,' I replied. 'Both our names are of eastern European origin.' I could tell he was furious by the tone of voice with which he summoned me to his house on Fifth Avenue.

It was a palatial mansion. A butler accompanied me on my way up in the elevator and I was ushered past magnificent tapestries into a long room bristling with signed photographs of the Prince of Wales, Winston Churchill, Woodrow Wilson, Franklin Roosevelt. There were also pictures of Baruch flexing his muscles. The atmosphere reeked of such egocentricity, I almost felt as though I had been wafted back in history into the presence of Mussolini.

For the first time in my life I found myself a visitor in the home of someone who failed to get up from his chair or offer me his hand. 'What do you mean we have a name in common?' he asked. I pointed out that he was the one who had raised the subject of names, not I; besides, I didn't think there was anything wrong with having an east European name. He proceeded to lecture me about the generations of Baruchs who had been loyal Americans, about his childhood in South Carolina, about the family's distinguished record of public service to the United States. Only after I assured him that nothing I had said was intended as a reflection on him or his family did he grudgingly agree to drop the subject; but from that day on he never referred to me by name, only as 'that man.'

Besides disliking Baruch's rigid negotiating style and the way he flaunted his wealth and power, I was amused by his naïve attempts to play up to the Soviets. When Andrei Gromyko, the Soviet ambassador to the United Nations and representative on the Atomic Energy Commission, was about to celebrate a birthday, Baruch decided that a good way to demonstrate his friendship would be to arrange a surprise birthday party complete with a huge cake, the appropriate number of candles, and a chorus of 'Happy birthday, dear Andrei' to be sung by all the guests. Gromyko, who thought he had been invited to discuss atomic energy with Baruch, was a picture of embarrassment when he found himself confronted with this bit of American folklore. He looked baffled, didn't know what to say or do, and presumably concluded that the cake, the candles, and the singing added up to yet another capitalist trick. In a way he was right.

Not that Baruch had a monopoly on running into embarrassing situations with Gromyko. Even General McNaughton, who tried hard throughout his stay in New York to be an apostle of peace and understanding, unwittingly succeeded in leaving the dour Russian temporarily speechless. It happened in March 1948, at a dinner party given by the Chinese president of the Security Council. Though more than two years had elapsed since the defection of Igor Gouzenko, a cypher clerk at the Soviet embassy in Ottawa, his revelations of widespread Soviet espionage activities in Canada were still fresh in the minds of the international diplomatic community. In the course of the evening, Gromyko complained bitterly about the artificiality of life in the United States. Everything was synthetic, he claimed, all the food was canned or prepackaged; it was next to impossible to find even such a simple item as a good fresh apple.

Henry Wallace, at that time Secretary of Commerce in the Truman cabinet, pointed out that American consumers, unlike their Russian counterparts, at least had a choice. If Mr Gromyko didn't like US-grown apples, he might find Canadian ones more to his liking. No doubt McNaughton could make some helpful suggestions. 'What are some of your favourite apple varieties?' Wallace asked, turning to the general. 'Mackintosh Reds and Northern Spies,' came the crisp reply. I wasn't there, but according to those who were, you could have heard the proverbial pin drop.

The next day the general worried that he might have offended Gromyko and actually considered writing him a note of apology, but I convinced him that wasn't necessary. Personally I thought the incident was funny, which is why I mentioned it to Mike Pearson during a telephone conversation. This upset the general even more. 'You know I don't like humour,' he said. It was one of the few times we had anything approaching a disagreement.

Though he didn't like to be crossed, McNaughton, like Hume Wrong, combined a forbidding appearance with an inner core of gentleness. His flashing brown eyes, topped by bristling eyebrows which protruded fiercely when he was angry, were often courteous and smiling, particularly in the presence of his wife, Mabel, or of children. After our son Michael was born, the general would not only play with him but mend his broken toys. Both Alison and I became so devoted to him that we decided to call our second son Andrew.

McNaughton's management style was that of a clan chieftain, a strict disciplinarian who expected absolute loyalty but not blind obedience from his subordinates. I admired his intelligence, his integrity, and his dedication to the cause of disarmament. He believed that the Acheson-Lilienthal proposals to create an international agency for the control of atomic energy were fundamentally sound; but he disagreed with Baruch's 'condign punishment' clause, which in effect meant war – the very thing we were trying to avoid – and he did all he could to bring about a compromise solution.

On the other hand, McNaughton was perfectly ready to admit that he was not a seasoned diplomat, and he was willing to accept my advice so long as I could back it up with a rational explanation. There was, for instance, the incident involving George Lawrence, an atomic scientist from Chalk River who had joined our mission as representative on the scientific committee. This committee had been formed for the exchange of information, and Lawrence, along with some of the other committee members, felt that the Americans' idea of exchange was pretty high-handed. He said so in a committee meeting, and McNaughton got up and announced: 'I disagree with what the Canadian representative has just said.' Of course all hell broke loose. I had to point out to the general that his position was completely indefensible, that he couldn't disavow in public a Canadian representative, let alone his own appointee on the committee. The general agreed, but it was too late as far as poor Lawrence was concerned. Quietly we had to change scientific advisers.

True to his military background, McNaughton had a quick eye for lines of communication, which was presumably why he located the first headquarters of the Canadian mission in the Biltmore Hotel, right above Grand Central Station. That was where Alison eventually joined me, once we persuaded External Affairs to lift its ban on wives of Atomic Energy Commission staff. The small hotel bedroom, which had to double most of the time as an office, was not an ideal home for newly-weds. Moreover, Alison was pregnant, and since there was no refrigeration for the daily bottle of milk she had been told to drink, she tried to keep it cool on the window sill. To our horror, the bottle slipped and hurtled down to Madison Avenue. We had visions of a diplomatic incident, but our reconnaissance walk around the Biltmore revealed no casualties and no trace of the bottle.

Our proximity to Grand Central Station was not much of a help when Canada was elected, late in 1947, to a two-year term on the Security Council and the general was appointed Canadian representative, in addition to his duties on the Atomic Energy Commission. The United Nations was housed at that time in a former factory building at Lake Success on Long Island, an hour's drive from our Manhattan quarters even under favourable weather conditions. Commuting back and forth made for a long day. However, it also provided junior officials like myself with an opportunity to discuss with superiors, on a more or less equal basis, some of the important issues of the day.

The Kashmir crisis, which came before the Security Council right after Canada took its seat, was a case in point. The gist of the controversy was that the majority of Kashmir's population was Muslim and therefore presumably anxious to join Pakistan, while the ruling maharajah declared Kashmir to be Indian. In a sense it was a conflict between a legalistic and a moral point of view, not unlike the one which arose many years later in Canada over the constitution. The Indians claimed that the head of state had the legal right to decide which way Kashmir was to go, whereas the Pakistanis argued that the overriding issue was a moral one: what did the people of Kashmir want?

McNaughton was president of the Security Council in February 1948 when the crisis came to a head. A cease-fire had been arranged between the Indian forces and the Paskistani 'volunteers,' but most council members clearly felt that the only equitable and lasting solution was to let the inhabitants of the country vote one way or the other. The Indian delegation threatened to walk out unless the debate was adjourned so they could go back to New Delhi for instructions. It was the first time in the short history of the Security Council that a non-communist delegation had issued such a threat, and McNaughton had to decide how the council should deal with it.

There was a sleet storm that evening, and when we tried to get back to the Biltmore we found that the Grand Central Parkway had turned into a skating rink. We skidded along for a while, but it soon became obvious that we couldn't make it. So we sat for about two hours, and that gave us time to discuss the pros and cons of all the possible courses of action the Security Council might take. I advised the general, and he agreed, that it was essential for him to take a strong stand and make it clear that no delegation had the right to leave the council. The United Nations charter clearly says that the Security Council has to be ready to meet in an emergency at *all* times; an item on the agenda may be suspended only long enough to allow for consultation.

By the time the sand truck arrived, we had worked out a solution. The next day, McNaughton announced that the Indians could go back to New Delhi for instructions if they wished, so long as they came back within a month; but Kashmir would remain on the Security Council agenda while they were gone and could be taken up at any time. He carefully avoided assigning blame for the conflict to either side, and emphasized that joint action was required for a satisfactory solution. Mr Ayangar, the Indian representative, was so impressed with his ruling that he came up to McNaughton almost in tears and said: 'You are a just man.'

At that point McNaughton suggested that Ayangar might try to persuade Prime Minister Nehru to agree that a plebiscite be held in Kashmir under international supervision. For a while it looked as though McNaughton might be asked to draft the conditions for such a plebiscite; but as far as I know, Nehru never said yes or no, and the situation has remained unresolved to this day. The maharajah has died but Indian claims to Kashmir have not, and Pakistani forces continue to occupy part of the country. After thirty-five years, UN observers are still monitoring the cease-fire.

Another crisis in which McNaughton played a crucial part was the decolonization of Indonesia. It was he who organized the conference at The Hague at which the Indonesian nationalists under Sukarno and the government of the Netherlands worked out a cease-fire which ended the civil war and led to a more or less orderly hand-over of the reins of government. I think the Dutch knew by then that their situation in Indonesia was hopeless, because there was such a well-organized, popular movement for independence and the Americans had made it perfectly clear that they had no intention of backing the colonial claims of European countries, in the Pacific or anywhere else. What was required was some international initiative which would enable the Dutch to accept the inevitable without making it appear that they were being driven out of Indonesia.

McNaughton was the ideal man for the job, not only because of his record as president of the Security Council but also because he had commanded Canadian forces; since the Netherlands had been liberated by Canadians, the Dutch trusted him and were willing to listen to his advice, so that he was able to play an extremely important role as a mediator. That was the time when I first met and worked with Joseph Luns, who later became secretary general of NATO. He was a counsellor on the Netherlands side and I was his counterpart on ours.

The third crisis with which the Security Council had to deal during McNaughton's presidency was the rape of Czechoslovakia. I had felt a particular affinity for Czechoslovakia ever since 1938, when I was a student in England and witnessed Neville Chamberlain's betrayal of that small outpost of democracy. I believed then, as I do today, that World War II might never have taken place had Chamberlain defied Hitler at their meeting in Munich and sided with the Soviet Union in defence of Czechoslovakia.

In 1947 I sat in the UN General Assembly listening to the Ukrainian representative denouncing Canada for supposedly giving sanctuary to fascist and nazi war criminals when suddenly I heard a soft but distinct voice behind me say: 'Canada is as fascist as Czechoslovakia is communist.' I turned around and saw that I was sitting in front of Jan Masaryk, Czechoslovakia's universally beloved and respected foreign minister, whose so-called suicide following the communist putsch shocked the civilized world. Those were the last words I ever heard him speak.

When the communists seized power in Czechoslovakia in February 1948, Gromyko claimed that this was the result of free elections, that the Czechs had chosen to rid themselves of the capitalist system, and that the United Nations had no business interfering in the internal affairs of a member country. I happened to be in the chair that day – McNaughton must have been away – and I moved that the voice of free Czechoslovakia should be heard on the subject; strangely enough, it was a call I was to repeat almost exactly twenty years later. The Soviets, of course, protested, but I asked for a vote, and as a result, the Czech representative of the democratic government, who was still in New York, was able to deny the Soviet version of what had happened.

But in spite of this token victory, there was no denying the fact that the coup in Czechoslovakia marked a watershed in relations between east and west and a major setback to the cause of collective security. It was the first tangible indication that the Soviets were willing to use force to tilt the balance of power in their favour, and that the United Nations was unable to do anything about it. I believe that the concept of a regional security pact and the eventual birth of NATO can be traced, more than anything else, to the communist take-over in Czechoslovakia. Had the Soviets realized what the western reaction was going to be, perhaps they would have let that little country go its own democratic way.

Another source of growing tension between east and west was the situation in Korea. In order to implement the Moscow agreement that an independent, united Korean state should be established after World War II, the United States representative on the UN Assembly's First Committee (the political committee) proposed that elections should be held under United Nations supervision in North and South Korea. It was in effect an attempt to prevent the country from becoming another Germany, permanently divided between two hostile camps. After a certain amount of haggling the First Committee adopted a modified form of this proposal, calling for elections to be held in Korea on a national rather than a regional basis, under the supervision of a United Nations temporary commission. This commission was to consist of representatives from every part of the world. Since the United States had armed forces in South Korea and therefore was not eligible for a supervisory role, Canada was to be the North American representative on the commission.

When the Americans first put the suggestion to me as the senior adviser to the Canadian delegation, I sensed that we might be heading for trouble. General McNaughton had warned me that Prime Minister King didn't want to be pushed into any international commitments, that he felt people in External Affairs such as Mike Pearson and Escott Reid were overly enthusiastic about 'this business of collective security.' I therefore put it to the Americans that they might be able to find some other formula for the composition of the commission and leave Canada out of the picture. But they insisted that Australia, China, El Salvador, France, India, the Philippines, and Syria had all agreed to serve, and that we were the only country eligible to represent North America.

So I passed the request on to Pearson, who in turn spoke to Ilsley, the acting head of our delegation. Both recognized that there might be a problem, but King was away in Europe at the time, and after consulting with St Laurent (then secretary of state for external affairs), they decided that serving on the commission was part of our commitment to the United Nations' peacekeeping efforts. At the crucial moment, however, just when the establishment and terms of reference of the commission were to come up for discussion in the First Committee, Ilsley decided he had to go to his Nova Scotia constituency to explain to the Annapolis Valley farmers why Britain had removed imperial preferences from Canadian apples. He therefore asked me to take his place on the committee.

Perhaps I had a premonition, or else I was just being my cautious self. In any case I suggested to Ilsley that it would be much more appropriate for a senior parliamentarian to speak for Canada rather than a civil servant. Joe Bradette, the Liberal member for Cochrane and chairman of the House of Commons standing committee on external affairs, happened to be in New York as a member of the Canadian delegation to the General Assembly. Why not ask him?

Ilsley agreed, on condition that I draft a statement for Bradette to read.

I drafted a rather innocuous statement which, while reaffirming our willingness to serve on the commission, pointed out how difficult it was going to be to hold elections in a country where armed forces of opposing ideologies were facing each other across a *de facto* border – particularly since the Soviets were showing no inclination to withdraw their troops. When Bradette read the statement, he threw in an aside about election results in communist countries always being ninety-eight per cent in favour of the government, and how he wished he knew how they did it because he could sure use that knowledge in Cochrane.

It was this remark which particularly infuriated Mackenzie King when he returned from England and found out what had happened. Not only had Canada entered into the kind of commitment which he was determined to avoid, but here was Joe Bradette, a man who according to King knew nothing about external affairs in general and Korea in particular, compounding the offence by making facetious remarks about this grave and potentially dangerous issue. Whether on the basis of extraterrestrial communications or just political instinct, the prime minister was convinced that Korea would lead to a major war and that the Americans were trying to involve Canada in the conflict. Rumour had it that he asked the cabinet: 'How many divisions are you prepared to commit to Korea?' Whatever may have been the source of this remarkably accurate premonition, I was glad I wasn't in Joe Bradette's shoes. Had I taken Ilsley's seat on the committee as he suggested, my diplomatic career might have come to an end much earlier than it did.

King may well have been right when he claimed that the Canadian delegation didn't know all the facts at the time we accepted the seat on the United Nations commission in Korea. But when he tried to argue that decisions taken in ignorance should not be considered binding, he precipitated a cabinet crisis. He had already sent Pearson to Washington to plead his case with President Truman. When Pearson returned empty-handed and King suggested that Canada should simply leave its seat on the Korean commission vacant, St Laurent and Ilsley both threatened to resign rather than go back on their undertaking. Dexterous politician that he was, the prime minister managed to resolve the crisis with a typically Canadian compromise. We were going to have a representative on the commission, but whoever was appointed would not take part in any substantive discussion and in the event of a vote would either abstain or leave the room. As a result, we had this ridiculous situation where the poor man always had to go to the john whenever he was called upon to cast his vote.

Unlike the Korean conflict, which started off as a seemingly harmless debate and took three years to escalate into warfare, the Palestinian situation had explosive implications from the very beginning. I was involved in discussions of the partition of Palestine from 1947, when the British dumped the problem in the lap of the United Nations. The Jewish Agency had no official status at the time, and since most of its members were of Russian origin, I acted as go-between and communicated their views to the United Nations. Two of the leading Jewish figures were Moshe Shertok, later Moshe Sharett, who was to become first foreign minister of the new state of Israel; and Jacob Epstein, who under his Hebrew name of Elahu Elath became Israel's ambassador to Washington and later London. Both came from Kiev and were familiar with my father's record first as governor of Kiev, when he put an end to anti-Jewish pogroms, then as minister of education, when he abolished all racial restrictions at Russian universities. They therefore assumed that I was their ally, which was essentially true.

Not that I was unsympathetic to the claims of the Palestinian Arabs or unaware of the contradictory promises that had been made to them and to the Jews before and during the war. Not for the first or last time, I wondered if the middle eastern problem might have been resolved if, way back in the nineteenth century, my grandfather had been able to persuade Britain to let the Turkish empire disintegrate and let the various nations under Ottoman rule exercise their right of self-determination. Apparently he pleaded his case so successfully with Lord Salisbury, who was Britain's representative at the 1877 Constantinople Conference and later became prime minister, that Disraeli was prompted to complain about Salisbury becoming 'more Russian than Ignatiev, plus Arabe que l'Arabie.'* Disraeli, of course, had the last word.

But in 1947 the humanitarian aspect of the problem – the horrors of the holocaust and the plight of Jewish refugees who had nowhere else to go – seemed to me to outweigh all other considerations. That was the way Pearson felt too. Unlike Ilsley, who kept groping for a judicial solution to the problem, who studied the Balfour Declaration and the writings of Lawrence of Arabia and all the literature I could assemble about the tangled history of Palestine, Pearson in his pragmatic way concluded that partition was a workable though admittedly imperfect way of dealing with a land which had been promised too many times to too many people. St Laurent agreed with Pearson; McNaughton tended to side with the Arabs.

Meanwhile we were making no headway with regard to control of atomic energy. Baruch was too rigid a negotiator even to contemplate a compromise, and his take-it-or-leave-it attitude cut no ice with the Soviets. When they turned down his plan for the creation of an international control agency, Baruch went before the Security Council and challenged all allies of the United States to have the courage to stand up and be counted.

Escott Reid, who was the counsellor to the Canadian delegation to the Assembly, found this so offensive that he went to see Baruch and told him it was highly inappropriate for a merchant banker to talk about courage to a general who had fought in two world wars and that he owed McNaughton an apology. This confrontation was followed by a stormy session at the Canadian mission, where Escott urged McNaughton to take a strong line with the Americans and vote against their resolution. I argued that we shouldn't allow ourselves to be swayed by sensibilities on an issue as important as the control of atomic energy, and that we ought to continue the search for a consensus. I urged the general to try to move the discussion out of the glare of publicity in the Security Council back to the Atomic Energy Commission and see if he could work out some sort of compromise, at least with regard to an early warning system to

*Robert Blake *Disraeli* (St Martin's Press 1967) 616

prevent the surprise use of what McNaughton called 'these horrible contrivances.'

After listening to our argument for a while the general phoned Mike Pearson in Ottawa – it was by then about 11 p.m. – and said: 'I am getting contradictory advice. What do you want me to do?' Escott and I were both asked to give our respective versions, after which Pearson told the general: 'You'd better take Ignatieff's advice.' He also asked Hume Wrong, our ambassador in Washington, to go to New York and see what he could do to sort out our differences. Though I didn't know it at the time, one of Hume's recommendations was that I be transferred to his staff in Washington.

Much though I liked and respected McNaughton, I was glad to leave New York. It was not just that I looked forward to working once again under Hume Wrong. Over and above that, I was anxious to put behind me the string of frustrations which had dispelled so many of my earlier hopes for international good will and co-operation. My involvement in the Baruch Plan negotiations had left me with a gnawing feeling of opportunities lost. With the benefit of hindsight I wish that, instead of opposing Escott Reid, I had joined him in advising McNaughton to vote against the Americans' UN resolution. But at the time I honestly believed that nuclear weapons were an effective deterrent to war; and since the Soviets had turned down what seemed to me like a constructive proposal for the control of such weapons, I felt the Americans were entitled to the support of their allies. Yet time was rapidly running out. That 1946–8 period was probably the last time when an agreement on nuclear arms control might have prevented the arms race that was to follow: some trade-off of non-proliferation in return for an exchange of information. Instead, there was all this posturing, as though America's nuclear monopoly was going to last forever, while spies were providing the Soviets with information the United States refused to share.

In all fairness I should add that Baruch was by no means the only influential American who opposed compromise solutions. When I visited Washington during that period, Hume Wrong introduced me to Dean Acheson, who looked at me with obvious disfavour. 'Are you one of the mice nibbling away at the noble edifice which

David Lilientahl and I so painstakingly built up?' he asked. I replied that I thought we were supposed to negotiate. 'You either accept the plan or come up with a better one,' he said. 'Nibbling away at it isn't going to resolve anything.'

On top of all that, there was the unsuccessful attempt in 1947 to continue in peace-time the co-operation on atomic weapons which had been worked out between Roosevelt, Churchill, and Mackenzie King at their Quebec City conference in 1943. The agreement stipulated, among other things, that the United States would consult Britain before ever using atomic bombs. King had already decided that Canada was only interested in atomic energy for peaceful purposes, so we were not involved in that part of the agreement.

When Senator Vandenberg, chairman of the Foreign Relations Committee, found out the terms of the Quebec City agreement, he insisted that any undertaking to consult with another government about the use of atomic weapons had to end. The way he saw it, no foreign power was going to tell the United States when it could use the bomb. The issue came to a head at a highly secret meeting in Washington, where I was secretary to the Canadian contingent led by Hume Wrong and Dr C.J. 'Jack' Mackenzie, head of our nuclear installation at Chalk River. Though we were not involved in the bitter argument between the Americans and the British, we were painfully conscious of its likely implications. We knew that the British had the capability to make their own atomic bombs, and we suspected that, if they did, France would probably follow suit. That is of course exactly what happened, so the 1947 conference marked the beginning of nuclear proliferation, at least among the western allies.

In the United States, the conference was followed in 1948 by the passing of the McMahon Act, named after Senator Brian McMahon who, in the words of Vandenberg, saw atomic weapons as 'the big club in the American defence closet.' According to this act, nuclear information could only be provided if it was in 'the national interest of the USA to do so in any given case.' This subjective criterion was destined to haunt Canadian governments in years to come.

All in all, it seemed that any opportunities that had existed for international control were being frittered away, that they were slipping beyond our grasp into a quicksand of suspicion and un-enlightened national self-interest. Many times since then I have searched my conscience and asked myself: was there anything we might have done to prevent the arms race which now threatens to engulf us? Had we raised our voice in the General Assembly, had we urged the Americans to work towards a compromise solution and warned of the consequences of failure, would any one have listened? The past record of the Cassandras of this world is not overly encouraging.

EIGHT

Golden age of Canadian diplomacy

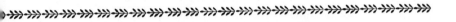

I was driving to Lake Success with J.L. Ilsley the day Mackenzie King announced that he had decided to retire from public life. Ilsley was acting head of the Canadian delegation to the General Assembly and, as General McNaughton's deputy, I had been assigned to be his adviser. We had known each other since the closing days of the war, when he was acting prime minister and I was duty officer at External Affairs. But he was a reserved man not given to small talk, and normally we would have passed the trip in silence.

The news of the day, however, gave me courage to speak up. 'I suppose many people would consider you a natural successor to Mr King,' I remarked. He shook his head: 'I haven't got what it takes to be prime minister,' he replied. I protested that he was widely respected as a man of outstanding intelligence and integrity, and that his record as wartime minister of finance was admirable by any standard. What other qualifications did a prime minister need?

'Well,' said Ilsley, 'I'll tell you a story which illustrates the difference between me and Mr King.' Early in the war, it seems, a delegation of prominent Montreal citizens came to see the prime minister and demanded that he put a stop to the proliferation of pornographic literature. After listening attentively to their presentation, King assured them that never since he entered public life had he heard a delegation plead a worthier cause. He wanted to thank each and every one of them for bringing this vital issue to his attention; and as he did so, he shook their hands and ushered them out of the door. Ilsley and Ernest Lapointe, both of whom were present at the meeting, asked King what he proposed to do about pornographic literature. 'Go back to work,' was the reply. 'That's something I just couldn't do,' Ilsley concluded. Without actually spelling it out, he was telling me that, if prime ministers had to be hypocrites who knew how to manipulate people, the job was not for him.

By that token, it shouldn't have been for St Laurent either. For all his old-world charm and courteous manner, St Laurent knew how to be outspoken when he thought the occasion called for it. I found out just how blunt he could be in the early days of the United Nations when, as secretary of state for external affairs, he decided to give a dinner party in honour of Ernest Bevin, foreign secretary in Great Britain's newly elected Labour government. At the end of the meal, Bevin got up and made a speech in which he praised Canada for standing beside Britain in her hour of need. His compatriots, he said, would never forget the way their cousins across the Atlantic had come to their assistance during the darkest days of World War II.

St Laurent was clearly nettled by the implication, real or imagined, that Canada had entered the war out of loyalty to the mother country rather than for reasons of principle. In his reply to Bevin he went out of his way to emphasize that Canada's declaration of war had been an independent decision made by the country's elected representatives, that it was prompted by the nation's determination to fight nazism and had nothing whatever to do with helping Britain. It was as though he had poured cold water on the proceedings. Bevin tried to break the tension by suggesting to Gladwyn Jebb, his senior adviser at the UN, that they sing a few popular folk songs, and St Laurent responded by asking Paul Martin to lead us in 'Alouette.' Perhaps he was trying to convey the message that, if Canada came to the assistance of any country, it was France as much as Britain.

In his insistence on Canada's sovereignty and right to make independent decisions, St Laurent was admittedly very much a disciple of Mackenzie King. But unlike King, who suspected any atttempt to involve Canada in world affairs as some sort of plot, St Laurent believed that most Canadians wanted their country to contribute to world peace and better understanding among nations. 'Our external policy shall not destroy our unity,' he told a University of Toronto audience early in 1947. He might have gone further and said that, as the son of a French-Canadian father and an English-speaking mother, he was determined to create for Canada a role in world affairs that Canadians of whatever origin or political persuasion could be proud of.

This was not always an easy task. There was, for instance, an embarrassing incident during the first meeting of the United Nations Assembly, when one of the issues under discussion in the back rooms of the UN was whether to bow to the wish of the east European bloc and pass a resolution condemning the Franco regime in Spain. St Laurent, who headed the Canadian delegation to the Assembly, invited Juan Negrin, the last president of Republican Spain, to dinner so he could sound him out on the proposal. In line with his conviction that Canada's foreign policy should be non-partisan, he also invited Messrs Bracken and Coldwell, leaders of the Conservative and CCF parties respectively.

On the subject of the proposed resolution, Negrin assured St Laurent most emphatically that it would be a terrible mistake for the United Nations to condemn the Franco regime. As he pointed out, the proud Spanish people remembered only too well the disastrous consequences of foreign intervention in the 1930s and would react violently against any attempt by an international organization – particularly one from which they were excluded – to meddle in their affairs. At that point Bracken suddenly perked up. 'Just what were all those foreigners doing in Spain in the 1930s?' he demanded to know.

In view of St Laurent's faith in collective security, his accession to the prime ministership and Pearson's entry into the cabinet as secretary of state for external affairs marked an important turning point in Canada's relations with the outside world. For the first time there was a sense of mission in our foreign policy, a conviction that, as a middle-sized power with a good deal of economic clout and international prestige, Canada had both an obligation and the ability to act as an architect of peaceful solutions to intractable problems.

For me personally, the change of command meant that two men

whom I admired and whose ideals I shared were now in charge of the government and the department which I served. This is not to say that I condone the contempt and ridicule which have recently been heaped on Mackenzie King. True, he was fussy and eccentric, he demanded a tremendous amount of service, and he was certainly not an internationalist. On the other hand he succeeded in assembling an impressive team of cabinet colleagues and public servants, he knew how to control a political situation, he dealt effectively with a series of crises that arose during the war, and when his powers began to fail, he had the good sense to resign. That is more than can be said for many politicians.

But I never felt close to Mackenzie King the way I did to St Laurent and Pearson. He was a remote character, even to those of us who were only vaguely aware of his spiritualistic pursuits. Pearson, on the other hand, was someone I had known since my student days. He had recruited me into the foreign service and I felt we operated on the same wavelength, especially since that memorable Sunday morning in 1943, when we had peered through the smoke-filled air at the devastation all around Canada House and agreed to dedicate our lives to a search for peace. Our friendship was reinforced when I married Alison, whom both Mike and Maryon Pearson had known for many years.

While I didn't know St Laurent nearly as well, I shared with him an attachment to the Eastern Townships, where he had been born and brought up. Compton, his home town where his family had a small grocery business, was not far from my parents' retirement home in Upper Melbourne. Time and again during my public service career, I have found that such local ties constitute a surprisingly solid basis for personal friendship.

St Laurent and, more particularly, Pearson tended to make decisions on the basis of intuitive judgment rather than some sort of consensus among their advisers or colleagues. This was another respect in which they followed in the footsteps of Mackenzie King, though they did not of course look to the spirit world for inspiration. This instinctive approach to problem solving did not make life easy for subordinates, as I discovered when Pearson was chairman of the United Nations commission charged with implementing the partition of Palestine, and I was appointed his adviser. On one memorable occasion I poked him in the ribs during a commission hearing and he turned on me with obvious irritation, 'How often do I have to tell you that when I want your advice I'll ask for it?' he snapped. 'I'm sorry, Mike,' I replied, 'but this is something rather important; I've just heard that Alison has given birth to our son in Toronto.' 'Well,' he said, somewhat apologetically, 'what are you sitting around here for? You should be in Toronto.'

The incident was typical of the way he operated. On the rare occasions when he did ask for my opinion, he never let on whether or not he agreed with me. He would simply listen and ask questions, and then leave me wondering what he thought of my answers. I never knew whether my advice was being accepted or rejected. In this respect Pearson was totally different from Hume Wrong, who always told me what he thought of any piece of work I had done for him, how he wanted it amended, and what he planned to do with it. As a chief, Wrong was a good deal more satisfying than Pearson.

On the other hand, I never had the slightest doubt that Pearson really had the golden touch where diplomacy was concerned. Unlike Wrong, with his highly disciplined, rational thought processes, Pearson relied on common sense and political instinct to come up with logical, practical solutions to seemingly insoluble problems. Just how effective an international statesman he was became fully apparent some ten years later during the Suez crisis. But even in those early days of the United Nations, his judgment and sense of fair play had already earned him the respect of most of his colleagues in the diplomatic community. The lone exception, to the best of my knowledge, was Australia's foreign minister Herbert Evatt.

I suspect Evatt may have resented being upstaged by Pearson, who at that time was still a civil servant and therefore technically ranked below a cabinet minister; or it may have been a simple case of personality conflict. Whatever the reason, the animosity was real, as I had occasion to discover during a 1947 session of the General Assembly. The cold war was heating up, and the Assembly was thrown into turmoil when an American state governor made a speech to the effect that the best way to deal with the Soviets would be to drop an atomic bomb on Moscow. This statement prompted Vishinsky to introduce a resolution condemning this kind of irresponsible talk and branding the United States as a warmonger.

Evatt decided that the only way to deal with the Soviet resolution was to vote it down. But a number of us in the Canadian delegation felt that the western nations would not look very credible if they refused to condemn statements inciting nuclear war. A much better idea, we thought, would be to see if we could amend the Soviet resolution and turn it into a reminder that United Nations members were committed to resolve their differences without resorting to force or the threat of force.

As Ilsley's adviser on the First Committee, I was put to work to find co-sponsors for such an amended resolution. I had no difficulty enlisting the support of the French delegation headed by Alexandre Parodi, a wonderful man who had been a leader of the Resistance against the nazis in Paris during the war. At that time, Couve de Murville was little more than a counsellor to Parodi, so I worked with Couve on the text of a joint resolution which condemned 'all propaganda in whatsoever country conducted, which is either designed, or likely to provoke or encourage any threat to the peace, breach of the peace or act of aggression.' The draft resolution also urged all member governments to promote, by whatever means may be available to them, friendly relations among nations and to 'encourage the dissemination of all information designed to give expression to the undoubted desire of all people for peace.'

But when I approached the Australians to see if they too would co-sponsor this resolution, Evatt exploded. 'This is a typical case of Pearsonian double talk,' he told me, and insisted that the only way to deal with the Soviets was to face them head-on. I pointed out that Vishinsky had a valid point, that threatening nuclear war was indeed contrary to the spirit of the United Nations charter. Besides, Vishinsky had done his homework a good deal better than Warren Austin, his American counterpart. When Austin tried to argue that the belligerent state governor was entitled to exercise his freedom of speech, Vishinsky countered by quoting outstanding American jurists, including Oliver Wendell Holmes, to the effect that freedom of speech has its limits, that it does not entitle anyone to raise false fire alarms or incite rebellion.

In the end, I was able to convince Evatt that, if he insisted on voting against the Soviet resolution, he risked going down to defeat. I had canvassed the other delegations, including the Latin Americans, and it was clear that, while they were willing to go along with a compromise, they were not likely to vote against the Soviets on that particular issue. In those days the United Nations had only fifty-one members, so every individual vote was important. Most reluctantly, Evatt finally agreed to join the French in co-sponsoring our resolution and, to our pleasant surprise, Vishinsky responded by withdrawing the warmongering charge against the United States. The compromise resolution was adopted unanimously by the General Assembly.

It was in reporting these negotiations that the press first dubbed me as 'peacemonger' – an appellation I have carried proudly ever since, even though I didn't feel fully entitled to it at the time. The strategy was Pearson's, and I had merely acted as his intermediary. Strangely enough, Evatt didn't hold the incident against me. In fact the following year, when he was president of the General Assembly, he asked me to be chairman of the Fifth (i.e., administrative) Committee, which was quite an honour for a thirty-four-year-old official like myself. But he continued to nurse his grudge against Pearson and at one point gave me quite an earful about Mike being overly cosy with the great powers instead of making common cause with middle-sized countries like Australia. 'He runs with the hares and hunts with the hounds,' was how he put it.

Evatt, however, was very much the exception, on the international as well as the domestic scene. I believe Pearson's outstanding accomplishments as a craftsman of Canadian diplomacy were acknowledged by all his External Affairs colleagues, including Hume Wrong who, though sometimes an outspoken critic, was also Pearson's close friend and confidant. I don't believe any of us spent much time wondering whether or not it was a good idea for a public servant to jump into the political arena.

I happened to be in Ottawa the day he was offered the external affairs portfolio, and I remember walking with him the short stretch from the East Block to the Château Laurier. 'How do you really feel about this appointment?' I asked him. He replied that it was, of course, a great honour and a wonderful opportunity to actually do things instead of merely advising the real decision makers. But he was clearly worried about the loss of security. As he said, 'I might find myself out on my backside after a year or two in office, and I haven't any financial resources to cushion the fall.' I tried to reassure him that a man of his ability and reputation would never lack opportunities for alternative employment should the need arise – which seemed to me most unlikely.

It was indeed a time for doing things, and whatever may be history's verdict on Pearson's performance as a prime minister, he was the right man at the right time in the External Affairs portfolio. The first of a series of wars had broken out in Palestine, the situation in Korea was deteriorating, Europe was divided into two hostile camps, and the United Nations was, as St Laurent so aptly put it in one of his speeches, frozen in futility. St Laurent was the first to say in public what a growing number of people were discussing in private: that the United Nations was not equipped to deal with an increasingly bitter cold war between two powerful groups of nations. Article 43 of the UN Charter provided for armed forces to be mustered by a military committee and put at the disposal of the Security Council whenever a member nation was threatened. But with the Security Council split wide open, no such force was likely to materialize. As St Laurent suggested in his 'frozen in futility' speech, western nations might have to look to regional defence arrangements for their collective security.

He was not alone in his search of a new approach to collective security. About the same time I had dinner with Gladwyn Jebb, the senior counsellor to Ernest Bevin, and he told me that the British were thinking of using the regional provisions of the UN Charter for some sort of European defence system, in the hope that the United States might be persuaded to participate. I reported this conversation to Pearson, and I understand it was the first indication he had that Britain was contemplating some sort of North Atlantic alliance.

St Laurent chose Remembrance Day 1948 to appeal to Canadians for support of the proposed North Atlantic Treaty Organization. 'Heaven helps those who help themselves,' he told a national radio audience. The choice, he said, was between 'isolationism with its certain weakness, and the hope through collective action of preventing another war.' Should war come, he warned, it would be fought by Canada's two powerful neighbours and would involve a conflict between 'the atheistic communist world and our democratic Christian civilization.' In such a war, Canada could not remain neutral.

Both St Laurent and Pearson agreed that to the extent that NATO involved pooling of military forces, it also implied sharing of control. As Pearson said in his first speech as a cabinet minister in September 1948, 'If obligations and resources are to be shared, it is obvious that some sort of constitutional machinery must be established under which each participating country will have a fair share in determining the policies of all which affect all.' Canada, in other words, was prepared to take on the obligations imposed by NATO so long as we had an opportunity to participate in its decisions. That was essentially the functional principle first expressed by Mackenzie King during the war, though it seems safe to say that King would never have sanctioned its application to the deployment of Canadian forces in peace-time Europe.

Part of my job as counsellor to Ambassador Hume Wrong in Washington was to negotiate the decision-making framework which would translate this principle into a practical mechanism. Out of these negotiations emerged the North Atlantic Council, which was to be the principal authority in the alliance, with responsibility for consultations on political and economic policies and supervision of all military and civilian agencies. It was to consist of the foreign ministers of member countries and was to meet once a year. Since a council which met so infrequently could not be expected to exercise effective control, it was agreed that there should be a permanent council of deputies reporting to the foreign ministers.

There was also to be a defence committee consisting of chiefs of staff, with an Anglo-American-French standing group to provide strategic guidance and act as the executive agency for the military side of the alliance. Canada decided not to press its claim to membership in the standing group for two reasons. One was that Italy, which wanted to be a member, agreed to stand down if Canada did likewise. But a more important reason was the fact that, although NATO strategy was based on the nuclear deterrent, the United States still had a nuclear monopoly and the McMahon Act prevented the Americans from sharing information on atomic weapons with their allies. For a non-nuclear power, membership in the standing group was therefore meaningless.

Throughout the planning stage, Canada argued that NATO should be more than a military alliance. As Pearson said at the signing of the treaty in April 1949, 'This treaty, though born of fear and frustration, must lead to positive social, economic, and political achievements if it is to live.' But this idea was not favoured by the United States, to whom NATO was primarily a means of bolstering European security, nor by such European statesmen as Paul Henri Spaak, who were afraid that a NATO concerned with economic and social issues would slow down Europe's march towards federalism. Had the broader concept of the alliance prevailed, NATO might have lived up to the hopes of its founders. As it was, a military partnership in which one of the players held all the trump cards inevitably led to suspicions and disagreements which undermined to some extent the effectiveness of the alliance.

The birth pangs of NATO coincided with the first head-on clash in the Middle East between the Jews and the combined forces of their Arab neighbours. The Security Council demanded and got a cease-fire; but what was to be the demarcation line between the opposing forces? Clearly the line contemplated by the UN partition plan had by then proved unacceptable to both Jews and Arabs. I had private talks in New York with Phil Jessup, one of the senior people at the State Department, and with Dean Rusk, at that time head of the department's UN Division. What was needed, we all agreed, was a UN mediator who would help the opposing sides arrive at a mutually acceptable compromise. But another school of thought at the State Department believed that the United Nations should establish a mandate over Palestine and enforce the partition plan, and that negotiations would never reconcile the differences between the Jews and the Arabs.

In the event, these discussions were overtaken by the unilateral declaration of the State of Israel and its recognition by most UN members outside the Arab orbit. In fact, I happened to be the member of our delegation to make the statement of recognition on behalf of Canada. At that point the Security Council did appoint Count Bernadotte of Sweden as its mediator, and when Bernadotte was assassinated, Ralph Bunche of the United States took his place. He established the first United Nations peace mission on the island of Rhodes, where the opposing parties came to negotiate and eventually established at least a provisional demarcation line.

Considering my intimate involvement in the Palestinian issue and the creation of Israel, I was delighted when I received an invitation to attend a reception at New York's Waldorf Astoria Hotel in honour of Chaim Weizmann, Israel's first president. Along with hundreds of other guests I joined the queue which wound its way towards the receiving dignitaries. When my turn finally came to be introduced, I held out my hand and waited in vain for Weizmann to grasp it. 'I will never shake hands with anyone by the name of Ignatieff,' he announced. I was stunned. Fortunately Elahu Elath, the Israeli ambassador to Washington, who was standing beside the president, came to my rescue. He quickly explained to Weizmann that he was apparently confusing two generations of Ignatieffs, that my father had been the governor of Kiev who put an end to anti-Jewish pogroms and the minister of education who abolished racial discrimination at Russian universities, not the minister of the interior who supposedly confined Jews to ghettos. By then I had recovered some of my composure. 'I believe we have a more personal connection, Mr President,' I said. 'My mother-in-law is the former Maud Parkin, whom you may remember from your research days at Manchester University where she was dean of women.' At that point he not only shook hands, he embraced me and said: 'To think that Maud has such a big son-in-law.'

Meanwhile, elections in South Korea had resulted in a *de facto* partition of the country, and when the communist north invaded the south, a Security Council resolution called upon UN members to help the Republic of Korea repel the aggressor. The resolution would have been foredoomed had the Soviet representative been there to exercise his veto. But because of a disagreement over the representation of China, Ambassador Yakov Malik had walked out of the Security Council, and in his absence the United States military command in Korea obtained the authority to act on behalf of the United Nations.

For Canada the Korean war had implications way beyond the participation of our forces in the Commonwealth brigade. The extension of the conflict north of the thirty-ninth parallel, the involvement of China, and General McArthur's apparent wish to transform a limited UN operation into an all out war all underlined the possibility that Canadians might find themselves involved in a major conflict whose objectives were at best peripheral to our own, under commanders who refused to share their responsibility for strategic planning with any of their allies.

The news in August 1949 that the Soviets had exploded an atomic bomb of their own did nothing to reduce the Americans' determination to hang on to their secrets and their exclusive responsibility for defence planning. If anything, that determination was reinforced by the arrest for espionage of Klaus Fuchs, a scientist employed in Britain's nuclear program, and the defection in 1951 of Maclean and Burgess, two foreign service officers previously on the staff of the British embassy in Washington. To Secretary of State Foster Dulles and his colleagues, these events simply proved that they had been right all along when they claimed that the security systems of other countries couldn't be trusted.

During my own posting in Washington I had known both Maclean and Burgess, as well as Kim Philby, the mysterious 'third man' who was unmasked as a KGB colonel years later, after he had fled to the Soviet Union. Philby was by far the most accomplished member of the infamous trio. He associated with all the right people, he delivered eulogies at memorial services to deceased patriots, he let it be known that he had been decorated by Franco during the Spanish civil war. The only thing that made me wonder about him was that Burgess, who was a repulsive, degenerate character, lived in his house. Burgess' heavy drinking, blatant homosexuality, and wild driving escapades were a constant embarrassment to Lord Inverchapel, the British ambassador, who unlike his successor apparently didn't know how to get rid of him. I couldn't help feeling that the only way Burgess could have been appointed to his position or managed to hang on to it was through a system of class privilege which was mercifully absent from Canada's public service.

Maclean, who was my opposite number in the British embassy, was a strangely tense person. We got off on the wrong foot the first time I met him, which was when Hume Wrong and I went to call on Lord Inverchapel. Maclean met us and said: 'I am afraid you'll have to wait. His Excellency has reached the pudding stage, and you know the importance we English attach to puddings.' I thought at the time that that was no way for a subordinate to speak about his ambassador. Unlike the so-called subversives unearthed by Senator McCarthy's un-American activities committee, the real spies never did attract the senators' suspicions.

I was in Washington when the committee first levelled its charges against Herbert Norman, at that time head of our liaison mission in Tokyo. Norman had been a member of some communist cell in his student days in the thirties and had openly admitted as much when he joined External Affairs. He was a gentle person, an idealist and a scholar, anything but a hard-nosed spy. Some five years later he rendered particularly valuable service to Canada and the world at the time of the Suez crisis, and I was horrified when the Americans' renewed charges of subversion drove him to suicide.

Unfortunately, the un-American activities committee turned particularly virulent in 1953, during the time when I was chargé d'affaires in Washington pending the arrival of Arnold Heeney as our new ambassador. What made me particularly resentful about the senators' allegations was that one of the people they wanted to investigate was none other than Mike Pearson. Apparently Pearson, at the time he was ambassador in Washington, conducted occasional staff meetings where confidential information came up for discussion. It turned out that a member of his staff had been a 'fellow traveller' and had fed tidbits obtained at these meetings to some sort of leftist group. With the help of their guilt-by-association tactics, the senators concluded that Pearson's own loyalty was therefore suspect.

I went to the State Department to protest in the strongest possible terms against having the reputation of a distinguished minister bandied around in this irresponsible manner. The State Department people were sympathetic but said there was nothing they could do to curb a congressional committee. I had no reason to doubt them. Indeed, ever since Eisenhower became president there had been a noticeable shift of power in Washington from the executive to the legislative branch of government, at least where external affairs were concerned. True to the military tradition of delegating authority to field commanders, Eisenhower gave Dulles almost complete freedom of action without apparently realizing that, by dissociating himself from the State Department, he was undermining its influence. As a result, when it came to dealing with the Americans on matters of mutual interest such as the St Lawrence Seaway, I found it was no longer good enough to rely on the State Department to interpret the Canadian point of view to other branches of government. Distasteful though it might seem to diplomats of the old school, we would have to do our lobbying among influential members of Congress if we wanted results.

As for the McCarthyites, their witch hunt escalated to the point where they announced they wanted to go to Ottawa to question Herbert Norman and other suspicious Canadians. Of course we refused, and I informed the committee that it was not up to them or anyone else to investigate whether Canadians were or were not un-American. I said we were quite prepared to hold hearings on un-Canadian activities, which might include the kind of character assassination the senator from Wisconsin and his colleages were indulging in. By the time Arnold Heeney arrived in Washington, there had been an editorial in the *Globe and Mail* which claimed that Canada's relations with the United States had fallen to the lowest ebb since the Fenian riots. I remember saying to Arnold that at least he had nowhere to go but up.

After leaving Washington I spent a year at the Imperial Defence College in London before taking up my new duties as chief of the defence liaison division in the Department of External Affairs. When I returned to Ottawa, St Laurent asked for a complete study of the implications of nuclear weapons for Canada's defence and foreign policies. It was obvious to the prime minister that the two policies had to be interrelated if they were to make any sense, which is why he wanted the study to be conducted jointly by External Affairs and National Defence. But General Foulkes, who was chairman of our joint chiefs of staff, was clearly in no hurry to discuss the project. Finally, on a memorable day in 1955, shortly after I had been involved in a serious car accident, he sent word that he was prepared to see me. I arrived on crutches only to be told that divulging nuclear information given to him in confidence by his friends at the Pentagon would be contrary to the McMahon Act, and that he had no intention of letting External Affairs 'eggheads' jeopardize his relationship with Admiral Radford, his counterpart in Washington. To put it in a nutshell, there was going to be no joint study: 'Is that understood?' I said it wasn't understood because it was contrary to the wishes of the prime minister, and we kept on arguing for a while. But in my weakened state, I knew I wasn't making any headway and I ended up telling him that, under the circumstances, we would have to make our own assessment of the situation. We tried to do just that, but without the required information it turned out to be a pretty futile exercise.

At about the same time, Pearson tried to persuade Dulles at a North Atlantic Council meeting to use NATO as an instrument for internationalizing control over atomic weapons, and specifically to include Canada's northern approaches among the Alliance's defence responsibilities. As he pointed out, the safety of the Arctic was just as crucial to the collective security of NATO members as the integrity of western Europe. But Dulles was not interested in either of Pearson's proposals and neither, for that matter, was National Defence. As Pearson wistfully remarked in his autobiography, 'Our own service people also, I suspect, preferred bilateral dealings and arrangements with Washington.'

Pearson's attempts to bring military power under international control proved considerably more successful in the Middle East, where Colonel Nasser's decision to seize control of the Suez Canal precipitated yet another in a long series of crises. Negotiations were under way in October 1956 to defuse the situation when Britain, France, and Israel decided to take matters into their own hands and invaded Egypt.

To the rest of the NATO alliance as well as the uncommitted nations, the Franco-British ultimatum and subsequent landings came as a rude shock. Since Britain and France would obviously have vetoed any Security Council attempt to brand them as aggressors, the Yugoslav delegate called for a special session of the General Assembly, where he introduced a resolution calling on the invaders to withdraw from Egypt. Pearson on behalf of Canada abstained from voting on this resolution.

It was not that our government condoned the attempt on the part of the allies to settle their dispute with Egypt by force of arms; indeed Prime Minister St Laurent had made it perfectly clear what he thought of this modern version of gunboat diplomacy. But, as Pearson told the assembly, it was no use telling the Israelis to withdraw their forces without also saying where they were to withdraw to. To the original partition line? The war of 1948 had made it irrelevant. To yet another temporary armistice line? Surely the time had come to start working towards a more permanent solution which everybody concerned could live with. Such a solution would have to be based on two principles: recognition by the Arabs of Israel's right to exist within secure borders, and an Israeli undertaking to abandon any territorial claims beyond those borders. It was the first time anyone had articulated what was to become the essence of all subsequent attempts to bring peace to that turbulent part of the world.

Obviously the kind of settlement Pearson envisaged could not be negotiated quickly or under the pressure of constant border clashes. He therefore proposed that a United Nations peacekeeping force be set up to act as a buffer between the Israelis and their neighbours. It was characteristic of Pearson's pragmatic style of diplomacy that the idea of a peacekeeping force had come to him almost as a flash of inspiration when Anthony Eden, in his speech to Britain's House of Commons, claimed that the invasion of Egypt would not have been necessary had there been an international force in the area.

After the General Assembly had approved the proposal in principle, I was summoned from Ottawa to New York to help Pearson organize the peacekeeping force. The next few days were absolute bedlam. There was no modern system of communication at the time, so we were using the long-distance operator of the Hotel Drake, where Pearson was staying, and the hotel's overcrowded telephone circuits to place calls all over the world to statesmen whose co-operation he was trying to enlist. Every so often I would go rushing into a room where Pearson was talking to some foreign minister or ambassador to tell him there was a call on my line from President Nasser or Prime Minister Nehru.

At the same time I was in touch with Ottawa to find out what forces Canada might contribute to the United Nations force. With remarkable lack of sensitivity, National Defence suggested that we could send the Queen's Own Rifles and have them sail on the aircraft carrier *Magnificent*. To say that the Egyptians were unenthusiastic about this proposal would be an understatement. After the events of the past few weeks they didn't care if they never saw another aircraft carrier, and as for the Queen's Own Rifles, they sounded altogether too much like the British forces they had just finished fighting.

So it was agreed that Canada would send a transport unit equipped to maintain communications between the various UNEF components rather than trained for combat. The bulk of the force was contributed by such countries as Brazil, India, Yugoslavia, and the Scandinavian countries, whose neutrality the Egyptians perceived as being beyond suspicion. UNEF's first commander, however, was Canada's General Burns, who happened to be in the Middle East in an observer capacity and could therefore assume his new duties without delay.

There was nothing in the UN charter to provide for such a peacekeeping force, and Secretary General Dag Hammarskjold at first doubted that it could be made to work, particularly with the western powers so bitterly divided. In all fairness, some of his scepticism was to be vindicated ten years later. But at the time Pearson was able to persuade him in a series of private discussions that the alternative might well be Soviet intervention in the Middle East and the danger of an all out war.

Once Hammarskjold had been sold on the UNEF plan, he spared

no effort in persuading President Nasser to accept it. Herbert Norman, our ambassador in Cairo, played a key role in these negotiations and got himself completely exhausted in the process. I have no doubt his heavy work load and the strain associated with his responsibilities contributed to the depression which overtook him a few weeks later when the Americans renewed their charges against him and drove him to suicide.

As for the British and French, they decided to accept Pearson's compromise and withdraw from Egypt rather than face condemnation not only by the communist bloc and the uncommitted nations, but also by most of their allies. Some Canadian loyalists and political opponents later accused Pearson and St Laurent of betraying the mother country in her hour of need. Strangely enough, that was not the way the British saw it. Their representative at the special session of the General Assembly was Selwyn Lloyd, Eden's foreign secretary and one of the people who were in and out of the Hotel Drake all the time during those frantic days when Pearson was negotiating the composition of UNEF. Years later, when I was deputy high commissioner in London, I was sitting beside Lloyd at a dinner party when he turned to me and said: 'It's a pity that the British have never publicly acknowledged the debt they owe to Mike for his part in the Suez crisis, because he really saved our bacon; without the international peacekeeping force, we would have been simply ordered out of Egypt and that would have been mighty difficult to explain back home.' Pearson, he said, had really thrown them a lifeline by coming up with an acceptable compromise.

Even so, the Suez crisis had left NATO deeply divided at a time when mutual trust and collaboration seemed more important than ever. The Soviet occupation of Hungary and the launching in 1957 of the first Sputnik underlined the military and technological aspirations of the Kremlin and the need for western democracies to heal the festering rift left behind by Suez. Clearly ways had to be found to make sure no NATO government would ever again spring a similar surprise on unsuspecting members of the alliance.

To work out the details for such a fence-mending operation, NATO set up a committee consisting of the foreign ministers of Italy, Norway, and Canada. As the acknowledged leader among these 'three wise men,' Pearson took along to Paris Ed Ritchie and myself as his economic and diplomatic advisers respectively. Just why he wanted advisers for whose advice he seemed to have little or no use wasn't clear to either of us, or for that matter to Pearson's Italian and Norwegian colleagues. As I had had occasion to discover ten years earlier when the partition of Palestine was under discussion, Mike was essentially a one-man show. The lengthy drafts which Ed and I produced for him disappeared into his briefcase to be metamorphosed, in due course, into a compact report that owed virtually nothing to anyone other than its author.

As a means of keeping the alliance together, the consultative mechanism which Pearson recommended has never been improved on. The report was approved in December 1957 but never implemented. If it were actually in force, the world would not, for instance, be treated to the spectacle of the United States feuding with its allies over export restrictions imposed by the US government on European subsidiaries of American companies. The problem would have been discussed beforehand and a compromise would presumably have been reached.

While Pearson did not seem to require my services as an adviser, he trusted me sufficiently to share with me his concern over a dream he had during our stay in Paris. He dreamt, he told me, that he was attending his own funeral. What bothered him was not the thought of dying, but the sight of a gun carriage, muffled drums, and flags at half-mast – all the pomp usually associated with state funerals. What could it mean? 'Mike,' I said, 'you've had a premonition. Some day you will be prime minister, and when you die, the country will give you a state funeral.' He muttered something about talking nonsense and changed the subject.

What was it about Mike Pearson that made him such an effective diplomat? Partly it was his intuitive ability to spot an opportunity for a compromise and capitalize on it. Alone among all the delegates to the United Nations, he realized that Eden's apologetic line about the non-existence of an international peace force in the Middle East provided a perfect opening for the creation of such a force and a compromise resolution of the conflict. Equally important was his ability to inspire confidence in the people with whom he dealt;

everybody trusted him, from the Israeli prime minister all the way to Egypt's president, not to mention non-aligned statesmen in Asia, Africa, and Latin America. He really deserved the Nobel Peace Prize because it was his imagination, common sense, and powers of persuasion that produced a workable solution. Of course that solution crumbled ten years later. But ten years of peace in that explosive part of the world must be counted as a major accomplishment.

Though my own part in the Suez negotiations was insignificant, it did provide me with a ringside seat for a suspenseful drama whose next instalment was to involve me to a much greater extent. Suez taught me two valuable lessons. One was that international crises are not resolved by coming up with a grand design, a perfect solution where every piece fits neatly into its appointed slot. Pearson knew, and taught me by example, that the only way to preserve peace is by negotiating a series of admittedly imperfect and temporary, but nevertheless acceptable compromises.

The other lesson I learned was that even a diplomat of Pearson's calibre can only be effective if, in addition to all his talents, he also has political clout. In a crisis situation you have to be able to make instant decisions rather than dither and say, 'Well I don't know whether my government will agree.' Pearson had that kind of clout because he had the complete confidence of the prime minister. They trusted each other implicitly, each understood the other's thinking, they spoke to each other several times a day on the telephone. Whenever an issue came up which required cabinet approval, Pearson knew he could get St Laurent to go to his colleagues and come back with a quick decision.

In my opinion, the St Laurent-Pearson combination was every bit as important for Canada's foreign policy as the Macdonald-Cartier partnership was for Confederation. Later in my career I discovered personally just how productive this kind of relationship can be. Later still, I found out the extent to which lack of communication and absence of mutual trust between a country's representative and his government can turn diplomacy into a frustrating, soul-destroying experience.

NINE

Russia revisited

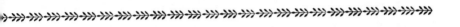

'A riddle wrapped in a mystery inside an enigma' is how Winston Churchill described the plans and future actions of the Soviet government in the early days of World War II. To western observers, the description seemed equally apt a quarter of a century later following the death of Joseph Stalin. Which of the so-called collective leaders was going to emerge as the dictator? Did the change of command in the Soviet Union constitute an increased threat to the NATO countries? What were the priorities, the concerns, the thought processes of these virtually unknown characters who were now governing the second most powerful country in the world?

It was in the hope of reaching at least tentative answers to some of these questions that Pearson accepted Molotov's invitation to visit the Soviet Union in the fall of 1955. The prospect of improved trade relations was an additional but decidedly secondary motive. The trip was essentially a voyage of reconnaissance into terrain where no Canadian foreign minister or, for that matter, any of his NATO counterparts had ever ventured before.

Since I was not dealing with Soviet affairs at the time, Pearson's phone call came as a complete surprise. 'I think it would be a good idea if you came with me to the Soviet Union,' he said. I replied that I was sorely tempted, that I found the prospect of visiting my native country almost irresistible. Nevertheless, I was bound to point out that there might be problems, that my Russian origin and tsarist connections might prove to be more of an embarrassment than a help to his mission. But he brushed aside my objections with a typically Pearsonian comment: 'George, if you're any trouble I'll simply dump you.'

I wasn't sure it would be that simple. Though little was known about the current interregnum in the Soviet Union, there was nothing to suggest a change in that part of the party dogma which claimed that anyone born in Russia was by definition a Soviet citizen. I discussed Pearson's invitation with Alison and told her frankly that, in my opinion, I would be taking a risk by going, that it was quite conceivable our hosts would stage an 'accident' or use some other means of preventing me from returning to Canada. A number of ex-aristocrats who had been invited to visit their home-land during the Stalin regime had in fact disappeared without a trace. But in the final analysis I reached the conclusion that I could never live with myself if I refused to go; that I would stand con-victed in my own eyes as a coward or, worse still, as someone who wasn't sufficiently sure of his Canadian identity to dare confront his Russian roots.

We arrived in Moscow in mid-afternoon on 5 October. Accom-panying Mike and Maryon Pearson were Mitchell Sharp, who was then deputy minister of trade and commerce, plus an External Affairs contingent consisting of John Holmes, Ray Crépault, and myself. There was also a flock of Canadian journalists, including an as yet obscure CBC reporter by the name of René Lévesque.

The visit did not start off on a happy note. Exhausted and suffer-ing from jet lag (the time difference between Ottawa and Moscow is eight hours), the Pearsons were looking forward to a quiet eve-ning and a good night's sleep at the Canadian embassy, where they had told the Soviets they wanted to stay. But we soon discovered our hosts had made different arrangements. No sooner had Pearson and Molotov exchanged formal greetings at the airport than all of us were whisked off to the expropriated home of a wealthy Moscow merchant, converted into a government hospitality mansion. It was furnished in the kind of heavy Edwardian plush which the Soviets apparently consider the height of elegance and bristling with staff, most of whom were obviously members of the protocol department or the secret police. The most efficient and certainly the most attractive member of the staff was a young woman called Tanya who was assigned to look after Maryon Pearson but also kept an eye on me whenever my own shadow, a young man called Georgi Alexandrovich, was off duty. In the light of subsequent events it might be deduced that I was supposed to fall for Tanya's considerable charms, though I am bound to add that she herself made no attempt to seduce me.

Though we had eaten *en route* and were not hungry, we were served a sumptuous supper complete with caviar, which, incidentally, became a staple part of our diet throughout our stay in the Soviet Union. Then we were off to the Bolshoi Theatre, where the Pearsons, seated beside Molotov in the imperial box, received an ovation from the audience. The dancing was beautiful, though it hardly seemed coincidental that the featured ballet for the evening was *Don Quixote*. This gave Molotov an opportunity to refer repeatedly to the 'tilting against windmills' that was supposedly going on in the west. Fortunately Pearson could take this sort of thing in his stride; he simply replied that every foreign office presumably had its Don Quixotes and its Sancho Panzas.

What the Pearsons found much more difficult to take were the massive quantities of food and drink which were served during each of the four intermissions. This kind of lavish hospitality, combined with the pomp of the imperial box and the orchestrated cheers of the audience, was obviously intended to impress the visitors. But the Pearsons, whose tastes were basically simple and who were desperately tired, found the whole evening, coming as it did on top of the Soviets' refusal to let them stay at the embassy, irritating and confusing.

Maryon Pearson's displeasure increased by several notches the following morning when she was confronted with breakfast. We found the table laden with bottles of cognac, mineral water, and pear cider, a large bowl of fruit, a bowl of yogurt, a plate of assorted sausages and ham, a plate of fish, an assortment of cheeses, hard-boiled eggs, black bread, sweet rolls, and a creamy cake, plus of course the ubiquitous caviar. 'Tell them all I want is orange juice, toast, and coffee,' she kept insisting. I tried to convey her wishes to the staff but discovered to my surprise that no one person seemed to wield enough authority to make that kind of weighty decision.

The Soviet Union may be a dictatorship of the proletariat at the top but, when it came to switching from caviar and cognac to toast and coffee, all they could do was argue among themselves, and nobody seemed able to issue the required instructions.

John Watkins, our ambassador in Moscow, joined Mike Pearson and his staff after breakfast and we all set out for a ten o'clock appointment with Molotov. Officers of what I took to be the Praetorian Guard, resplendent in sky-blue uniforms with vast quantities of gold braid, greeted us at the main gate of the Kremlin and ushered us into Molotov's equally ornate office. As for the talks, they were cordial in tone but short on substance. What Molotov said could be summed up in a single sentence: let's try to relieve international tensions by negotiating on those matters where there is hope of agreement, and leave aside for the time being those where there is no common ground.

The meeting was followed by a luncheon which Molotov gave for the Pearsons at Spiridonovka Palace, a rather pretentious-looking baronial house formerly owned by the sugar king Morozov. I was intrigued to find that one of the halls had its ceiling and walls decorated with fleurs-de-lis on a blue background. The luncheon provided us with our first opportunity to meet Malenkov, Stalin's protégé, who had succeeded his mentor as premier in 1953 but appeared to have subsequently begun to slide down the hierarchical ladder. He was very short and rather stout, with decidedly more bourgeois manners than any of the other Soviet leaders we met. His face was alert, yet there was a benign quality about him which reminded me of a medieval monk. Had it not been for the decline in his fortunes, I might have been tempted to suspect that the Soviet system was mellowing. According to *Pravda*, the meal 'went off in a friendly atmosphere,' which, as far as I was concerned, was another way of saying that I was expected to drink the innumerable toasts 'like a Russian,' that is bottoms up. The trip was clearly going to prove hard on my constitution.

After touring the Kremlin in the afternoon we went on to the Canadian embassy, where John Watkins and the Pearsons were hosts at a huge reception for the Soviet establishment. It was a mark of the importance attached to Pearson's visit that six members of the Politburo – Kaganovich, Malenkov, Molotov, Pervukhin, Saburov, and Shepilov – attended the reception, as did several cabinet ministers and the chiefs of the army and air staffs. Also there were several artists, writers, and performers, including Plesetskaya, the prima ballerina we had seen dance the previous evening at the Bolshoi.

Being so to speak on home territory, I let down my guard during the reception, and first thing I knew, I found myself separated from the rest of our party and surrounded by a flock of Russians, with my back against the table. A writer named Mihalkov, clearly the spokesman for the group, told me that he was, like myself, an aristocrat by birth but was nevertheless happy and successful under the Soviet regime. He had even won the Order of Lenin before being admitted, more recently, to the Communist party. Surely, he said, I must realize that, having been born in Russia, I remained by law a Soviet citizen. I replied that I was nothing of the kind. 'There is one facet of communist ideology that I agree with,' I said, 'and that is the doctrine that environment is more important than heredity; though I happen to have been born here I left Russia as a small boy; I grew up in Canada and I consider myself a Canadian.'

Did I have any relatives in Russia I would like to visit, some of the KGB men around me wanted to know. What about the widow of my father's cousin, the general who had become quite a celebrity as inspector general of staff colleges? I said I had never met the lady and could see no reason why she would want to see me. As for any cousins I might have in the country, it would surely be pointless to pay them an unsolicited visit and possibly expose them to the charge that they were fraternizing with western imperialists. 'Just as a matter of interest,' I asked when they kept up the pressure, 'how do you think I might earn a living in the Soviet Union?' They weren't quite prepared to admit that the information with which I would presumably supply them would be worth my keep. 'You could write books,' was the somewhat hesitant reply. I told them I'd much rather be a Canadian diplomat. 'Moreover,' I said, 'if you don't leave me alone, I'll have to inform my minister that an attempt has been made to subvert a member of his staff.' Though I subsequently received many invitations to visit the Soviet Union and many assurances that the country's current rulers consider any descendant of Marshal Kutuzov as a kind of soul brother, I was never again subjected to an overt attempt to enlist my services on behalf of their cause.

Later that evening we all went to the Central Theatre to see Obratsov's remarkable puppet show. On the program that night was *The Devil's Mill*, an adaptation of a Czech folk tale which deals with human temptation. Homogenized by Soviet ideology, the story led to the inevitable conclusion that soldiers have the moral fibre to stand up to the devil's enticements, whereas monks are more than likely to succumb. I found myself cast in the role of translator for the benefit of Maryon Pearson as well as the accompanying newspapermen, including Mr Paré of *L'Action Catholique* and I. Norman Smith, the editor of the *Ottawa Journal*. After the show we toured Obratsov's museum of puppets, then went on to the embassy for drinks. I finally got to bed at half past one; Pearson, who had found the afternoon reception particularly exhausting, left the theatre early and managed to get some sorely needed sleep.

The following morning was devoted to trade talks. Kabanov, the Soviet minister of foreign trade, started off on a cordial note but didn't waste much time getting to the crux of his argument. While the Soviet Union was prepared to buy substantial amounts of wheat from Canada, they wanted something more than the 'most-favoured-nation' treatment in return. Specifically, they were looking for some sort of commitment on our part that we would relax or even dissociate ourselves from NATO restrictions on the sale of strategic materials. Mitchell Sharp, who did most of the negotiating on our behalf, made it clear that we were not prepared to renege on commitments we had made to our allies. It looked as though we might be heading for a stalemate, though by late afternoon we detected indications that the Soviets had decided to buy Canadian wheat, even if they could not get any concessions in return.

While Sharp was negotiating, Pearson decided to take a few hours off to visit the Moscow Agricultural Exhibition and asked me to go along as an interpreter. We were met by the director, Academician Tsitsin, who explained to us that the exhibition served mainly educational purposes. Farmers from all over the country came there and received a week's free board and lodging while they learned how to improve their techniques in experimental plots and machine shops. To me this was one of the most impressive and imaginative glimpses of contemporary Russia. Less impressive was the director's predilection for utterly irrelevant statistics. I couldn't imagine, for instance, why it was important for us to know that, if all the photographs taken of the exhibition were sewn together, they would cover six hectares.

By late afternoon I had developed a sore throat and was feeling too miserable to accompany the Pearsons to the Dynamo Stadium to see a soccer game. But at half past eleven we were off to the railway station to take the 'Red Arrow Express' for Leningrad. We passed through what had been the royal waiting room, and the Pearsons boarded a special car, obviously of tsarist vintage, which might well have carried the last empress on her way to visit her husband at the front. There was a bathroom complete with full-sized tub and fittings that looked suspiciously like solid gold, a private salon, and, of course, the inevitable buffet with the usual spread of caviar, smoked fish, and sausages, plus suitable liquid refreshments to wash down all this nourishment.

Ray Crépault and I had been assigned a compartment in a separate, modern sleeping car. I was running a temperature, and my shadow, Georgi Alexandrovich, was all for wiring ahead to have a doctor meet me when we reached Leningrad. But I suspected that this was just another attempt to separate me from the ministerial party and possibly confine me to a hospital, so I told Georgi that in Canada we didn't call doctors to treat common colds. He finally relented on condition that I let him feel my pulse. It was a deal, though having my hand held on the night train to Leningrad by a man who was presumably a secret police agent was not an experience I had bargained for when I decided to visit the USSR.

Leningrad was clearly out to show that, when it came to welcoming Canada's foreign minister, the city was not to be outdone by Moscow. Crossed Canadian and Soviet flags decorated the station and the acting mayor was on hand with other civic officials to do the honours. Maryon Pearson was presented with three huge bouquets of flowers, which left me staggering as I carried them down the platform. The assembled spectators clapped as we emerged from the station.

The Pearsons were taken to another one of the government's hospitality mansions while the rest of us were lodged in the Hotel Astoria. Once again we found that, in matters of taste, time seemed to have stood still since the revolution isolated Russia from western Europe. Everything about the hotel – the furnishings, the servants, the entire atmosphere – seemed to have been frozen for the past thirty-eight years and revived for our benefit. On the desk in my bedroom I found little silver figurines of a bear and her cubs and for the first time since my arrival in the Soviet Union, I felt a strange stirring of childhood memories; I was sure I must have played with identical knick-knacks on my father's desk when I was a little boy in this same city.

When the civic officials heard that I had been born in Petrograd, they went out of their way to be helpful. The city architect personally showed me the house where I was born, on a street which runs through an arch in what used to be the Imperial Senate. The Senate building overlooks the garden with the famous equestrian statue of Peter the Great, which is still one of the country's national monuments. I also saw the house where we lived when father was minister of education, and which now serves as the city's Palace of Marriages. Appropriately enough, mother's boudoir has been set aside for any last-minute adjustments to the brides' finery, while the grooms use my father's study for the same purpose.

Our tour of Leningrad included what one of the Soviet officials described as a 'barbarously short' visit to the Hermitage, with its priceless treasures of Italian, Flemish, Dutch, French, English, and German art. In a way the Hermitage epitomized what, to my mind, was so sad about Leningrad as a whole: one of Europe's most beautiful cities cut off, to all intents and purposes, from the civilizations which had inspired its founder and given it meaning.

Only two parts of the Hermitage are not western in character. One is the Romanov throne room, which to my surprise has been preserved intact, complete with the imperial coat of arms; the other is a vast chamber dedicated to the 'First Patriotic War.' It is dominated by a life-size portrait of Marshal Kutuzov, and as we came through the door I exclaimed: 'That is one of my ancestors.' Our guides were tremendously impressed. Kutuzov is considered a national hero not only for leading the Russian army against Napoleon but for inventing guerilla warfare as the most effective weapon against a technically superior enemy. Rather than wasting Russian lives in pitched battles, he decided it was much better to retreat, harass the enemy by hit-and-run attacks, and let the Russian winter do the rest. Tsar Alexander I never forgave him for abandoning Moscow, which of course made it easier for the Bolsheviks to claim him as one of their own. During World War II, when guerilla tactics proved once again so devastatingly effective, the Order of Kutuzov became one of the two highest awards for military valour. All in all, being a descendant of this almost legendary figure was considered quite a status symbol.

All too soon we had to rush off to a civic reception at the City Hall, formerly the Marinsky Palace. In my experience official visits are invariably too long on formal (and boring) events such as receptions and banquets, and too short on things of real interest. This particular banquet was better than most because the guest list included, in addition to members of the Leningrad Soviet, a number of the city's intellectuals and artists. I sat beside a civic official who told me about the appalling conditions during the wartime siege of the city, when those who were either too young or too old to fight were virtually cut off from any source of supply. About a million people died of hunger and cold during the nine hundred days the German army besieged Leningrad. Though he didn't tell me anything I didn't know, hearing these horrors described by someone who had actually lived through them was a profoundly moving experience.

We took the overnight train back to Moscow and arrived just in time to attend the Sunday morning service at the Patriarch's Cathedral. Tanya explained that, while she was not a believer, the Soviet regime had adopted a tolerant attitude towards the church and she therefore proposed to accompany me. I told her I was a believer and that I needed no help to worship, but she announced she was coming anyway. It turned out to be quite an experience. We drove up to the cathedral in a government car with its MVD driver, only to find we couldn't get anywhere near the main door because of the throngs of people. We only managed to get in by being ushered through the clergy's entrance beside the altar.

The church was packed with people of all ages and from all walks of life, some of them in uniform. Perhaps the fact that many Moscow churches had been closed accounted to some extent for this spectacular turn-out. To me, the highlight of the service came when the Metropolitan of Moscow led the congregation in repeating the Credo, rather than following the traditional practice of having it sung by the choir. It was as though he wanted the world to know that, regardless of the agnosticism of the regime, there were people in the Soviet Union who were not ashamed to 'confess the faith of Christ crucified.' After the service Tanya, who knew that none of the visiting Canadians had been provided with any spending money, bought me a candle to place before one of the icons, so I could pray for her salvation as well as that of my family.

I spent most of the afternoon working on a memorandum about questions Pearson still needed to discuss with Soviet officials before leaving Moscow. In the evening we all went to the Bolshoi to see Glinka's patriotic opera *Life for the Tsar* renamed *Ivan Susanin* by the Bolsheviks. It was a lavish production with superb singing and dancing. The grand climax came at the end of the final act when two heroic Russian army leaders rode on horseback onto the stage to the sound of the Kremlin bells peeling a triumphant and, to me, poignantly familiar tune. As a child I had often heard my father sing it, while my uncle Kolya and his son-in-law stood at attention. It was the imperial anthem.

The feelings of nostalgia stirred by the opera were reinforced later that evening when I went to bed, still suffering from my cold and a slight temperature. Much to my surprise, one of the elderly maids attached to the hospitality mansion came into my room with a glass of hot milk mixed with mineral water and two aspirins. She tucked a voluminous eiderdown around me, thrust the glass into my hand and said 'Pej,' the Russian word for drink. It was as though my old nanny had come back to nurse the little boy I had been almost forty years ago.

I woke up next morning feeling much better, which was just as well, because the day turned out to be particularly demanding. In the morning Pearson, Holmes, and Watkins had another meeting with Molotov while I sat in with Mitchell Sharp on further negotiations with Ivan Kabanov, the minister of foreign trade. Once again, Sharp explained that we were prepared to enter into an agreement on a most-favoured-nation basis, so long as it did not include any items on the 'strategic list' drawn up by NATO. The talks culminated in an agreement on the sale of hundreds of tons of Canadian wheat – the first of many similar sales negotiated since then.

I drafted a report on the trade talks to be sent to Ottawa, and then we were off to Pearson's farewell luncheon at the Canadian embassy. I sat beside Kaganovich who, I thought, looked like an ogre. As an opening gambit he informed me that the Canadian smoked oysters, which were being served as hors-d'oeuvres, tasted like cod liver oil and felt like rubber. Though it was not exactly the kind of comment I would have expected from a guest, I couldn't help agreeing with him. However, the conversation soon turned from food to a theme which seemed uppermost on the minds of the Soviet officials, namely Canada's role as a bridge, an instrument of co-existence between the United States and the Soviet Union. Pearson told Molotov that, while the Canadian government was conscious of the country's delicate geographic position and anxious to play the part of peacemaker, the two super-powers had to realize that, far from resolving their differences, nuclear war would bring about nothing but wholesale death and unthinkable devastation. Malenkov, who was sitting across the table from me, looked pointedly at Kaganovich and said: 'Did you hear that?' The tone of that brief remark seemed to confirm information we had from our own sources, that Malenkov was at odds with the Soviet leadership in opposing strategic dependence on nuclear weapons.

In the course of the luncheon, Pearson also made it clear that 'nothing is more exhausting than friendly pressures.' It was his way of telling the Soviets that he was not impressed by all the fuss they were making over him, that giving him too much to eat and drink and telling him what a grand guy he was wasn't going to affect his views about Canada's foreign policy. Once again, Malenkov clearly agreed. 'That was a shrewd remark,' he said to Kaganovich.

After lunch John Holmes and I went to the Foreign Office to wrestle with the draft communiqué to be issued simultaneously in Moscow and Ottawa. As we soon discovered, we had to be extremely careful, because the Soviet officials kept trying to slide into the Russian text words or phrases that were not part of the English version and that modified its meaning. For instance, where the communiqué said that we would endeavour to ease international tensions, they inserted 'in the spirit of Geneva,' implying a reduction in our defence establishment; where the communiqué dealt with bilateral trade, they added that we would work towards the elimination of 'discrimination,' meaning strategic controls. Since my Russian was considerably more fluent than John's, it was up to me to spot these discrepancies and insist that they be removed.

We broke off in the late afternoon to attend a final reception Molotov gave for the Pearsons and the rest of the Canadian party. Once again all the members of the Politburo were there, except Khrushchev and Bulganin, whom we were to meet later in the Crimea, and Mikoyan and Zhukov, who were out of town. The reception was a vastly different affair from our own party at the Canadian embassy, where all guests were considered equal and rubbed shoulders with each other. Here in the Spiridonovka Palace, the élite (consisting mostly of Politburo members and visiting Canadians) were segregated from the common hordes by a table laden with food and drinks. Some selected guests, such as the British and Indian ambassadors, were escorted to our table so they could exchange a few words with Pearson. It was the way the tsar might have received favoured subjects in days gone by. I noticed that the chiefs of staff, though present at the reception, were not part of the charmed inner circle; the Communist party leaves the military in no doubt as to who is boss in the Soviet Union.

In the evening, John Holmes and I had to pass up an opportunity to see Ulanova dance at the Bolshoi in order to resume our haggling over the communiqué. At one point, when the Soviet officials insisted on putting in a sentence about the gradual removal of strategic controls, I told them that I couldn't possibly go along with their wording without consulting my minister. Even though it was almost midnight, I phoned Pearson and reported to him that we were deadlocked. He backed me up completely and said that, unless they accepted the position we had maintained throughout the negotiations, he wouldn't sign the communiqué. In the end the Soviets agreed to leave out the contentious clause, on the understanding that the text would be referred to Khrushchev for final approval.

At six o'clock the following morning we left for the airport, where a Soviet military aircraft was waiting to fly us to Stalingrad. The flight was comfortable enough except for an extraordinarily powerful compressed air ventilating jet in the toilet which turned the use of that facility into a somewhat hazardous exercise. In Stalingrad we were greeted by the mayor, who was also a delegate to the Supreme Soviet, and a rather forceful woman who turned out to be one of the city's three deputy mayors. She wasted no time informing me that her particular responsibilities were social welfare and education, that all schools in Stalingrad had their own resident doctors, and that the children received free medical care. What about Canadian schools? I did my best to assure her that Manor Park school in Ottawa, which my sons attended, was also reasonably progressive.

Driving into the city we noticed rows upon rows of suburban houses, some of them no more than shacks, but nevertheless models of privacy compared with the huge communal apartment complexes we had seen in Moscow and Leningrad. Our escorts explained that these homes had been built by their occupants after the war, with the assistance of government loans and materials. Apparently this concession to the spirit of free enterprise was a measure of the authorities' gratitude to the people of Stalingrad for the bravery they had displayed during the long and desperate battle for their city during World War II.

Everywhere we went we were reminded of the terrible cost at which that decisive battle had been won. Memorials in the form of monuments, museum exhibits, and beautiful gardens on the embankment of the Volga all paid tribute to the 160,000 soldiers and 100,000 civilians who died fighting for Stalingrad. Pearson agreed to lay a wreath on one of the monuments, and our hosts obligingly led him to one which looked perfectly appropriate to the uninitiated. Fortunately I realized, only just in time, that this particular monument had been erected to commemorate 'the victims of the white guardist executioners,' in other words Bolsheviks who died fighting the White Russians during the civil war. No doubt a photograph of Canada's foreign minister paying tribute to the Reds would have made the front page of *Pravda* the following day. As it was, we pointed out to the Soviet officials that there had apparently been a slight mistake, and Pearson ended up laying his wreath on a ridge which had changed hands many times during the epic World War II struggle for Stalingrad, and where 36,000 identifiable bodies were found when the battle was over.

In the afternoon we flew to Sevastopol, another city which had suffered heavy damage during the war but had since been largely rebuilt. Being a naval base, Sevastopol is normally out of bounds to foreigners, but apart from some MIGs on the air strips and a squadron of ships in the harbour, the only military hardware we saw were some relics from the Crimean War. During a sightseeing tour our guide pointed out to us the narrow gorge where the Charge of the Light Brigade took place and the location of the Russian batteries which mowed down the oncoming British cavalry. To me it was just one more reminder of the abysmal folly of wars and the stupidity of some of the men who wage them.

Later the same day we drove along a winding and sometimes precipitous coastal road to Mishkor, a Black Sea resort about five or six kilometres from Yalta. We were housed in a 'rest home,' a luxurious mansion set aside for vacationing Soviet officials, with a full medical staff in attendance. A female doctor was determined to give Pearson a complete examination before prescribing a remedy for the cold that plagued most of us during our visit to the USSR. But Mike insisted that all he wanted was a gargle to restore his vanishing voice, and, after a bit of an argument, he got his way.

Chuvahin, the Soviet ambassador to Canada who had accompanied us to the USSR, informed us that Khrushchev and Bulganin would see us at any time convenient to the minister, and we agreed we'd be there at 7.45 p.m. This barely gave us time to change before setting out for the most momentous meeting of the entire trip. There were six of us: Pearson, Watkins, Crépault, Chuvahin, Alyosha (a male friend of Watkins' whose function was ill defined), and myself; the rest of our party had stayed behind in Moscow. Government Villa No. 4, the country home of the Khrushchevs, turned out to be one of the many palaces formerly owned by the Yousoupov family, whose scion, Prince Felix Yousoupov, acquired international fame by murdering Rasputin. Judging by what little we could see in the twilight, the exterior of the palace had not been affected by the change of ownership; even the Yousoupovs' heraldic crest was still at the door, along with a huge stone lion. A bevy of plain clothes policemen guided us through the large grounds and ushered us into the presence of our hosts.

They were a study in contrasts: Khrushchev, the archetypal Ukrainian peasant with his compact, powerful frame and shambling walk, obviously intelligent and bubbling with energy, but deliberately crude in language and behaviour, as though determined to advertise the fact he had once been a swineherd; and Bulganin, slightly reminiscent of Napoleon III in appearance, with a quiet, dignified manner and hints of inner reserves of strength, but cold, expressionless eyes. As we discovered in the course of the evening, Khrushchev was given to violent, irrational outbursts, particularly when the conversation turned to Foster Dulles or Senator McCarthy. It may have been this impulsive side of his personality, as exemplified years later in the Cuban adventure, which finally led to his downfall. Russians like their leaders to be more predictable.

Both Khrushchev and Bulganin were obviously aware of my Russian origin, though Khrushchev's information was not as accurate as I would have expected. He said he knew all about me, that my father had served under Kerensky in the provisional government. I told him he was mistaken, that my father had never served anyone other than the tsar. 'You know, Nikita Sergeyevich,' Bulganin chimed in, 'he is the son of Count Paul Ignatieff, the former minister of education.' From that point on Khrushchev persisted in addressing me as 'Count' or 'ex-Count' until I felt compelled to point out that, as a Canadian, I preferred to be called plain Mr.

The official talks between Pearson and the two Soviet leaders, which lasted about two hours, revolved almost exclusively around Soviet relations with a divided Germany. Khrushchev made it abundantly clear that, in so far as West Germany had been admitted to NATO under the Paris Agreements of October 1954, reunification was out of the question. Unless the Federal Republic of Germany were excluded from the western alliance, East Germany would be rearmed and the Soviet government would take whatever additional measures it considered necessary to safeguard its own security and the security of its allies.

Pearson tried to explain that, so long as the Red Army remained in the heart of Europe and the Soviet government engineered coups d'état such as the one in Czechoslovakia, the west could not afford to relax its defences. He also pointed out that a Germany rearmed under the auspices of NATO was the safest option available to the Soviets, since any weapons and troops located in that country would be under NATO rather than German command. But that argument didn't cut any ice with Khrushchev. He kept on ranting against NATO and the capitalist system in general, and assured us that communism was bound to prevail against the decadent west. As for Canada, he warned us that next time round we would not escape the ravages of war. 'We know what war is. You Canadians and Americans don't know,' he repeated time and again. The only reassuring part of the conversation was his admission that nuclear war was unthinkable, that some other means would have to be found to resolve our differences.

At about ten o'clock Khrushchev announced that it was time to eat and led the way to the banquet room, past several washrooms which he was careful to point out to us. The significance of this hospitable gesture became disconcertingly clear once we sat down to eat, and our hosts proceeded to propose a seemingly endless series of toasts. Once again I was informed that I was expected to drink 'like a Russian,' and it didn't take me long to realize what was the objective of the exercise. 'Your husband is trying to get me drunk,' I said to Mrs Khrushchev, who had joined us for dinner and was sitting beside me. She was a pleasant, mild-mannered woman, a former schoolteacher with none of her husband's bluster. 'What would you like me to do about it?' she asked. 'If you can't stop him,'

I replied, 'at least get me some black bread and butter; it will act as a blotter for all that vodka.' She did as I asked, but no amount of bread could soak up all that undiluted liquor. Khrushchev and Bulganin kept their eyes fixed on me as they proposed one toast after another, making sure my glass was refilled the moment I emptied it. I was munching bread furiously and I tried to spill some of the drink over my shoulder as I drained each glassful but Khrushchev immediately spotted my stratagem and announced that the Count ('or should I say ex-Count?') was trying to cheat.

I counted eighteen vodkas, fortified with red pepper, before heading for one of the washrooms Khrushchev had so thoughtfully pointed out to us earlier in the evening. I was violently sick, then returned to the table, where my absence had apparently gone unnoticed, and joined in the drinking all over again. Determined to prove that I could hold my own in this nightmarish test of competitive co-existence, I proposed a toast on behalf of the visiting Canadians to the Khrushchevs, 'our gracious hosts.' Bulganin announced that he wanted to associate himself personally with this toast and came over to drink with me. He then proceeded to inform us that he and Nikita Sergeyevich were close friends, that they had been comrades under Stalin, and that he hoped they would always remain friends. Was he trying to mask his fear of an incipient split in the collective leadership? Obviously Khrushchev was already the first among equals. Within a matter of months Bulganin would be relegated to a figurehead role while Molotov and Malenkov would be banished to obscure postings in Outer Mongolia and Siberia.

Throughout the evening Khrushchev and Bulganin concentrated all their unwelcome attention on me and, to a lesser extent, on 'that wily Frenchman' Ray Crépault. Pearson had made it perfectly clear that he was not going to drink more than the minimum the circumstances required, and though Watkins and Alyosha were also present, our hosts paid absolutely no attention to them. I mention this because, according to a recently published book, Khrushchev teased Watkins in the course of that evening about his homosexuality. I was there and I can testify that nothing of the kind took place. What's more, if Pearson in his capacity as foreign minister had heard the head of another country make an insulting remark about the Canadian ambassador accredited to that country, he would undoubtedly have protested and, more than likely, removed the ambassador. As a matter of fact, I didn't know Watkins was a homosexual at the time, and I suspect Pearson didn't either, though I suppose we might have guessed. While I admit that, under the circumstances, it was indiscreet on his part to accept the Moscow appointment, I resent having Watkins' loyalty questioned at a time when neither he nor his relatives are around to defend him. I shall always remember him as a scholar, a man whose encyclopaedic knowledge of Viking history and traditions was a source of constant amazement to me. I am not aware of any indication, let alone evidence, that he was ever disloyal to his country.

Shortly after midnight I told Khrushchev and Bulganin that Pearson was suffering from a sore throat, that he had a busy day ahead of him, and that we ought to be on our way. After 'two more for the road' we thanked our hosts and marched out of the banquet hall with our heads held high and the dubious satisfaction that we were in marginally better shape than some of the people we left behind. I barely made it back to our quarters before I was sick all over again. Years later René Lévesque, who had accompanied us to Yalta, told my wife that, the last time he saw me, I was having 'a wonderful time with Khrushchev' while he was just an underling with steerage accommodation. When Alison asked him what made him so sure I had such a good time, he said he could tell by the number of times I flushed the john.

Terrible though I felt, I couldn't go to bed until I had telephoned Moscow, got hold of our press attaché, and confirmed to him the wording of the communiqué which Pearson and Khrushchev had approved earlier in the evening. It was without any doubt one of the most difficult phone calls I ever made. My head was spinning, and though I propped myself up in an armchair, the floor seemed determined to come up and meet me. I woke up next morning with all the symptoms of an acute hangover which neither the glorious view of the Black Sea nor the warm sunshine could dispel. Looking out of my bedroom window I spotted a clutch of middle-aged, pyjama-clad men, whom an instructor was putting through the calisthenic routine to the sound of an accordion. I had no wish to join them.

Fortunately the guest-house dispensary was well equipped with remarkably effective pills designed to deal with my particular ailment. Even so, the four-hour drive which followed turned out to be an ordeal, what with precipitous coastal roads which made us feel as though we were hurtling along in the front seat of a roller-coaster. At one point we stopped to admire a monument, and Ambassador Chuvahin explained that we were standing on the exact spot where Marshal Kutuzov lost an eye fighting the Turks. Pearson commented wryly that, a couple of hairpin turns back on the same road, the Soviets might like to commemorate the place where Canada's foreign minister lost his stomach.

All of us were relieved to see the RCAF C-5, with the rest of the ministerial party on board, waiting for us in Sochi, the airfield used by Churchill and Roosevelt when they attended the 1945 Yalta conference. We took off early in the afternoon on 12 October and flew to Basra on the Persian Gulf, where the aircraft refuelled before carrying Pearson and most of his entourage on to Karachi. I was left behind in Basra to make my way to the nearest Canadian mission and transmit to Ottawa a report on Pearson's talks with Khrushchev and Bulganin. While I felt somewhat chagrined at being dumped in the middle of nowhere once I had served my purpose, I at least had time to collect my thoughts and to sort out my impressions of the eventful week I had spent in my native land.

I guess what had come to me as the greatest revelation was the soul-searing effect which four decades of uninterrupted suffering had had on the Russian people. It was not that I was unfamiliar with the facts. But up until then I had thought of Russia's terrible losses in World War I, the revolution and civil war, the collectivization of farmland, the Stalinist terror, and finally the death of twenty million people in World War II as a sequence of tragic events rather than interlocking pieces of one monstrous scourge. It wasn't until I visited the Soviet Union that I became fully aware of the cumulative impact of this catastrophe on the Russian psyche.

This realization has had a deep and lasting effect on the perspective from which I view the Soviet threat. I understand, though I don't necessarily condone, their obsession with security, their intransigence with regard to a rearmed Germany, their pride in the country's achievements. They were then, and probably still are, too isolated from the outside world to realize how comparatively modest those achievements are. When Khrushchev told Pearson that the Soviet Union was about to overtake the United States in terms of living standard and technology, he may well have believed what he was saying. Certainly he and his colleagues were convinced that the Soviets had earned their place as one of the world's two great powers and that the division of Europe into two spheres of influence was their legitimate reward for their contribution to the Allied cause. No matter how much the west may regret this aspect of the Potsdam and Yalta agreements, the Soviets have made it clear time and again that, as far as they are concerned, this is one bargain which is not open to renegotiation.

While our hosts had made no secret of the fact that in their eyes I remained a Russian, I can honestly say that I never felt more Canadian than during the week I spent in their country and that my return to Ottawa was a home-coming in the truest sense of the term. Yet I had also become aware of the fact that my perspective of the Soviet Union was probably different from that of many Canadians. Short though it was, the trip had bolstered my conviction that Russians – whether red or white – are too much of a conglomerate to be lumped together into some sort of monolithic, bloodthirsty monster. Still less am I prepared to go along with the notion that political, economic, or social differences can be resolved by force of arms.

I should add that, generally speaking, Soviet diplomats have treated me with consideration and a kind of warmth which I have occasionally found more difficult to deal with than the crude KGB tactics to which I was subjected in Moscow. Take, for instance, Amasasp Aroutunian, an outstanding economist who was Soviet ambassador to Canada at the time I was assistant under-secretary of state for external affairs. One day, after we had caught some Soviet spies, I summoned him on behalf of the under-secretary and told him what we thought of their activities. He looked at me sadly and said: 'You know the system, there is nothing I can do about it.' I knew this to be true but nevertheless felt compelled to point out that this sort of behaviour was unacceptable. 'Let's talk about something more pleasant,' he suggested, 'such as education.'

When I was later appointed ambassador to NATO, Aroutunian phoned to congratulate me and said he'd like to throw a party for me to celebrate the appointment. 'That's very kind of you,' I said, 'but can you imagine what TASS would say about a Soviet ambassador giving a party in honour of an imperialist reactionary and his appointment to the hostile alliance?' Still, he obviously meant well and I suggested that, if he'd like to invite Alison and me at a time when nobody else was around, we'd be glad to come. So the four of us had dinner together in the Aroutunians' kitchen, and his wife, who turned out to be the daughter of a famous Armenian poet, recited some of her father's poetry. It was a delightful evening, and one which awakened in me unsuspected feelings of nostalgia.

But nostalgia was far from my mind in Basra, as I watched the RCAF plane take off and pondered the challenge of making my way from the Persian Gulf to the nearest Canadian mission with machine cypher facilities, so I could report to Ottawa on Pearson's talks with Khrushchev. That meant going to Bonn, which in 1955 was no easy assignment. I had to wait two days to catch a flight to Cairo, then fly via Rome and Geneva to Frankfurt, where I was grounded by fog. By the time I got hold of a car and reached my destination, I was more convinced than ever that the lot of Mike Pearson's subordinates was not an easy one.

TEN

Ambassador to Yugoslavia

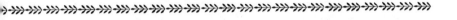

In 1956 I heard a rumour that I was about to be made an ambassador and posted abroad. I can't say I was happy about such a prospect: the defence liaison work I was doing was interesting and very much in line with the expertise I had built up first as secretary to the post-hostilities planning committee, then during the negotiations of NATO, and finally during the year I spent at the Imperial Defence College in London. Also, I was working with Jules Léger, who had become not only a trusted colleague but a close friend; and last but by no means least, I was happy to be back in Canada and able to sink some roots for a change. We had just built our house in Ottawa, so we had absolutely no wish to move.

But in my experience foreign service officers were seldom consulted about their wishes. One day Jules told me that my name had gone forward to cabinet, though I had no idea where I was supposed to be going until the cabinet had approved the appointment. Given a choice, I doubt whether I would have picked Yugoslavia. During my student days I had spent a year in the Balkans and I had recollections of a country racked with internal problems where our lives would be subject to all kinds of restrictions. Besides, it hardly seemed like an ideal place to bring up two small children.

On the other hand, I had every reason to be happy about the way I was briefed for my duties as 'Ambassador Extraordinary and Minister Plenipotentiary.' In those days there was a very close relationship between the government and officials who had been appointed to head missions abroad. Once the under-secretary had informed me where I was going and given me my letters of instructions, it was Mike Pearson and, after him, the prime minister who explained to me personally why I had been chosen for that particular job.

Mr St Laurent told me that I was being sent to Yugoslavia for two main reasons. First, I was to give the government my assessment of Soviet intentions: were the invasion of Hungary and the suppression of the Hungarian uprising simply a reaction to internal events in that country, or were they part of a broader scheme of Soviet expansion? Yugoslavia seemed like a good vantage point from which to attempt to answer that question. The second reason was that the government wanted to establish a closer relationship with this unorthodox socialist country which was trying to free itself from Stalinism and, in the process, embarking on all kinds of interesting political and economic experiments. I was to explore the possibility of developing trade not only with Yugoslavia, but possibly also with other Balkan countries.

Mr St Laurent suggested that I discuss this aspect of my mission with C.D. Howe, the minister of trade and commerce. Howe was a notoriously busy man, but he too found time to see me and discuss with me the trade contacts which already existed, the establishment of a Massey-Ferguson plant in Yugoslavia, and the possibility of developing markets for farm machinery, cattle, agricultural seeds, and rolling stock in Rumania, Bulgaria, and Hungary.

In my thirty-three years in the foreign service, that was the only time when the prime minister and members of his cabinet took the trouble to explain to me what they expected me to accomplish or made me feel they were interested in my mission. I was forty-three years old and though my background was never mentioned by either Pearson or St Laurent, I was frankly proud to be the first foreign-born Canadian to be appointed ambassador. Mr St Laurent went so far as to present me with a photograph of himself inscribed 'To my friend and colleague, George Ignatieff.' That may seem like a token gesture, but as I was to discover, there is nothing that impresses government officials of a foreign country, particularly a small country, more than this kind of proof that you are a friend of your prime minister. Mr St Laurent obviously knew this, and it was typical of him that he wanted to do whatever he could to help me.

In February 1957 we were off. In those days, heads of missions travelled in style, so we sailed first class on the *Queen Elizabeth* from New York to France, where we boarded the famous Orient Express. When it left Paris it was an impressive train, complete with wagon-lits and restaurant cars and all kinds of uniformed attendants making sure the passengers were comfortable. This lasted as far as Trieste. Then suddenly all these people disappeared and we were hooked on to a local train which stopped absolutely everywhere, so passengers could get on with their chickens, pigs, sheep, and every other conceivable kind of baggage. To make matters even more interesting, the train soon became permeated with sulphurous fumes produced by a low-quality fuel called lignite widely used in Yugoslavia.

We arrived in Belgrade around 4.30 a.m. and we were met by the first secretary, who was the chargé d'affaires, and by the chargé d'affaires of the British Embassy. At this point Bert Hart, the number two man at the Canadian mission, told me he was very sorry but the official car had been in an accident and my chauffeur was in hospital. The second car was not available either because that chauffeur was in jail, so would it be all right if he drove us in his own car? It seemed like an inauspicious beginning.

Another surprise awaited us at the embassy: the pre-revolutionary owner of the building, which had been expropriated by the Yugoslav government, was claiming title to her property. Only a few days before our arrival she had moved furniture into the house to establish her claim and had told the servants that she intended to get us out. Apparently she was a prima donna at the state opera and had informed the government that she would not sing again until she got her house back.

If there were other aspects to this story, it did not seem wise for a newly arrived diplomat to enquire into them. Besides, I had no wish to resist the return of property to its rightful owner, though I did insist that the Yugoslav government provide us with alternative accommodation. So a house being built for a general was reassigned to the Canadian embassy, and we moved in time to celebrate Canada's national holiday in our new quarters.

The house stood on a lovely site in Topcider park, but apart from a few neglected fruit trees there was no garden. In response to my request for some flowers for the Dominion Day reception, there appeared a gentleman who asked me, in impeccable English, whether I wanted an English or a French garden. Where, I asked, had he acquired his Oxford accent? 'At Trinity College, Cambridge,' came the reply. 'The accent is something we share with Oxford.' He went on to explain that, as a botanist, he had worked his way up to become director of greenery in the city of Belgrade – a job which involved the supervision of all state property within the city limits as well as the public parks.

At my request he installed an English garden, complete with flowering shrubs, roses, and a variety of other flowers, all in two days. All I had to do was await my official rating at the Dominion Day reception. In Yugoslavia ambassadors know where they stand with the regime according to the number of Central Committee members who turn up for their national holidays and the number of lines they rate in *Borba*, the official party organ. Starting near the bottom, Canada's rating improved moderately over the years.

A few days after our arrival in Belgrade we were invited by the US ambassador to an informal dinner. James Riddleberger was one of the first-rate people produced by the State Department – a man who really knew his job, liked it, and put everything into it. He gave me an excellent overview of the situation in Yugoslavia, stressing that Tito's decision to assert his independence from the Soviet Union was, in the American view, an event of major historical significance. It was his government's policy to help the Yugoslavs in their struggle for independence by providing them with military as well as economic aid.

Our friendship with the Riddlebergers was firmly established from that first meeting. Mrs Riddleberger, who was of Dutch origin, was a woman of great intelligence and charm, as well as a superb hostess; we liked both of them tremendously. Even so, we were surprised when we got another dinner invitation to the American embassy only two or three days after the first one. Apparently we had hit it off even better than we thought. When we turned up Riddleberger looked rather surprised. 'But you came to dinner just a few days ago,' he said. 'This is a dinner for the new

French Ambassador.' Fortunately I had slipped our invitation in my pocket, so I was able to show it to him. 'Oh dear,' he said, 'my secretary must have fouled things up; but do come in, I'm sure Millie can put some water in the soup.' Ever since, I have made a point of taking along my invitation whenever I attend a social function.

Finally the day arrived when I was to present my credentials to Marshal Tito. Meeting this man who had literally become a legend in his own lifetime was an intriguing prospect. Riddleberger had warned me that Tito regarded himself as a historic figure and expected to be treated accordingly. But what was it about Tito's personality that had enabled him to become his country's symbol of both independence and social change? How had he been able to defy Stalin's attempts to extend Soviet rule into the Balkans and at the same time devise a new brand of socialism for his country?

Presenting my letters of credence turned out to be an even more interesting experience than I had expected. To begin with, Tito, who owned a fleet of all kinds of cars, sent a Cadillac to pick me up and drive me to the meeting. Apparently this particular car was a gift from those of his compatriots who had settled in Canada after the war but chose to return to Yugoslavia after Tito's break with Stalin. Tito told me he thought it was appropriate for me to travel in a Canadian car; it was, I suspect, his way of reminding me that some people preferred life in Yugoslavia to the political and economic climate of a capitalist country.

Equally surprising to me was the formality of the affair. I had not expected such bourgeois trappings as a morning coat with striped pants, which I had been advised to wear for the occasion; but, as I was to discover, Tito's insistence on protocol transcended anything to be found in the west. Diplomats were warned to address him always as Mr President or Marshal and to make sure their own clothes were at least as formal as his own. Before any kind of meeting, you always had to phone and find out what the marshal was planning to wear. It was the only time in my career when I needed the full wardrobe of a diplomat – striped pants with short jacket, striped pants with long jacket, the whole works; they have been mothballed ever since.

The man who received me in the former Palace of the Kings in

Belgrade looked more like a prosperous businessman or an Austrian baron than the gaunt partisan leader pictured in wartime photographs. He was immaculately dressed, manicured, beautifully turned out; I never saw Tito any other way. Call it vanity if you like; he certainly was vain in the sense that he dyed his hair to make himself look younger than he was, and, judging by his current wife, I assume he had a penchant for young, attractive women. But he was also an exceptionally astute politician whose authority rested not only on his remarkable military record but also on his intuitive ability to gauge and respond to public opinion. If he behaved at times more like a monarch than a communist, it was not because he had undergone some sort of ideologicial conversion. Rather, my impression was that he believed the country needed strong leadership and that, in the minds of most Yugoslavs, leadership was historically associated with monarchy.

Tito and his colleagues were, of course, well aware of my Russian origin and intrigued with the fact that I had been appointed Canadian ambassador to Yugoslavia. There were few people in the Balkans who had not heard about the exploits of my diplomat grandfather or of his involvement in the San Stefano Treaty, so the Ignatieff name carried strong connotations in that part of the world. Indeed, shortly after my arrival in Belgrade the Soviet ambassador had suggested that, considering my family's past association with parts of Yugoslavia, it would be appropriate for him to launch me in the city's diplomatic circuit with a formal dinner party. I declined, politely but firmly.

To dispel any misapprehensions Tito might have on the subject, I assured him that my background had nothing whatever to do with my appointment, though the fact that I spoke Russian might have been considered an asset. 'If I may give you a piece of advice,' said Tito, 'play down your Russian roots and your ancestry.' Russians, he said, were highly unpopular in Yugoslavia; people were suspicious of them. Canadians, on the other hand, were well liked, and as Canadian ambassador I would be welcome wherever I went. All this was said in Russian, which he spoke more fluently than I, but he made it clear that it was not the language of his choice. 'I speak Russian with you today,' said Tito, 'but the sooner you learn Serbo-

Croat, the better; in the meantime, I suggest you use English or French – anything other than Russian.' I promised that I would speak Serbo-Croat to him before I left Yugoslavia, and I kept my promise.

Another memorable incident during that first meeting concerned a diamond ring Tito was wearing. It was so huge it literally flashed at you. 'I see you're looking at my ring,' Tito said to me. 'I am looking at it with great curiosity as well as admiration,' I replied. 'I don't believe I have ever seen such a large diamond.' Tito then explained that before World War II, when he was travelling around Europe as an underground Comintern agent, the two possessions which he found most useful were a false Canadian passport and his diamond ring. The passport, he said, was relatively easy to come by because of Canada's lax regulations: 'I chose a foreign sounding name so that, when I was crossing the French border, I'd say that I was a Canadian of German origin and when I was crossing the German frontier, I pretended to be a Canadian of Balkan origin; I speak a little of all these languages, so I got by.' As for the diamond ring, it was a safety device to provide him with instant cash in case of an emergency; the emergency never arose (though I gathered there had been some close scrapes), but he kept the ring as a memento of his service to the Comintern cause.

I was interested to hear that Tito had been aware, way back in the thirties, of Canada's linguistic diversity, because multiculturalism and economic regionalism were two important features of national life which our two countries had in common. That was one of the factors which made my posting to Yugoslavia so fascinating. There you have in the north Slovenia and Croatia, both of which were previously part of the Austro-Hungarian Empire; their population is predominantly Roman Catholic, culturally advanced, and western in orientation. On the Adriatic coast there is Dalmatia, which at one time was under Venetian and later under Italian rule and therefore has a strong maritime tradition. All these provinces are fundamentally different from Serbia, Hercegovina, Macedonia, and Montenegro – the inland areas which suffered a long and cruel domination by the Ottoman Empire and whose people are widely known as fierce freedom fighters. While the majority religion in most of this region is Orthodox and the official alphabet is Cyrillic, there is also a strong Muslim component.

Culturally and economically, the inland remains relatively underdeveloped; yet it was Serbia which first achieved independence and became the focus of a sovereign Yugoslavia. The divisive forces within this country are potentially much more serious than anything to be found in Canada: an area not much larger than Nova Scotia and New Brunswick encompassing not only several totally different languages and traditions but two alphabets and three deeply entrenched religions. Yet Yugoslavia seemed remarkably united under Tito. He had tried, in much the same way we do in Canada, to overcome economic disparities by insisting that new industries be located in the poorer parts of the country such as Macedonia, though he was careful not to go so far as to alienate the Slovenes and the Croats. Another thing that reminded me of Canada was the way Tito chose members of the Presidium, which could be loosely described as the equivalent of our cabinet. He always made sure that all regions of the country were represented among the members.

But what seemed to hold Yugoslavia together more than anything else was Tito himself. It was not just his wartime record as an almost legendary leader of the partisan struggle for national independence. Equally important, it seemed to me, was his ability to relate to people. Whenever a problem arose anywhere in the country, he did not rely on bureaucrats to resolve it; he went and dealt with it himself. For instance, when students who were building autoroutes complained that they were being used as unpaid labour, he personally went and told them they should consider themselves lucky that they didn't have to suffer the kind of hardship the partisans had undergone during the war; it was now their turn to contribute to the welfare of the country. After that, there was no further trouble.

During my subsequent meetings with Tito we did talk about some of these problems, but he would not discuss politics with an ambassador, certainly not a Canadian one. There was a definite pecking order within the diplomatic corps, and while I made out rather better than most of my western colleagues, Tito definitely favoured the representatives of India, Egypt, and Burma. He had an excellent relationship with Nehru and Nasser, particularly the former, and so it was the Indian ambassador who provided me with insight as to Tito's political views. On the international scene Tito's number one objective was to maintain Yugoslavia's non-alignment, to keep the country outside the sphere of Soviet imperialism. Particularly after the events in Hungary, he believed there was a real threat of Soviet military intervention in Yugoslavia, which was why he was anxious to get all the help he could from the United States. As for his domestic policies – and this he did say to me personally on one occasion when we were talking about the balance between east and west – he was convinced that the so-called revisionism which he was introducing in Yugoslavia was following the direction in which communism or socialism had to move in order to survive, that ideology had to be sufficiently flexible to adjust to changing circumstances.

But if you tried to discuss Tito's ideas with him in detail, he became evasive. I remember once, after returning from a visit to Macedonia, I told him that revisionism in Yugoslavia seemed to date back to the twelfth or thirteenth century. 'What do you mean?' he asked. I explained that the Byzantine church had laid down strict rules as to the way the figure of Christ, the Virgin Mary, and the holy saints were to be depicted. 'It came to me as a surprise,' I said, 'to find that the first departure from these rules, the first attempt to endow saintly figures with human form, is to be found in your country, in beautiful murals painted long before the Renaissance legitimized that kind of art in Italy.' He said, 'That's very interesting, but it has nothing to do with communism,' and he changed the subject.

I guess Tito did not really want to discuss his political views with diplomats, though he was perfectly willing to let me travel around the country and talk to other people. This was particularly useful after I had learned to speak Serbo-Croat so that I could communicate directly with officials such as presidents of local communist organizations. What politicians say privately is often quite different from the kind of pink mush they feed to an interpreter; besides which, interpreters sometimes superimpose their own bias on top of the original. Of course the communist official will still give you the party line, but in a direct conversation you don't get the same kind of deliberate ambiguity which is so often compounded by an interpreter. Talking to people in their own language enabled me to get a great deal of information which I am sure would not have been available otherwise.

I remember, for instance, talking to Janez Stanovnik, a Slovenian who subsequently became director-general of the Economic Commission for Europe. We discussed Yugoslavia's modified brand of Marxism, including the decentralization of government, the creation of workers' councils, and the introduction of incentives into industry and agriculture. 'Why not take the next step,' I asked, 'and allow opposition parties to put up candidates for the National Assembly?' That, he replied, was out of the question; the Communist party's political monopoly was an inviolable part of the system.

The irony of it was that, had Tito allowed free elections, I am convinced he would have won; most people approved of the way he was running the country, and it was a measure of his talents as a leader that he offered Yugoslavs sufficient economic concessions at home and independence abroad to forestall any concerted demand for political change. Unlike the Hungarians in 1956, the Czechs in 1968, or the Poles in 1981, most Yugoslavs were willing to settle for non-alignment rather than the substance of freedom. Those who didn't were allowed to emigrate.

Of course I had to exercise common sense and not attempt to establish contact with the more conspicuous or outspoken opponents of the regime. For instance, I warned Canadian visitors that it was unwise to be found in possession of a book by Djilas, the articulate dissident who was in jail at the time. On the other hand, I was free to meet with survivors of the old regime or people who had refused to join the party. Included among the former, as it turned out, was Prince Geroge Karageorgevic, the eldest son of Serbia's late King Peter I and an uncle of the exiled King Peter II.

This member of the royal family lived on a state pension in a villa provided for him by the government next door to the Canadian embassy. He had been granted these privileges by President Tito in appreciation of his refusal to collaborate with the occupation forces during World War II. He had also been offered a car and chauffeur but refused on the grounds that this was a luxury which most of his compatriots could not afford.

One cold winter day I asked who was the erect, distinguished-looking man spreading sand in front of our residence. 'Why, that's our king,' said Ciko Spiro, the old man who looked after the garden and the yard. 'Then why do you let him do work you should be doing yourself?' I enquired. 'He always does it for himself and for others. That's why people respect him so much,' explained the old man.

Much though I wanted to meet Prince George, I was afraid of breaching royal protocol by making the first move; besides, I had been warned that he had a quick temper, and I didn't want to find myself at the receiving end of it. I needn't have worried. A few days later, the prince marched into my office and demanded to know what he had done to offend the ambassador. I quickly assured him that I had wanted to pay my respects to my royal neighbour but didn't know how to go about it in a country which no longer recognized royalty. The prince replied that, since I was an emissary of Her Majesty the Queen, it was for him to pay the first call, and so we proceeded to arrange two meetings – one just for the two of us and another which was to include our wives.

During the first meeting, the prince spoke very frankly about the events which caused him, the Crown Prince, to renounce his claim to the throne. Apparently as a young man he had instructed his valet, during an acute political crisis, to deliver a message to the prime minister. When he discovered that his instructions had not been carried out, he flew into a rage and, unaware that the valet was suffering from a hernia, he kicked him so hard that the man died. Once he realized what he had done, the prince went to his father and informed him that he was not fit to rule with the blood of one of his subjects on his conscience.

He told me that he had decided to stay in Yugoslavia under its communist regime because, as a member of the royal house of Karageorgevic, he was determined to share the fate of his people. He never had betrayed the monarchy and never would, and he asked me to convey this message to the queen. Oddly enough, he refused to discuss family matters in the presence of his wife, who accompanied him for our second meeting and who, incidentally, was a qualified lawyer. 'Chuti [shut up]!' he said to her abruptly when she made what he considered an inappropriate comment.

As I became more accustomed to life in Yugoslavia and got to know people in different walks of life, I gave a number of parties to which I invited communist officials as well as professors, artists, or technocrats who had remained faithful to the church and therefore, by definition, were not communists. On one such occasion, one of our guests who was a member of the National Orchestra sat down at the piano and started playing rock 'n' roll. This kind of music was of course a symbol of dissent among young people in Yugoslavia, along with blue jeans and other manifestations of a bourgeois orientation. Next day I got a call from one of my communist friends who said it was a wonderful party, but he suggested that in future I should be more careful in selecting my guests. Apparently rock 'n' roll was pushing revisionism beyond permissible limits.

Shortly after my arrival in Belgrade in the spring of 1957, I got a message from the bishop of Karlovci that he would be pleased to receive me during Lent for my devotions. I said I'd be happy to come and asked the messenger what I might bring the bishop as a gift. 'English beer and pretzels,' came the surprising reply. It turned out that the bishop had studied theology in Cambridge before the war, and beer with pretzels therefore seemed to him a fitting way to end his Lenten fast. I was glad to oblige and was rewarded with some excellent Karlovci wine from the bishop's cellar. During subsequent months I became a frequent visitor at Karlovci, where the bishop was doing his best to restore the historic eighteenth-century cathedral, badly in need of repairs following its wartime occupation by German troops.

The highlight of my mission and the incident which, more than anything else, established my cordial relationship with Marshal Tito was the part I played in resolving the Hungarian refugee problem. After the Soviet troops had occupied Hungary and cut off the escape route to Austria, some of the freedom fighters who had held out to the bitter end fled across the border to Yugoslavia. The Yugoslav authorities were clearly in a quandary. On the one hand, they didn't want to send the refugees back to Hungary, where they would almost certainly face Soviet firing squads. Quite apart from any humanitarian considerations, they were afraid that this would upset the Americans, who by then were providing Yugoslavia with substantial economic and military aid. On the other hand, the government was not exactly anxious to let the Hungarians go free and allow them to infect Yugoslavia's youth with their violently anti-communist ideology.

When I first heard about the problem from people who were working among Hungarian refugees in Vienna, I asked a Yugoslav Foreign Office official if I could be of any assistance. As usual in such situations, he looked blank and pretended he didn't know what I was talking about. But eventually I managed to convince him that I was not asking out of curiosity, that I was genuinely anxious to help, and that it was conceivable some of these people might be allowed to go to Canada.

Suddenly out of the blue, Ministry of the Interior officials approached me and asked whether I was really interested. When I assured them I was, they took me to what amounted to a concentration camp in the wilds of Slovenia. There I found some two thousand Hungarian freedom fighters crowded into barracks which had been built during the war for two or three hundred Italian soldiers. Yugoslavia was clearly not the country of the refugees' choice. I was deeply moved to find that an artist among them had covered the whitewashed walls of the barracks with pictures of angels carrying visas to Canada, Australia, and the United States.

I immediately cabled Jack Pickersgill, the minister of immigration, whom I happened to know, and asked him whether he would consider sending one of the Canadian teams who were processing Hungarian refugees in Vienna to the camp I had visited. Within days the Canadian immigration officials arrived on the scene, and with a minimum of red tape several hundred refugees received the coveted Canadian visas.

There was, however, one more stumbling block to be overcome. I was told that I would have to arrange transportation for the Canada-bound Hungarians, and that the man to see about shipping was Edo Jardas, the mayor of Rijeka and president of the city's

Communist Party Committee. It so happened Jardas had spent several years before the war in Canada, where he had been a member of the Central Committee of the Communist Party. When Tito turned anti-Stalinist Jardas broke with the leadership of the Canadian party and returned to Yugoslavia, along with a boatload of his compatriots.

I approached Edo with considerable trepidation, on the assumption that an ex-member of Canada's Communist Party would not be kindly disposed towards a Canadian ambassador. I couldn't have been more wrong. Edo welcomed me like a long-lost friend and assured me that his quarrel was exclusively with Tim Buck, the leader of Canada's Communist Party, not with the government. 'Your country took me in as an immigrant,' he said, 'so I have nothing but affection for Canada and Canadians. I'll do anything I can to help.' He invited me to his home, which was guarded by electric wires, police dogs, even a shark fence on the water front. 'The damn Stalinists are out to get me,' he explained. 'They'll never forgive me for breaking with the party line in Canada.'

He was as good as his word. Government ships were made available and soon the refugees were on their way to Canada. Before they sailed I made a little speech and told them that I too had been a refugee at one time. Canada, I said, does not look upon newcomers as foreigners; quite possibly they too would become ambassadors or serve their adopted country in some other way. It was a thrilling occasion for all of us.

Once Canada had set an example, other countries quickly followed suit. The United States, Australia, the United Kingdom, Norway, Sweden, Switzerland, and France all accepted some of the refugees, and in no time at all a potential problem and source of embarrassment to the Yugoslav government had disappeared. But because Canada led the way, we got the pick of the crop and most of the credit. From then on I never had any trouble with the powerful Ministry of Internal Affairs. On one occasion we needed permission for overflights in connection with another refugee operation. The normal procedure would have been for me to go to the Ministry of Foreign Affairs, which in turn would contact the Ministry of Internal Affairs – all of which would entail endless delays. Instead I simply phoned a Yugoslav friend who had worked with me on the Hungarian refugee problem, and we were given immediate clearance. On another occasion I phoned the ministry about a Yugoslav girl who had been waiting for months for permission to join her family in Canada; again, whatever difficulties there had been suddenly disappeared.

Perhaps as a reward for his involvement in the Hungarian refugee episode, Edo Jardas was appointed to the cabinet as minister of tourism. He promptly set out to raise the standards of efficiency and sanitation in a country which was not conspicuous for either, and as a first step, he told his staff that there were two things a tourist agent should do: he should shave, and he should make sure the plumbing worked. Not a bad start, but Jardas knew that was not enough. If Yugoslavia was to develop its tourist industry, it would have to supplement the country's natural beauty with modern roads and hotels.

Once again I was able to help. One of the friends I had made in Washington was Johnny Miller, who at that time was European representative of the World Bank. When Johnny and his wife came to stay with us, I introduced him to Edo and other Yugoslav officials concerned with tourism. Loans from the World Bank soon followed. I remember telling Johnny that in my opinion trustworthiness was not so much a matter of ideology as of national character. The Yugoslavs were honest people and I was sure they would repay their debts. They didn't let me down.

In recognition of my services, Edo Jardas made available to me a yacht in which to tour the beautiful Dalmatian coast and Adriatic islands. The yacht had two captains, one a communist who was in charge of navigation and the other a non-communist who attended to our comfort and our sightseeing wishes. Though this typically Yugoslav compromise made me feel a little nervous, it worked surprisingly well.

Something else I found surprising was the close relationship between the Dalmatians and the Italian tourists who even then were crowding the beaches. Considering the wartime occupation of the country by Italian troops, plus the post-war confrontation between the two governments over Trieste, I would have expected, if not hostility, at least a certain amount of animosity. Instead, there was an obvious affinity between the two nations which extended beyond tourism to such matters as joint ventures in shipbuilding and agreements for the export of electricity.

When I asked a leading Dalmatian communist about this strange friendship, he explained to me that he and his compatriots liked Italians because they had something very important in common: they all loved children! Apparently the Italians came during the war to arrest him and, since he was a communist as well as a partisan, his prospects seemed dim, to say the least. But at the last moment he grabbed his child and, as the police burst through the door, pinched the baby and made him cry; at which point the Italians became so busy soothing the poor *bambino*, they forgot why they had come and let the father go free.

The Yugoslavs were less kindly disposed towards German tourists, but at least, I was told, 'the Germans are well disciplined and you know where you stand with them.' The people they really disliked were the Russians, largely, I think, because towards the end of World War II the Soviets kept their best troops for their attack on Berlin and sent the dregs to the Balkans. I heard endless horror stories about the behaviour of the 'liberators' – the rape, plunder, and drunken brawls. Apparently the Russians would drink anything so long as it was alcoholic.

Since I had no trade commissioner, it was up to me to do whatever I could to promote closer trade relations between Canada and Yugoslavia. Occasionally this involved me in situations which most people might not associate with the glamorous life of an ambassador. I particularly remember the visit of an Ontario farmer by the name of Ernie Warwick, who walked into my office with the challenging question: 'Are you one of those goddam ignoramuses from Ottawa who don't know the difference between a bull and a cow?'

Apparently he had been told by customs officials at Heathrow airport in London that tubes of semen intended for artificial insemination of Romanian cattle were not admissible under British law; if he wanted to go into London, he would have to leave them at the airport. In an effort to apply some pressure he telephoned Canada House and explained to the telephone operator that he had just landed with some semen for Romania and that the customs were giving him a hard time. Without a moment's hesitation the operator said: 'One moment please, I'll connect you with the naval attaché.'

Once I had convinced Mr Warwick that I had spent part of my childhood on a farm and therefore did know how to distinguish a bull from a cow, he asked that I make an appointment with the minister of agriculture so he could try to sell some Landrace pigs. I thought my function at the meeting would be confined to interpreting, but when the minister displayed a distinct lack of enthusiasm for the proposed transaction, Ernie rose to the occasion by having me model as a pig. Slapping his own voluminous waist and hips, he explained that he would make a bad ham and bad bacon; on the other hand, the leaner waist and thighs of a pig such as me would yield excellent pork products. While Ernie's marketing efforts left me feeling a bit deflated, I am bound to admit that they were effective. He sold his pigs.

Science was another area where both Tito and Ottawa were hoping to develop closer ties. As it happened, a conference on energy problems in non-aligned countries was to be held in Belgrade shortly after my arrival, and since I knew that my friend Jack Mackenzie, head of the National Research Council and of the Chalk River Atomic Energy Project, had recently retired, I suggested that he attend the conference as our guest.

One of the main speakers at the conference was Homa Bhabha, the head of India's nuclear project. He was describing the Indian nuclear reactor and everyting it could do by way of producing energy for countries which were short of hydro power, when his eye caught Dr Mackenzie sitting in the audience. 'Why should I be talking about the uses of atomic energy,' he said, 'when the man who taught me everything I know is right here among us?'

Jack Mackenzie was promptly surrounded by people who wanted to meet him, and that night, for the first and last time in my diplomatic career, we found ourselves entertaining twice the number of dinner guests we had invited. They just came and said they wanted to talk to Dr Mackenzie. The end result of this unscheduled meeting was that Canada helped Yugoslavia acquire an atomic energy pile for research purposes. I may say that I personally heard Dr Mackenzie explain to the Yugoslavs the dangers of radiation and the strict precautions which would have to be observed. Nevertheless, their inquisitiveness got the better of them, and some of their scientists removed the top of the calandria of the zero energy pile they had purchased to see what exactly was going on inside. Five of them suffered serious radiation poisoning, and though they were all rushed to a specially equipped hospital in France, one of them died. Tito was very upset when he heard about this tragic incident; had I not been able to assure him that we had done everything we could to warn the Yugoslavs about the dangers of radiation, it might have seriously damaged our relationship.

Contrary to my expectations, bringing up children in Yugoslavia turned out to be easier than in any other foreign country in which I ever served. Our neighbours' children played freely with our two sons in the streets of Belgrade – there was very little traffic in those days – and they swarmed all over the house and the garden. Though I had given orders to the militia who guarded our residence that children were to be allowed to come and go as they pleased, I was a little taken aback one day when I found all the spring flowers had disappeared from the garden. However, the explanation turned out to be perfectly reasonable: some of the youngsters had picked the flowers to present to their parents on their Saint's Day.

Where we did have a problem, at least during the early part of our stay, was in the selection of staff. When we arrived in Belgrade we found two servant girls who had been engaged by my predecessor. Whether he had not left enough money for them or whether they just got bored during the six weeks between his departure and our arrival, I don't know; but whatever the reason, they had decided to supplement their income by offering their services to soldiers in the military barracks across the street. Though my sons remember watching with fascination the constant procession of soldiers in and out of the house, I personally did not tumble to the truth until I had learned enough Serbo-Croat to make sense of the constant telephone calls the girls were getting from prospective clients. I promptly informed our two entrepreneurs that the Canadian Embassy was not to be used as a brothel, and we parted company.

After this episode we managed to reorganize the staff around some of the most lovable individuals I have ever known. They really became members of the family and were all at the airport when the time came for us to return to Canada. Of their many farewell gifts, the one I remember most vividly is a pair of very dead partridges in a bloodstained bag. We really hated leaving Yugoslavia, and we were deeply moved by the display of Slavonic emotion on the part of the staff. Janos, our devoted chauffeur, clasped me in his arms, and we both wept.

The news of my transfer had come without advance warning. The Liberal government of Louis St Laurent had been defeated in the 1957 federal election, and another election in 1958 resulted in a landslide victory for John Diefenbaker and his Progressive Conservatives. All of a sudden, after less than two years in Yugoslavia, I found myself summoned back to Ottawa to participate in the change of administration.

A few days before I was due to leave, I was informed by Dalibor Soldatic, the chief of protocol at the foreign office, that President Tito would receive me and my wife on his island retreat in Brioni. I knew by then that this was a high mark of favour – getting invited to Brioni was much more difficult, for instance, than getting an invitation to Buckingham Palace. Soldatic made a casual remark to the effect that the president wanted to show his appreciation for the part I had played in improving relations between our countries. In order to forestall a potentially embarrassing incident, I replied that Canadian government regulations would not permit me to accept any foreign award. In any event, an opportunity to visit the president was all the honour I could hope for.

On the appointed day, one of Tito's automobiles called for Alison and me early in the morning and drove us to an aircraft of the president's flight. Though it was an ordinary six-passenger plane, it was equipped with extremely comfortable tilt-back chairs. After breakfast we landed in Pula in Istria and transferred to one of the president's yachts, which took us to Brioni. Tito's *maître d'hôtel* escorted us to the president's guest-house, which, I gathered, had been the home of the Austro-Hungarian owner of the island before it was taken over by the Yugoslavs. He informed us that the president would receive me alone at noon, and that he and his wife would then expect Alison and myself to join them for a private luncheon at the president's villa. It was now about half past ten; what would we like to do in the meantime?

'I'd like to take a walk and look around,' I said. But he pointed out that Brioni was a defence area, and though he did not say it in so many words, I gathered that my invitation did not include walking around. However, he did offer to provide us with a sightseeing tour, and in no time at all a horse-drawn carriage, presumably of royal vintage, pulled up in front of the guest-house. In addition to a coachman and a guide, there were two men with umbrellas at the back of the carriage to shelter us from the unsettled November weather.

There certainly was plenty to see. Diplomats serving in Yugoslavia had apparently tipped off their governments that the gift most likely to please Tito was the rarest animal capable of surviving in Brioni. The evidence was all around us: different varieties of deer and antelopes as well as peacocks, pheasants, and other exotic birds were wandering around the beautiful gardens and among the Roman ruins. The only place where I had ever seen anything like it was Woburn Abbey, the duke of Bedford's estate where I had my wartime encounter with an ostrich.

There was this strange paradox in Tito's character. He really loved and understood animals; yet once a year he invited the diplomatic corps to a hunting party where, I understand, half-tamed birds were driven by beaters across the path of the visiting diplomats so each of them could shoot a pheasant. I never went because I don't like shooting animals.

At twelve o'clock sharp I was received by the president in his new, modern, air-conditioned villa, presented to him, he said, by 'a grateful people.' There were marble staircases, a heated swimming pool (at a time when heated pools were a rarity even in North America), and all kinds of exotic birds chirping in the background. The interview lasted an hour and was conducted entirely in Serbo-Croat. I reminded Tito of the good advice he had given me at our first meeting, to de-emphasize my Russian ancestry, and I took advantage of the opportunity to enquire about Yugoslavia's relationship with the Soviet Union – the kind of political question he normally did not discuss with members of the diplomatic corps.

Tito replied that there was a clear distinction between Soviet and Yugoslav socialism, just as there was a world of difference between Soviet imperialism and Yugoslav non-alignment. Communism, he said, had been his school, his university, his whole life; he would die a communist. But Yugoslavia, unlike the Soviet Union, had rejected the autocratic brand of socialism in favour of a democratic regime, complete with workers' councils and determined steps towards self-management. The Soviet Union, in his opinion, would have to institute similar changes before it could claim to be a socialist people's democracy in the true sense of the term.

As for imperialism, Tito said he considered any kind of foreign interference unacceptable, especially when it was accompanied by the use or threat of military force. I gathered that he believed the Soviet Union's objectives were directed towards Asia and the Middle East rather than Europe; that was why he had worked so hard to develop the non-aligned group of nations. He said he would continue to work towards a balance between Soviet and American imperialism, though he seemed more concerned about the Soviet variety than its American counterpart.

In answer to his question about my impressions of Yugoslavia, I told him that one of the things I found most interesting was that, in order to improve productivity, he had returned most of the land to the peasants and allowed them to sell their produce on the free market. He also required industries to show a profit; if they failed, they would be shut down and the workers would be transferred to some other activity.

Another thing that impressed me was Tito's approach to the distribution of consumer goods. All communist dictatorships practise a form of indirect rationing by restricting the number of retail outlets to a bare minimum. Yugoslavia was no exception until 1957, when there was a trade fair in Zagreb and the Americans had the brilliant idea of exhibiting not earth-moving machinery or steel furnaces but a self-serve supermarket; they flew in fresh fruits and vegetables every day from Italy, and the Yugoslavs went wild with enthusiasm. When Tito saw the exhibit and the sensation it was creating, he said, 'That's what we're going to have.' Implementing that decision involved a total reorganization of the food distribution system, including the provision of previously non-existent facilities for refrigerating and conserving perishable food products. But by the time I left Belgrade, at least two supermarkets were doing a booming business.

Tito thanked me for my contribution to the improved relationship between Canada and Yugoslavia. He singled out the Hungarian refugee problem, the promotion of cultural and scientific exchanges, and the development of tourism as areas where I had been particularly helpful; and he said he hoped this was only the beginning of a continuing *rapprochement* between our two countries.

Lunch was served by liveried, white-gloved servants. Tito looked tough, fit, and self-assured, while his wife, Jovanka, was, as usual, all smiles and appropriately deferential to her husband, some thirty years her senior. The only time she stepped outside her purely decorative role was when a large tray with drinks was being passed around, and she reminded Tito that he was supposed to be on a diet.

As we rose to leave, Tito said he understood that I was not allowed to receive any mark of recognition from a foreign government, but this presumably didn't apply to Alison or her efforts to promote interest in Yugoslav culture among her fellow Canadians. He therefore presented her with a painting depicting, as he put it, 'a study on the theme of human vanity': two women at two windows, each examining herself in a mirror against a background of roses. He went on to explain that this gift had been selected by his advisers; his personal choice was a beautiful gold bracelet with his initials, which he proceeded to place around Alison's wrist.

Finally, Tito said he hoped that we would return to Yugoslavia. I assured him we would, and I kept my promise. In 1973, when I was leaving the foreign service and returning from Geneva to Canada, the Yugoslavs invited me back to take leave once again. They gave a dinner in my honour at the Hotel Yugoslavia in Belgrade, and the minister of foreign affairs asked me whether I remembered the building. I said it looked vaguely familiar, but I couldn't identify it. 'It was the headquarters of the Cominform before we broke with them,' he explained, 'and it is now a hotel for tourists. Don't you think that's a distinct improvement?'

ELEVEN

In London
with the Drews

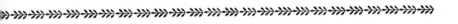

I first met John Diefenbaker in December 1957 while I was still ambassador to Yugoslavia. The new prime minister and Sidney Smith, his recently appointed minister of external affairs, had decided to take advantage of a NATO conference that was being held in Paris to meet Canada's diplomatic representatives in Europe. They also wanted first-hand reports on the views of the various governments to which the diplomats were accredited concerning Canada's participation in NATO.

The only other time I had seen Sidney Smith was in 1952 at the funeral of my brother Nick, who was warden of Hart House when he suffered a fatal stroke at the age of forty-eight. Smith was president of the University of Toronto at the time, and it was no secret that he and Nick had fundamentally different views about the meaning and administration of educational institutions. What was not generally known was that they'd had a flaming row just a couple of days before Nick collapsed in front of Hart House on the university campus. I can only assume that it was the disturbing memory of these two events and the nagging suspicion that there might have been a cause-and-effect connection between them that prompted Smith to single me out for special attention in Paris.

Though I was junior to several of the assembled heads of mission, the minister asked me to launch the discussion with a report on Yugoslavia's attitude towards NATO. I interpreted to the best of my ability what Tito had said to me on more than one occasion: that he considered NATO a threat to world peace because it perpetuated the division of Europe into two armed camps, each sheltering under its own nuclear umbrella. The way the Yugoslavs and, presumably, other non-aligned governments saw it, the militarization of western Europe gave the Soviets a welcome excuse to do what came to them naturally, namely turn the Warsaw Pact countries into an armed fortress and an arsenal for communism.

George Drew was furious. Not only did he consider himself, as high commissioner to Britain and former head of the Conservative party, several notches above the likes of me; he also made it clear that he found my remarks offensive and inappropriate. The Diefenbaker government's first priority, he said, should be a resounding declaration of support for the western alliance. He for one was not interested in the anti-NATO views of communist dictators. But, much to my surprise, Sidney Smith came to my defence. Canada's government, he said, had no intention of following blindly in the path plotted by its predecessors. It was determined to examine all available options, acquaint itself with the viewpoints of non-aligned governments, weigh the evidence, and then decide what Canada's foreign policy ought to be. He even suggested that Canada might consider following Mexico's example and pursue a more independent relationship with the United States, rather than tying ourselves hand and foot to our neighbours' defence policies. Needless to say, Drew didn't like it. His flushed complexion and twitching nose, I was soon to discover, were tell-tale signs of intense annoyance.

At a reception later that day, I was surprised when Sidney Smith made a point of introducing me to the prime minister. Though Diefenbaker had a bad cold and clearly was not in a party mood, he asked me to help him meet my diplomatic colleagues. I had no way of knowing that this brief encounter would turn out to be the gateway to three of the most important appointments in my diplomatic career. During the next few years I came closer to the seat of power than at any time before or since. The experience was exciting at times, intensely frustrating at others.

After the Paris meeting I returned to Belgrade, where I expected to spend another two or three years. But within a few months I was summoned back to Ottawa, where Sidney Smith asked me to accept an appointment as George Drew's deputy in London. I was dumbfounded. Judging by our far from cordial meeting in Paris, I didn't think Drew and I would make a particularly harmonious team. My doubts must have been written all over my face because Smith put his arm around my shoulders and said: 'Do it for Nick's sake.' On that basis, I could hardly refuse. However, I did ask for time to travel with my family across Canada, so I could renew my feel for the country and find out first-hand how people felt about some of the issues that were facing Canada and the world in the late 1950s.

In those days, heads of mission got passes on Canadian railroads so they could get to know the country they were supposed to represent abroad. But in spite of my ambassadorial rank my pass didn't include travel on the CPR's transcontinental 'Canadian' which was faster, more comfortable, and more expensive than other trains. This turned out to be an unexpected stroke of luck. Instead of hurtling non-stop across the continent, I journeyed with my family through the Crow's Nest Pass to the Kootenays, where I had spent two happy summers as a fledgling Canadian working on the railway. We then took the one-coach dayliner from Nelson to Vancouver and when the trainman heard that I had worked on the construction of the line linking Kootenay Lake to the Kettle Valley railroad, he invited us into the engineer's compartment up front, where we had a magnificent view of the Rockies as the train wound its leisurely way towards the coast. The whole trip was like a tonic, exactly what I needed to fortify me for whatever lay ahead. Unfortunately these diplomatic railway passes have since been discontinued.

My first few weeks in London in early 1960 seemed to confirm all my worst apprehensions. Drew treated me with obvious reserve, owing no doubt at least partly to his conviction that I was what Diefenbaker used to call a 'Pearsonality.' This intense suspicion of appointees of the Liberal administration, particularly those who had served under Pearson in External Affairs, seemed to be one of the few points of agreement between Diefenbaker and Drew. In introducing me to the assembled heads of federal departments represented at Canada House and to the provincial agents general,

Drew explained that I was to do only those jobs which he had specifically assigned to me; in other words, I was to have none of the discretionary power exercised by my predecessor, Sydney Pierce. Obviously that made my situation rather difficult. Every time I raised a point or suggested a course of action, I could see some official wondering: 'Has that job been assigned to George or hasn't it?'

Fortunately the problem soon resolved itself, thanks largely to the influence of Fiorenza Drew and her excellent relationship with Alison. These two highly intelligent, sensitive women took to each other from the very beginning and proceeded to demonstrate the constructive role wives can play in the professional lives of their husbands. A striking, cosmopolitan woman with a broad educational background, Fiorenza had been brought up in Italy and later lived in New York with her father, the Canadian tenor Edward Johnson, who by then had become head of the Metropolitan Opera. Her mother had been a Portuguese aristocrat. It was a vastly different background from that of George Drew, the dashing World War I hero and provincial politician whose outlook on world affairs at the time of their marriage was firmly rooted in Anglo-Saxon Ontario.

Whether they were together or apart, Fiorenza seemed to bring out the best in her husband. I remember a meeting at Canada House when we were discussing immigration with the provincial agents general. Our man from Ontario, a Drew appointee who obviously assumed he was operating on the same wavelength as his chief, deplored the fact that Italian newcomers were pouring into Canada in ever-increasing numbers while immigration from Britain was slowing down. 'What's wrong with that?' Drew asked with a chill in his voice. 'Italians make excellent citizens and Ontario should be happy to have them.' I could tell that Fiorenza was there in spirit if not in body.

Though Drew had recovered almost completely from the illness that had forced him to relinquish the Conservative leadership, he was not yet strong enough to bear the full load of social obligations imposed on Canada's high commissioner in London. As his deputy I had to represent him at many of the dinners given by every conceivable organization, from foresters to anaesthetists, and attend on his behalf some royal functions such as receptions for President de Gaulle or the Shah of Iran. A particularly memorable occasion was a Buckingham Palace dinner in honour of de Gaulle, to which we were invited because the Drews had been called home to the deathbed of Fiorenza's father. Alison, who is congenitally nervous of horses, was somewhat discomfited to find herself seated beside a courtier with the impressive title of Master of the Horse. 'Do you come here often?' he enquired by way of conversational gambit. Apart from stand-ins like ourselves, most of the guests were distinguished wartime colleagues of de Gaulle's, including Winston Churchill, in a wheelchair but still mentally alert. When Prime Minister Harold Macmillan asked him whether he had noticed much change in the general, Churchill replied: 'Yes. His profile used to remind me of a bottle of hock; now it's more like a bottle of burgundy.'

As the Massey's niece, Alison had been presented at court together with Maryon Pearson in 1937 and knew how to handle ceremonial or 'high society' functions. Fiorenza soon realized that she had acquired in my wife a valuable partner, someone with whom she could share her own responsibilities. It took George Drew a little longer to reach the same conclusion about me, but once he had decided that I was not an undercover agent of the Liberal party and that he could trust me, he accepted me as his deputy in the broadest sense of the term. Instead of confining my authority to strictly defined assignments as he had at the time of my arrival, he proceeded to delegate to me practically all his responsibilities other than a few he specifically reserved for himself. These included the Law of the Sea Conference, which represented the first attempt to find an international consensus for the conflicting claims and interests of the world's coastal countries. The issue was obviously of tremendous importance to Canada, and as an experienced politician and lawyer, Drew was the obvious person to represent his country in these negotiations. Education and personnel were two other areas which he carved out for his personal attention. Education had remained one of his abiding interests since the days when he held the education portfolio in the Ontario cabinet, and as a World War I veteran, he felt a keen commitment to the welfare of his 'troops.'

But beyond that, he let it be known that I was in charge and that people should turn to me for guidance. That gave me plenty of scope. At the time Drew first arrived in London to assume his duties as high commissioner, he found some seventeen or eighteen Canadian government departments scattered in various high-rent quarters all over the city, with next to no co-ordination between them. The Film Board, for instance, operated as a power unto itself, and if Canada House wanted to show a Canadian film it had to wait its turn like any other customer. Drew decided to consolidate all these bits and pieces under one roof on Grosvenor Square, where he had persuaded the Diefenbaker government to buy the building formerly occupied by the American embassy. He was also determined to reduce the number of officials – there were literally hundreds of them – living in London at the Canadian taxpayers' expense.

The implementation of these plans, with all their inevitable problems, became part of my responsibilities. Another part of my job was to act as glorified salesman and promoter for Drew's campaign to divert fifteen per cent of Canada's export trade from the United States to Britain. He fully subscribed to the Conservative government's view that this was the answer to the growing continentalism of the United States, that Canadians could emerge from their status as hewers of wood and drawers of water simply by developing closer economic ties with the mother country.

It would have been no use pointing out to him that the British government was far from enthusiastic about increasing its huge trade deficits; absorbing an additional fifteen per cent of our exports would merely aggravate the country's economic problems. Indeed, my contacts at Whitehall made no secret of the fact that Britain was already in the process of loosening her commonwealth ties and moving towards some closer association with Europe. But such views were anathema to Drew, and anyone who wanted to get along with him knew better than to challenge his faith in Canada's role as the brightest jewel in the crown of the British empire.

So we mounted this high-powered campaign designed to sell to

Britons everything from household goods to pickles, from costume jewelry to rain coats. We even tried, God help us, to sell rye whisky to the Scots. 'I'll give it a bash, ma'am,' said the sergeant-major of the Royal Scots regiment when Alison dutifully presented him with a case of Seagram's VO. That evening a bottle of Glenlivet was delivered to us at the Edinburgh hotel where we were staying. Attached to it was a note from the sergeants' mess, telling us in effect that a bottle of good scotch was fair exchange for a case of rye.

The rest of the trade drive was considerably more successful, particularly in its early stages when the British public seemed to consider Canadian imports an interesting novelty. Personally I thought some of the low-priced, shoddy stuff we were exhibiting and pushing on the British market was far from representative of Canada's manufacturing industry and did little credit to the country of its origin. But Drew was as determined as any Soviet commissar to fulfil his self-imposed export quota, and the fuse to his temper began smouldering whenever anyone suggested the fifteen per cent target might be overly ambitious. He actually fired a public relations officer who had dared argue that the real sales figures were one or two percentage points short of the goal.

Part of the problem was that Drew refused to see the Suez fiasco for what it was, a blow to British imperialism from which it was never going to recover. It was a time when Britain's Conservative party was still deeply split between those who believed the only thing wrong about the Suez adventure was its failure and some of the younger party members, such as Sir Edward Boyle, the minister of education in the Macmillan cabinet, who condemned the Anglo-French invasion of Egypt as a totally unjustifiable exercise in gun-boat diplomacy. Hostility between the two factions permeated official as well as social contacts. I remember mentioning Boyle's name in the course of a conversation with one of the party stalwarts in our house. 'Oh yes,' he said with palpable contempt, 'he is the man who chews his finger nails and who ratted at Suez.'

As an ex-premier and party leader, Drew considered politicians the most reliable sources of information, particularly if they happened to share his outlook on world affairs. He was very much under the influence of Lord Beaverbrook and those of his colleagues who still saw Canada as the hub of the Empire and tended to dismiss as a temporary phenomenon the emergence of African nationalist leaders such as Nkrumah and Kenyatta. He had little contact with a younger generation of Tories such as Heath or Maudling, and no use at all for what he called the 'junior officials' at Whitehall, who to my way of thinking had more reliable information and a more realistic appraisal of current events than the members of Drew's old boys' club.

My diplomatic training was put to a crucial test when the prime minister came to Britain on an official visit and I was assigned to act as his aide. It didn't take any great insight to realize that Diefenbaker and Drew had no use for each other. Not that there were any fundamental policy differences between them. Both were totally committed to the British connection; indeed a closer relationship with the mother country had been an important part of Diefenbaker's election platform, and his government had launched the British trade drive which Drew was pursuing with such vigour. Yet Drew clearly could not forget that, had it not been for his serious illness following the pipeline debate in 1956, he would have led the Conservative party into the 1957 election and would, presumably, have become prime minister. No doubt he felt that, under the circumstances, he should have been given a senior cabinet portfolio rather than being fobbed off with a diplomatic posting which looked to all the world like a consolation prize. Diefenbaker, for his part, saw in Drew the personification of all the mysterious and, in his mind, insidious Bay Street forces of big business and finance which he was determined to strip of their influence in the Conservative party. To me, watching their personality clash was like reliving Mackenzie King's 1941 visit to London and his icy relationship with Vincent Massey.

Even the cordial facade which Diefenbaker and Drew maintained for public consumption occasionally showed obvious cracks. Drew tried to be a good host and, conscious of the prime minister's devotion to Conservative traditions on both sides of the Atlantic, he arranged a luncheon at the Carlton Club in the room used by Disraeli for his 'kitchen cabinet' meetings. In his speech of welcome he drew the attention of the guests, including the provincial agents general, to the historic significance of the room. He also pointed out that, while Quebec had no agent general in London at the time, he hoped that this situation would soon be corrected and that Quebec House, which had been closed as an economy measure, would be able to reopen.

In his reply, Diefenbaker ignored completely the historical references to the kitchen cabinet. As for the absence of a Quebec agent general, he said he was relieved that he didn't have to speak French since that was not one of his strong points.

Fortunately Diefenbaker's dislike of Drew did not rub off on me. To the extent that I had come to Canada as a refugee and had worked on the railway in the west, I apparently epitomized to him what he considered to be the backbone of the country, the ethnic immigrant who uses manual labour rather than Bay Street connections to get ahead in the world; and he chose to disregard those aspects of my background which didn't fit this populist image of a good Canadian.

We saw a great deal of each other during his stay in London. The highlight of the visit was his address in support of the British Empire, delivered at a mammoth rally in the Royal Albert Hall. Lord Beaverbrook, who sponsored the event, made sure that his newspapers gave it appropriate publicity. 'The Great British Commonwealth Statesman Speaks – you only have ten more days to buy your ticket,' proclaimed a headline in the *Evening Standard*. The speech was a great success, and as Diefenbaker basked in the applause, he saw nothing to suggest that within a few months Britain's Conservative government would be asking Canada to support its application for membership in the European Economic Community.

Also on the prime minister's agenda were meetings with all kinds of dignitaries and groups, including such unlikely ones as an association of Ukrainian Canadians living in London. They invited Diefenbaker to a reception at the Savoy Hotel in the hope that they could persuade him to speak out in public in favour of Ukrainian independence. When I turned up ahead of time to check the arrangements, they all converged on me and informed me that, as one of their own, I'd have to plead their cause with the PM. I tried to explain that I had been born in Russia rather than the Ukraine, that I had come to Canada as a young boy, and that I had no wish to involve my adoptive country in conflicts which my family had been only too glad to leave behind in Europe. But they pointed out that my father and grandfather had lived in the Ukraine; as far as they were concerned, that made me the next best thing to a native son. I finally agreed to suggest to the prime minister that he encourage the CBC to add Ukrainian broadcasts to its international service – a recommendation which he was glad to accept.

Another important visitor to London in 1960 was Howard Green, who had been appointed secretary of state for external affairs following the sudden death of Sidney Smith. The first time I met him was when he came into my office and asked whether he could borrow it for a day. I assumed he had an appointment with some VIPs and asked him did he wish any special arrangements to be made. He replied that he wanted three cups of tea and 'if possible some biscuits.' The following day he turned up with two old ladies, who, he told me, had looked after him while he was recovering from his wounds during World War I. I couldn't help but be impressed by the man's modesty and basic decency. Here he was, a key cabinet minister on an official visit to London, and the thing that was uppermost in his mind was to express his gratitude for an act of kindness extended to him more than forty years before.

We hit it off from the very beginning. The fact that I knew the Arrow Lakes and the Kootenay country where he came from and where his mother still lived, that I had taken my family there to visit before coming to London and had seen one of the old paddle-wheelers being used as a museum gave us something in common. To my mind, part of an official's function is to help a cabinet minister relax when he is off duty by steering the conversation into congenial channels. When a minister has been making difficult decisions all day, the last thing he wants to do is to rehash the same problems over the dinner table or at the end of a tough day. Throughout my diplomatic career I found that, where I had a good relationship with ministers – St Laurent, Pearson, Green, Martin – it was at least partly because we had this kind of geographic link or some area of mutual interest. By the same token, I found it difficult to relate to those ministers with whom I had nothing in common outside our working relationship.

Shortly after the Diefenbaker and Green visits, I was surprised to learn that I was to be transferred to Ottawa as an assistant under-secretary of state for external affairs. I had been in London for less than two years, and now that we were getting along so well with the Drews I had no wish to leave. Besides, I had seen enough of the prime minister to realize that, though he obviously liked me, serving under him in Ottawa wasn't going to be easy. I would have been considerably more apprehensive had I suspected just how difficult it would in fact turn out to be.

TWELVE

Ottawa
under Diefenbaker

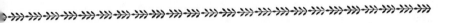

Shortly after I arrived back in Ottawa in January 1961, I was summoned by the prime minister and told that I was to report to him regularly as his adviser on national defence policy in general and the implications of nuclear weapons in particular. It would have been useless to point out that a great deal had happened in the five years since I had last been involved in defence planning, or that the appointment would put me in a highly embarrassing position vis-à-vis Norman Robertson, the under-secretary of state, who, according to all the rules of the hierarchical game, should have been Diefenbaker's choice as adviser. Indeed it was no secret that, in Diefenbaker's eyes, Robertson's long association with Mackenzie King and Mike Pearson made him hopelessly suspect as a closet Liberal. As I was about to discover, the prime minister was also uncomfortable with Norman's fantastic intellect and his ability to perceive aspects of a problem which a less erudite observer would inevitably overlook. What Diefenbaker wanted was clear, black and white position statements, the kind of arguments a lawyer could use to win his case, not the subtle shadings which were more characteristic of Norman's style.

In a broader sense, the situation in which I found myself reflected a recurring problem in Canada's governmental system, namely the ambiguous relationship between the bureaucracy and cabinet ministers. It is all very well to say that public servants are non-political, that they are honour bound to serve their ministers regardless of political affiliation. This is perfectly true. Yet it would be unrealistic to deny that when one party has been in power throughout the working lives of most public servants, when deputy ministers have spent many years acting as advisers to their political masters and have developed relationships of mutual trust, not to say friendship, a change of government may leave them feeling mildly schizophrenic.

It is therefore hardly surprising that, on the few occasions in living memory when the Tories have formed a government, they have treated the so-called mandarins with profound suspicion. Yet, in a democracy the orderly transfer of power from one party to another does not coincide with an equally orderly transfer of the knowledge and experience required to exercise that power. Men and women whose previous public life has been confined to the opposition benches have, by and large, been starved for information by an administration which had no wish to groom its opponents for the succession. Suddenly confronted with the responsibilities of government, they are desperate for reliable advice but uncertain where to find it. Americans, who face the same dilemma whenever there is a change of administration, resolve it by letting the newly elected president replace his predecessor's advisers with candidates of his own choice and political persuasion. In Canada such a partisan bloodletting has always been considered unacceptable. Though a few deputy ministers closely associated with the previous government may find themselves out of jobs, new prime ministers and their cabinet colleagues are more inclined to resolve the problem by bypassing the most senior echelons of the bureaucracy and looking for confidants lower down the hierarchical ladder, to people who presumably have developed no personal ties with previous ministers and therefore may have no personal stake in the *status quo*.

This was the unenviable role in which I was cast by John Diefenbaker early in 1961. Though he had by then been prime minister for three and a half years, he was only just beginning to realize that, by signing the North American Air Defence agreement in the early days of his administration, he had entered into commitments whose implications he had neither explored nor understood. He simply accepted the advice of General George Pearkes, the newly appointed minister of national defence and close friend of the chiefs of staff, who assured him that NORAD had passed through the channels of cabinet approval and that signing it was just a matter of confirming defence arrangements that had existed for years. As General Charles Foulkes, chairman of the Canadian Chiefs of Staff Committee, later put it, 'the decision for a joint air defence was taken in 1946, not 1958 [sic] as some of the critics claim when discussing NORAD.'

This was at best a one-sided interpretation of the facts. It is true that military leaders in both Canada and the United States had advocated some sort of continental defence system ever since the late 1940s, and more particularly after it became apparent that the Soviets had developed the capability to mount a nuclear air attack against North America. The Canadian government had acknowledged the need for such a joint defence system when it agreed to participate in the establishment of early warning lines in northern Canada, to be manned by both Canadian and American forces. But when it came to actually integrating these forces under a single peace-time command, senior air force echelons of both countries agreed to keep their plans under wraps because, as the Americans put it in February 1956, 'this subject is very sensitive in Canada' because of its sovereignty implications, and therefore 'it is important there should be no leakage of information . . . to the press.'* A year later, however, these sensitivities had apparently been allayed, and the integrated command was to have been discussed by the cabinet defence committee on 15 March 1957. At the last moment it was removed from the agenda, and the Americans were informed that there would be no decision until mid-June. A federal election was called for 10 June.

Had the matter come up while Pearson was secretary of state for external affairs, I am convinced he would have insisted that any continental defence agreement must include an explicit commitment by the United States to consult Canada before taking any

---

*Chairman, Canadian Joint Staff (Washington) to Secretary, JCS, 27 February 1956, reprinted in JCS 1541/104, 27 February 1956, 'Note by the Secretaries to the JCS on Integration of Operational Control of the Continental Air Defenses of Canada and the United States in Peacetime.' Documents released as a result of Freedom of Information Act, as quoted by Joseph T. Jockel in *The American Review of Canadian Studies* vol. XII, number 3, Fall 1982.

action that might lead to war. That was the advice he received from his senior officials, and it seems inconceivable that he would have settled for less. Indeed I know for a fact that Pearson had grave misgivings about any bilateral agreement outside the framework of NATO. His viewpoint, which I shared, was that NATO had been created for the collective defence of all its members, whether European or North American, and that it was therefore up to NATO to counter any threat to Canada or the United States. He had actually tried to argue the point with John Foster Dulles, but the secretary of state told him, in essence, what the American chiefs of staff had already told their secretary of defence, namely that any European involvement in the defence of North America was 'militarily unacceptable.'*

But whatever misgivings Pearson had became irrelevant in the wake of the 1957 election. The Liberals had been defeated, and when NORAD came up before their last cabinet defence committee meeting, the committee decided that the issue was too important to be dealt with by a government that had been voted out of office. So when Diefenbaker was told, once he became prime minister, that NORAD had been before the cabinet defence committee, that may have been the truth but it was certainly not the whole truth.

Neither did the new prime minister's advisers bother explaining to him that, unlike the agreement to place Canada's NATO contingents in Europe under the command of non-Canadians, NORAD amounted to a decision to give a foreign power control over our air defence forces in Canada. From the point of view of the minister of national defence and the military, that may well have been the logical culmination of the cosy relationship between General Foulkes and his friends 'Brad' (General Bradley) and 'Rad' (Admiral Radford) in Washington. But in terms of the relationship between two sovereign countries, it was what politicians would describe as a totally new ball game. One of the inevitable side-effects of the integrated air defence command was that Canadians would have little or no

*Memorandum, JCS to Secretary of Defense, 11 June 1954; approved in JCS 1541/94, 11 June 1954, 'Proposed North American Continental Defense Organization.' Quoted by Jockel in ibid.

say in the choice of strategy or weapons. The decision to equip our northern defences with the surface-to-air Bomarc missiles was just one in a chain of military hardware purchases made not on the basis of what's best for Canada, but rather what is for sale in the United States.

By the time I arrived in Ottawa the consequences of these earlier decisions were coming home to roost. The Bomarcs had been delivered and installed but, without warheads, they were sitting like so many guns without ammunition on our northern approaches. Though American pressure on Canada to accept the nuclear warheads had been mounting for some time, the debate had been conducted with considerable decorum so long as Eisenhower was president of the United States. But almost as soon as John Kennedy was sworn in, it became obvious that the new president had no patience with an ally whose reluctance to accept nuclear warheads he interpreted as an attempt to evade his responsibilities. By the same token, Diefenbaker looked down on Kennedy as a callow young man who had somehow landed in the White House by mistake, and who failed to show the appropriate respect to a statesman of his maturity and stature.

It became my unenviable task to brief Diefenbaker on the events that led up to NORAD and the implications of what he had done. Without putting it in so many words I tried to make him understand that, by committing Canada to an integrated North American defence system, he had accepted a subordinate role in a strategy based almost entirely on the nuclear deterrent. Whether it was true, as the prime minister claimed, that he had been misled into believing that the Bomarcs could be equipped with conventional warheads, was almost beside the point. The crux of the matter was that the day he approved NORAD he embarked on a course which led to the acceptance of nuclear weapons. In my opinion he was left with a choice between two alternatives: either accept the warheads or negotiate his way out of NORAD and opt for a conventional role within NATO, similar to that of Norway and Denmark.

But making clear-cut decisions was not part of Diefenbaker's nature. Instead he had an unfortunate tendency to personalize issues, blame his advisers for letting him down, and, if at all possible, play them up against each other. Though I was never at the receiving end of these tactics, I hated seeing some of my friends badgered by the prime minister. One of his favourite targets was Air Marshal Hugh Campbell, whom I had known and admired ever since I first met him at RCAF headquarters in wartime London. During one cabinet session which I was asked to attend Diefenbaker attacked Campbell so viciously that Douglas Harkness, who by then had succeeded Pearkes as minister of national defence, finally intervened and said that this kind of abuse of a senior air force officer was unacceptable. For my part, while I shared Diefenbaker's conviction that the armed forces had manoeuvred him into signing NORAD, I had no wish to become involved in his personal vendettas. Besides, he had only himself to blame for making such a momentous decision without discussing it with his cabinet or any External Affairs official, let alone submitting it to a parliamentary debate.

Being obliged to witness attacks on selected officials was only one of several reasons why I was anxious to reduce to the inescapable minimum my briefing sessions with the prime minister. For one thing, it was becoming increasingly clear that he was using me mainly as a sounding board for his own ideas, and that he found any advice I had to offer of little use as ammunition against his political opponents. For another, I had been a public servant long enough to be aware of the pitfalls that lie in wait for an official who, in the eyes of the bureaucracy, tries to leap-frog over the shoulders of his superiors into the entourage of the prime minister. Even though the minister of external affairs, Howard Green, and his deputy, Norman Robertson, had both told me that I had no choice but to comply with Diefenbaker's wishes, and though I had been careful to keep them informed about our conversations, there was no denying that the situation was, to say the least, awkward.

Fortunately, the potentially explosive problem was defused by the understanding attitudes of Green and Robertson, plus the fact that the three of us were in fundamental agreement about most external policy issues. Unlike the prime minister, Howard Green was a great admirer of Robertson's intellect and integrity, not to mention his British Columbian roots. Above all Green, stirred by memories of the horrors of World War I, found in Robertson as well as myself enthusiastic allies in his determined fight for arms control and against the proliferation of nuclear weapons.

Jointly we searched for some means of bridging the gap between National Defence and External Affairs, and I met repeatedly with Robert Bryce, the secretary to the cabinet, in an effort to come up with a mutually acceptable solution. During one such meeting, which we held over dinner in a Hull restaurant, the proprietor, Madame Burger, handed me a note on which she had written: 'You are being overheard.' I glanced over my shoulder and saw Pierre Sévigny, the associate minister of national defence, sitting at the next table.

The incident was symptomatic of the atmosphere of intrigue which permeated the relationship between the two departments. Little had changed since the time when General Foulkes told me that he wouldn't allow External Affairs eggheads to interfere with defence planning. Though Air Marshal Frank Miller, who had succeeded Foulkes as chairman of the chiefs of staff, was somewhat more diplomatic in his choice of words, his meaning was the same. As far as he and his National Defence colleagues were concerned, NORAD had been signed, there was an implicit commitment to equip our armed forces with nuclear weapons, and that commitment was not negotiable.

Faced with this kind of stone wall, we came up with our own formula for defusing the government's nuclear dilemma. According to this formula Canada would accept nuclear warheads on two conditions: the weapons would have to be under joint American/ Canadian control, and their acceptance would have to be preceded by an all-out effort to reach a disarmament agreement. Unless it could be shown that all attempts to reach such an agreement had proved fruitless, it would be neither desirable from our point of view nor consistent in the eyes of the world for Canada to preach non-proliferation to other nations while accepting nuclear weapons on our own soil.

To the beleaguered prime minister, this compromise solution was a welcome peg on which to hang his own indecision, and he clung to it even after it became obvious that it wasn't strong enough to save his government. We knew all along that the proposal was no more than a holding action, that the Americans would never accept joint control with regard to the use of nuclear weapons.* But in the mean time it did enable Howard Green to wage a number of successful campaigns on behalf of the one cause which, in his mind, overshadowed all others in importance, namely arms control.

One of his major concerns was the radiation hazard caused by nuclear testing on both sides of the Iron Curtain. He put a number of us to work drafting United Nations resolutions to curb such tests, monitor any radiation unleashed in the atmosphere, and provide for an international exchange of information on the subject. Next we were conscripted to find co-sponsors for the resolutions, to be proposed both at the General Assembly in New York and at the Disarmament Commission in Geneva. I accompanied Green to New York, where Charles Ritchie was our permanent representative, and I witnessed the relentless pressure with which Green made us pursue potential co-sponsors, all the way to the washroom if necessary. In large measure as a result of his tireless efforts, United Nations opinion became aroused to the extent where the Soviet Union, the United States, and the United Kingdom ended up signing a treaty that banned all nuclear tests other than the underground variety. More than one hundred UN members, including Canada, subsequently added their signatures to this treaty.

Another achievement which owed a great deal to Green's initiative was the agreement to refrain from using outer space for military purposes. Green first raised the issue in 1961 at the conference of the committee on disarmament in Geneva, when he asked for an assurance that satellites would not be equipped with nuclear weapons that might be launched by remote control against an unsuspecting adversary. The Americans were furious because, the way they saw it, they should have been consulted before Canada put forward such a proposal. But a number of other delegates decided to back the concept, and eventually the Soviet Union and the United States signed such an agreement. Of course satellites have always

---

*Contrary to a widespread misconception the so-called two-key system deals with technical safeguards, not the actual decision whether nuclear weapons should be used.

been used for spying, or surveillance, to use a more polite term; but at least up till now outer space has not been turned into a launching pad for nuclear time bombs.

In line with his faith in the United Nations and his determination to loosen Canada's dependence on the United States, Green was forever on the lookout for opportunities to develop closer ties with third world countries. Many a time in the hall of the United Nations I watched him buttonhole Afro-Asian delegates, sit them down for a talk, and try to find out how Canada could help them resolve some of their problems. More often than not he ended up inviting his newfound friends to Ottawa, with results which at times had more in common with a bedroom farce than the lofty world of diplomacy. I was in London at the time when Patrice Lumumba, the mercurial prime minister of the newly independent republic of the Congo, paid a visit to Ottawa, but External Affairs was still buzzing when I returned with vivid accounts of Lumumba's requests for 'girls' to be sent to him at night. In his innocence Green interpreted this to mean that his African visitor wanted stenographers to help him catch up on his correspondence after a day's work, and he issued instructions accordingly. I don't know whether it was the stenographers or Lumumba who let it be known that there had been some sort of misunderstanding; either way, arrangements were made to meet the wishes of the Congolese prime minister the following night. When it came to accounting for the expenditure, some imaginative External Affairs official decided it should be identified in the books as 'flowers.'*

As it turned out, the trip to Ottawa may have been Lumumba's last hurrah. Within a matter of weeks a chieftain called Moise Tshombe, backed by Belgian mining interests, led the rich province of Katanga in an attempt to secede from the Congo and plunged the country into civil war. The Lumumba government had no army other than the half-trained gendarmerie left behind by the Belgians at the time of their hasty exit from their former colony. In the absence of any established authority capable of maintaining law

---

*In his book *You Can't Print That!* (Hurtig 1983, pp. 188–9) Charles Lynch tells a slightly different version of the same story. This is the way I heard it.

and order, the country was plunged into total anarchy, compounded by racial and tribal hatreds. When Belgium responded to reports of widespread rape and massacres as well as an invitation from Tshombe by sending its forces back into the Congo, Lumumba appealed to the United Nations for assistance 'against the present external aggression which is a threat to international peace.'

By then Secretary General Dag Hammarskjold had become convinced that the only hope of bringing the situation under control was to dispatch an international peace-keeping force to the Congo. Howard Green supported this plan wholeheartedly and immediately agreed that Canada should contribute a non-combattant contingent to such a force. The Canadian communications unit which went to the Congo under the command of Colonel Dextrase (later General Dextrase, head of the joint chiefs of staff) did a wonderful job, under frightful conditions of physical discomfort and in the absence of any protection from local authorities. Several times in 1961 I went to New York to discuss with Hammarskjold incidents where our men had been attacked by undisciplined mobs. I can't claim that I got to know Hammarskjold well; unlike Pearson, who established a really close friendship with him, I found it difficult to relate to his Arctic smile or his scholarly, precise manner. Yet I was tremendously impressed not only with his intellect, but with his obvious sense of mission, his determination to have the United Nations become the instrument of a global society for the protection of small countries against the imperialist ambitions of their powerful neighbours.

When it came to searching for peace, Howard Green didn't care what the political complexion of any particular government was so long as it was willing to negotiate rather than fight. His friendly if somewhat strange encounter with the foreign minister of the People's Republic of China, for instance, may well have helped pave the way for the formal exchange of diplomatic representatives between our two countries some nine years later. Green and Chen Yi had both come to Geneva in 1961 to attend a conference that had been called in an attempt to persuade the Soviet Union, the United States, and China to recognize the neutrality of Laos and thereby stop the war in Vietnam from spreading beyond its borders. Green found this objective all the more appealing since Canada was part of the international commissions (along with Poland and India) which had been trying to observe and report on events in Indochina ever since the French pulled out in 1956. It had been a difficult, often frustrating assignment, given the lack of co-operation on the part of the belligerents, and it seemed clear the commission system would not survive unless its members could move freely around Laos and make sure its neutrality was being observed.

The conference got off to an inauspicious beginning when Howard Green, accompanied by Chester Ronning and myself, pulled up at the Palais des Nations only to be told that the British and Soviet co-chairmen had been unable to agree either on an agenda or a time when the sittings were to begin. We were in fact the only ones to arrive, other than a peacock which hopped onto the minister's car and proceeded to relieve itself. I understand this is considered a bad omen in the Far East, but it did not affect Green's determination to attend the conference, even if he had to sit there all alone.

It did not come to that. Even though Prince Sihanouk of Cambodia, who had been invited to act as chairman, was somewhere on the French Riviera and could not be found, the conference did eventually get under way and, somewhat to the surprise of everyone concerned, actually reached a compromise agreement concerning the neutralization of Laos and the continued existence of the international comission. In retrospect it was a hollow victory, soon to be overshadowed by actual developments in Indochina, but at the time, it seemed like a minor triumph.

Throughout the conference, the Canadian and Chinese delegations sat side by side, but, given the state of non-recognition between their governments, each delegation pretended that the other didn't exist. In fact the Chinese didn't participate in any way in the conference proceedings so that, up to the last day, no one knew where they stood with regard to the Laotian issue. Then just before we were to leave Geneva, I noticed in the *Journal de Genève* an item to the effect that the Chinese foreign minister had paid a courtesy call on Canada's minister of external affairs. I pointed this out to Green and told him that, translated into ordinary language, this undoubtedly meant such a call was about to take place. Just then the doorbell announced the arrival of Marshal Chen Yi along with two other Chinese officials.

Fortunately Chester Ronning, who had been brought up in China by missionary parents, spoke fluent Mandarin and was able to act as interpreter. Chen Yi said he had come to thank Canada's repre-- sentative for the shipment of wheat which our government had sent to China in the wake of his country's severe drought; and he added he appreciated what we had done all the more since he understood that we had encountered problems in obtaining Ameri-can unloading equipment, which was so vital to the prompt delivery of the wheat. Actually the problem had been blown out of all proportion by the Canadian press. While it was true that United States legislation at that time forbade the use of American equip-ment for trade with mainland China, this was one instance where the US government made a real effort to accommodate Canadian interests. However, the scare headlines in our newspapers had clearly been brought to the attention of China's foreign minister. 'We too have alliance problems,' he said, 'as you apparently have yours.' It was a fascinating comment, coming as it did at a time when rumours about an ideological rift between the Soviet Union and the People's Republic of China were yet to be confirmed.

Being somewhat out of his depth in the realm of diplomatic subtleties, Green turned the conversation to more mundane mat-ters. Why, he asked in his typically ingenuous way, had Marshal Chen Yi come all the way to Geneva if he was going to sit through the entire conference in stony silence? 'Why, to play tennis,' replied China's foreign minister. He was perfectly serious. Apparently he had trouble finding enough time for his favourite game in Peking, what with all the interruptions. As for the large delegation that had accompanied him to Geneva, he explained he had brought these subordinates along so they could study languages and diplo-matic protocol.

Encouraged by Chen Yi's apparent sincerity and sudden commu-nicativeness, Green asked him whether he would like to come to a reception the Canadian mission was holding that evening. Chen Yi enquired which Americans were going to be there, and when told that both Secretary of State Dean Rusk and Averell Harriman, the head of the US delegation to the Geneva conference, were expected to attend, he announced: 'I'll come. I'll speak to Harriman.' He did just that, and following his conversation with Harriman that evening he told the conference that China was ready to accept the neutralization of Laos. The incident illustrates the importance of the personal contacts for which New York and Geneva provide such an ideal setting. Long before Henry Kissinger made his widely touted journey to Peking, high-level representatives of the United States and China made contact at a party given by Canada's foreign minister in Geneva and took the first step in breaking the diplomatic log-jam between their countries. Chen Yi, incidentally, was to become a victim of the cultural revolution and, though eventually rehabilitated, he never regained his health or his position.

On at least one occasion Howard Green's dogged determination to bridge differences between governments and their political systems got him and me into trouble. It all started when he asked me what I thought about inviting Yugoslavia's foreign minister, Koca Popovic, to Ottawa for an official visit. I told him that my reaction to such an invitation was decidedly mixed. I did agree, of course, that Canada should do everything possible to maintain good relations with the only member of Europe's communist bloc to have asserted its political, military, and economic independence from the Soviet Union. Moreover, I was delighted at the prospect of renewing my friendship with the most cultured, brilliant, and stimulating official I had met while I was ambassador to Yugoslavia. The son of a wealthy Belgrade merchant, Popovic had studied in Paris at the Sorbonne in the 1930s and presumably was recruited into the Communist party about the same time that Maclean, Burgess, and Philby were joining the party in England. He fought in the Spanish civil war and rose to become an artillery captain in the International Brigade before returning home in time to see his country invaded by the Germans and Italians. He joined the partisans, and his bravery as one of Tito's top generals soon became legendary.

But while his record as a freedom fighter undoubtedly earned him the respect of his party comrades and the position of foreign minister, I was much more impressed with his sharp mind and the variety of his interests. He was a connoisseur of literature and art as well as sports, wine, and good food. He not only spoke impeccable French, he wrote poetry in French as well as his native Serbo-Croat. His favourite hobby was deep-sea diving (long before its current popularity) and the study of underwater fish and plant life. He played an excellent game of tennis. All in all, Popovic was a highly civilized, fascinating human being who, I always suspected, felt just a little ill at ease with his more proletarian comrades.

On the other hand, I warned Green that an official visit by a high-ranking Yugoslav official, no matter how personally attractive, would not sit well with those new Canadians who had suffered at the hands of Yugoslavia's communist regime. There might be demonstrations and even threats against the visitor's life, which was exactly why the St Laurent government had never invited Marshal Tito to Canada. Such an invitation had been discussed several times, but the risks had always outweighed the potential benefits.

However when one of Howard Green's projects was at stake, it was next to impossible to dissuade him. He issued the invitation, and next thing we knew, a delegation of Yugoslav Canadians requested a meeting with the prime minister and informed him that, should he receive this 'communist murderer', no Canadian of Yugoslav extraction would ever again cast a vote for the Progressive Conservative party. Diefenbaker promptly informed Green that he was not going to meet Popovic during his stay in Canada.

I told Green that going ahead with the visit without having the foreign minister meet the head of our government was simply inconceivable. He would have to either persuade the prime minister to change his mind or make up an excuse and call the whole thing off. But rather than accept my advice, Green and Diefenbaker came up with a typically Canadian compromise. According to their scenario, the president of the Senate would host an official government luncheon in honour of Mr Popovic. Meanwhile, Diefenbaker, ostensibly on his way to the House of Commons, would pass the Senate chamber and rustle the curtain as a signal, rather like Polonius in Hamlet. At that point I was to say to Popovic: 'I believe that's our prime minister passing by. Let me take you over and introduce you.'

It was one of the most embarrassing episodes in my entire diplomatic career. The curtain rustled on cue, I mumbled the prearranged lie and rushed Popovic in the direction of the rustle. There was the prime minister of Canada, shaking his jowls at the mystified visitor. He said, 'Welcome to Ottawa,' and promptly took his leave. Later that day during a visit to the National Research Council, Popovic's curiosity got the better of him. 'Come clean,' he said, 'what on earth is going on? Why did your prime minister behave in this extraordinary way?' All I could do was appeal to our long-standing friendship. 'I'd rather not explain,' I said. 'You have your domestic problems to which I never referred while I was in your country; please don't ask me to talk about ours.'

To top off this memorable day, there was an evening reception given by Howard Green in honour of his visitor. Popovic told his host how glad he was that Canada was a bilingual country because, while he spoke very little English, he was perfectly at home in French. 'You do speak French, Mr Minister?' he enquired almost as an afterthought. 'Pity pooh,' replied Green with a benign smile, and went on to explain that the only French he had learned while he was overseas during World War I was 'quarante-huit chevaux and eighteen hommes' (the capacity of boxcars used to transport troops and horses). All in all, the Popovic visit was not much of a success as far as I was concerned. The Yugoslav ambassador to Canada had made it clear to me that he considered me personally responsible for the foreign minister's safety, and though I persuaded the RCMP to pull out all the stops to prevent any incident, I heaved a sigh of relief when my friend was back on his way to Belgrade.

But if Green's naïveté and lack of sophistication led to some embarrassing incidents, these shrank in significance beside his self-less pursuit of world peace and the determined, often imaginative way in which he explored solutions to international conflicts. There was a widespread assumption in External Affairs that Diefenbaker had chosen Green as foreign minister for two reasons. One was that Howard knew nothing about world affairs and would therefore be easily guided by the prime minister; the other was Diefenbaker's wish to inflict a scourge on a department which he considered a hotbed of 'Pearsonalities.' If that was indeed his motivation, he failed on both counts. True, Green knew next to nothing about the niceties of diplomacy when he was appointed to the portfolio. But he had very definite views not only about disarmament, which was his pet cause, but also about the need to develop stronger ties with the emerging countries of Africa, Asia, and Latin America and about the importance of the British connection.

What's more, he was determined to learn, and he looked to the intermediate echelons of the department as a source of new ideas. It wasn't that he distrusted Norman Robertson or me; after all, the three of us were on the same wavelength, certainly where disarmament and Canada's relations with the third world were concerned. But Green liked to deal directly with the desk officers who were going to do the actual research and implement his instructions. Though this was highly unorthodox, both Norman and I felt it made a great deal of sense for these junior officers to provide the minister with direct advice, rather than have it percolate up the hierarchical channels, with all their roadblocks and built-in biases. The meetings the desk officers attended, the opportunity they had to brief the minister and to discuss various initiatives, generated a sense of involvement which was unique in the public service. Green for his part became a devoted fan of External Affairs and its people. 'I'd like to make them all ambassadors,' he once said to me in a burst of enthusiasm.

There has been nothing like it since. After the change of government it soon became clear that henceforth there was to be no breach of the hierarchical chain of command. Years later, following the fall of the short-lived 1979 government of Joe Clark, Flora MacDonald complained that, as minister of external affairs, she had been denied access to anyone within the department other than the under-secretary of state. Ironically enough, the under-secretary of state at that time was Allan Gotlieb, one of the bright young men whom Howard Green had identified as rising stars in an era of more open and less formal communications within the department.

THIRTEEN

Ambassador to NATO

Jules Léger was Canadian ambassador to NATO when he suffered his first heart attack late in 1961. I was sent to Paris in January 1962 to pinch-hit for Jules while he was convalescing in southern France, and it didn't take me long to become aware of the pressures under which he had been working. On the domestic scene, de Gaulle's decision to renounce all claims to Algeria had brought France to the brink of civil war, and though the worst of the crisis was over, the nation was still torn apart by that agonizing decision and the sense of betrayal it engendered in many Frenchmen. I arrived in Paris to the sound of bombs exploding in nearby streets and the sight of policemen armed with machine-guns. At the same time, NATO was traumatized by the situation around Berlin, where the Soviets were delaying convoys laden with supplies and generally defying international agreements concerning free access to the city. Watching helplessly the ups and downs in the Algerian and Berlin crises, members of NATO Council sometimes felt as though they were riding a roller-coaster that was out of control.

Though I returned to Ottawa after a couple of months, it soon became obvious that Léger was not recovering his health as quickly as had been hoped. Green therefore decided to transfer him to the less demanding post of ambassador to Italy and to appoint me his successor as Canada's permanent representative on the North Atlantic Council.

From my point of view it seemed like an ideal posting. I had been associated with the planning of NATO way back in 1948 while I was at the United Nations in New York and with the establishment of its political and military structure during the time I spent on Hume Wrong's staff in Washington. After the Suez crisis, when Mike Pearson went to Geneva as a leading member of the committee of 'three wise men' appointed to work out a consultative mechanism to prevent future rifts in the alliance, he took me along as one of his advisers, or 'the little wise guy' in Pearsonian lingo. Not only did I know a good deal about the North Atlantic Alliance; I sincerely believed in its mission as a deterrent to war and an instrument of economic and political co-operation among western nations. Being associated with that mission as Canada's emissary seemed to me both a challenge and an honour, all the more so since all my predecessors in this responsible post had ranked as deputy ministers in our public service. With the ghost of Algerian decolonization finally laid to rest, the prospect of living in Paris and immersing myself in French culture beckoned like an additional bonus. All in all, I arrived at my new posting in July 1962 with a sense of enthusiasm and great expectations.

My one regret was that the move would mark the end of my close association with Howard Green, whom I had come to regard not only with respect, but with genuine affection. I therefore should have been pleased when he persuaded the prime minister shortly after my arrival in Paris to let me join them in London, where both of them were attending a commonwealth conference. Actually I responded to the summons with considerable apprehension because, as I tried to tell Green the moment we met, I wasn't at all up to date on commonwealth issues. But he brushed my objections aside. Prime Minister Harold Macmillan had just informed the assembled statesmen that Britain intended to apply for membership in the European Economic Community, and Green, to whom the announcement had come as a profound shock, wanted me to analyse its political implications. How was he to explain to his constituents in Vancouver-Quadra that the mother country, for which so many of them had fought and bled in two world wars, would rather be part of Europe than the British commonwealth? Where did that leave the Conservative party, for whom the British connection had always been a source of strength and inspiration?

I told him these were political questions which he should discuss with a British cabinet minister, and I proceeded to make an appointment for him with Duncan Sandys, the commonwealth secretary. Next day I couldn't resist asking him how the meeting had gone. 'Well,' he said, 'at least Sandys was frank. He told me I should explain to people in Vancouver that mum's children are grown up now, and she has decided she wants a divorce so she can get married again.'

My concern as to my ability to assist Green at the conference itself proved fully justified when I found myself sitting beside the minister in a committee on 'temperate food stuffs' – an important subject, no doubt, but one about which I knew absolutely nothing. The prime minister of Australia's coalition government, Robert Menzies, launched the discussion with a bland statement to the effect that he was confident Britain would negotiate with the EEC terms that were favourable to the empire and the commonwealth. But this wasn't nearly good enough for his deputy, 'Black-Jack' McEwen, whose rural constituency was a traditional supplier of fruits to the British market. He demanded to know just what Britain proposed to do to help his constituents, who had been assured when they planted their orchards that they would enjoy imperial preferences. When he was told he should simply rely on the good faith of the British government, he brought his fist down right in front of my nose. 'I know what the good faith of the British is worth,' he shouted. 'You've sold us down the river any time your interests clashed with ours, and you'll do it again.'

After a few seconds of dead silence, Howard Green turned to me and asked, 'What shall we say?' I suggested he'd better ask Jake Warren, who had been summoned from his post in Geneva to advise the minister on economic matters; and we all listened as Jake coached Green to tell the committee that Canada expected to be consulted about any arrangements to be negotiated in lieu of imperial preferences. Quite obviously my presence on the temperate zone food stuffs committee was redundant, and I hurried back to Paris.

My maiden speech to the NATO Council was not a resounding success. I took my cue from a recent address of the prime minister to the UN Assembly, in which he pointed out that the Soviets were hurling charges of imperialism at western countries such as Britain, France, and Portugal while practising the most blatant kind of imperialism in Hungary, Poland, Czechoslovakia, and the Baltic states. Diefenbaker may well have had the ethnic vote in mind when he made that speech. But I certainly agreed with him that the western democracies, which had, reluctantly or otherwise, divested themselves of their colonies after World War II, should not allow themselves to be branded as imperialists without telling the Soviets what they thought of the ruthless subjugation of their satellites.

To say that my remarks got a chilly reception would be an understatement. Of all the council members, the only two who said they agreed with me were the Greek and the Turk, both of whom represented fairly extreme right-wing governments at the time. As for the rest, their reaction was summed up by Paul-Henri Spaak, the former secretary general of NATO who had reverted to his role as Belgium's foreign minister. An ardent admirer of Pearson's diplomacy and peacekeeping efforts, Spaak said he never thought he would find himself in such profound disagreement with a spokesman of the Canadian government. Apparently he considered it inconsistent for the delegate of a NATO country whose foreign minister had journeyed to Moscow and pioneered personal contacts with the Soviet rulers to denounce the contradictions between the public pronouncements and the policies of the Kremlin.

Personally, what seemed to me inconsistent was the schizophrenic attitude towards national defence and foreign relations displayed by some of our allies. On the one hand they resented the clout of the Americans within NATO and tried to counterbalance it with a policy of *détente* towards the Soviets. That was why my reference to Soviet imperialism was anathema to their ears. There was a widespread hope among the European members of the alliance that, if only NATO refrained from doing or saying anything to offend the Khrushchev regime, they might reach some sort of accommodation, avert the danger of war, and at the same time put the Americans in their place.

On the other hand, these same governments were content (at least until the Cuban crisis) to depend on American nuclear power as the ultimate deterrent to another war and got extremely upset whenever there was the slightest indication that the United States might withdraw some of its forces to other parts of the world. Any suggestion that western Europe should build up its own conventional forces to the extent where it could repel an attack without resorting to the nuclear deterrent was invariably countered by the argument that the war-torn democracies couldn't afford such vast military expenditures, that they had to use their resources to rebuild their economic and social structure. They didn't seem to understand that, by refusing to live up to their conventional defence commitments, they were lowering the nuclear threshold, that is to say increasing the danger that NATO would resort to the use of nuclear weapons in the event of an armed conflict.

Exacerbating the debate were some deep-rooted historical and emotional traumas which were haunting individual NATO countries. In the case of Germany, it was the partition of the country and the realization that, as Khrushchev had told Pearson during his Moscow visit, the Soviets would never permit reunification so long as there was a NATO presence in Germany. In the eyes of many Germans the alliance therefore represented an obstacle to the realization of their most cherished dream, while many others suspected that disarmament and unification would eventually reduce them to the status of a Soviet satellite. In France, the defence issue was intertwined with the trauma of having served as a battlefield during two world wars and the suspicion that the Americans might be plotting a similar scenario in the event of another European conflict. When, for instance, the US secretary of defence, Robert McNamara, came up with the 'flexible response' concept, according to which a Soviet attack would be met not by the 'massive retaliation' conceived by Foster Dulles but rather with conventional weapons, to be followed if necessary by tactical nuclear weapons and only as a last resort by strategic intercontinental missiles, French critics interpreted this strategy as an indication that the United States was willing to sacrifice London or Paris but not Washington or New York on the altar of democracy. Personally I have always found the assumption that a nuclear conflict could be confined to the use of 'tactical' rather than 'strategic' weapons totally unrealistic. It seems obvious to me that, if one side or the other were to unleash a nuclear missile of whatever description, the conflict would inevitably escalate into a total holocaust.

What lent the debate a good deal of urgency when I took up my duties at NATO was the continuing crisis around Berlin, symbolized by the construction of the hideous wall between the east and west parts of the city. Even while the various governments were talking about *détente*, their representatives on the North Atlantic Council discussed contingency plans that might be activated to convince the Soviets that, as far as NATO was concerned, any attempt to isolate Berlin would be an act of war.

Some of these plans were pretty bizarre, to put it mildly. There was, for instance, the shot-across-the-bow scheme, which called for a nuclear weapon to be fired as a warning from a NATO ship, should the situation in Berlin become critical. I pointed out that it was preposterous to suggest you could use a nuclear weapon the same way you would fire a shot across the bow of a rum-runner. Where would we explode this nuclear weapon, and how would we communicate to the Soviets that this was just a warning to which they were not supposed to respond in kind? Equally weird was a plan designed to provide the non-American members of NATO with a sense of participation in the nuclear deterrent. This was to be achieved by having ships camouflaged as ordinary freighters armed with nuclear weapons and manned by multinational crews: Turks, Greeks, Germans, Italians, I suppose even Canadians. It seemed rather unlikely to me that these so-called freighters would escape the attention of Soviet fishing trawlers which were already engaged in surveillance activities all over the seven seas. It also occurred to me as we sat around the council chamber that, considering what a motley crew we were on the ground, we wouldn't make much of a team at sea.

On top of everything else, the plan failed to allay the fears of those NATO members who felt they were not masters of their own destiny so long as the American finger was the decisive one on the nuclear trigger. Just how valid these concerns were became abundantly clear during the Cuban crisis in the fall of 1962. News about the impending confrontation between the two superpowers came to NATO Council just as unexpectedly as it did to the rest of the world. We knew nothing about the installation of Soviet missiles in Cuba, or about the American decision to retaliate with a naval blockade of the island, until a few hours before President Kennedy's television address, when former Secretary of State Dean Acheson came to brief us.

Along with all my NATO colleagues, I found the evidence, in the form of reconnaissance photographs, totally convincing, and I said so in my report to the Canadian government. But the prime minister, who was being briefed that same afternoon by the former US ambassador to Canada, Livingston Merchant, suggested that an impartial team of UN observers be sent to Cuba to investigate the charges. I believe Canada was the only ally to question the authenticity of the reconnaissance photographs; or perhaps it wasn't so much a matter of doubting the evidence as annoyance on Diefenbaker's part at being presented with a *fait accompli*, without prior consultation. In any event, he refused to sanction Canada's participation in a continental air alert until National Defence Minister Douglas Harkness took matters into his own hands and gave the required orders.

Meanwhile, in the absence of any instructions from Ottawa, I was obliged to sit in silence while I listened to unequivocal declarations of support for the United States from every single council member. Even the French announced that they stood foursquare behind the Americans. I have seldom felt more uncomfortable or isolated. Finally, after five days or so, the prime minister made a general statement in the House of Commons to the effect that, in the event of hostilities breaking out, there should be no doubt where Canada stood. It wasn't much, but at least it gave me something I could quote.

The only thing which made those few days remotely tolerable was the attitude of the American delegate, a man of extraordinary judgment, experience, and sensitivity. Tom Finletter and I had been friends since my days at the Canadian embassy in Washington when he was secretary of defence for air, and when he realized the awkward situation I was in, he went out of his way to make me feel at ease and to include me in informal consultations. We discussed, for instance, Khrushchev's argument that there was no reason why the Soviets should not station missiles in the western hemisphere so long as American missiles were based in Turkey, right at the Soviet Union's back door. Since some of the American missiles were obsolete, would it be an idea to remove them as a trade-off for the Soviets' withdrawal from Cuba? In the end, the Americans decided that the only concession they were willing to make was an undertaking not to invade Cuba, and the Soviets backed down.

Though the world heaved a collective sigh of relief, the Cuban confrontation had in a sense reinforced some of the worst fears of many NATO members, including Canada. When the chips were down and decisions were being made that might plunge the world into a nuclear holocaust, all NATO could do was hold its breath while Washington took whatever steps the president and his military advisers deemed appropriate. For all the ringing declarations of solidarity made around the NATO table during that week when peace and possibly the survival of millions of people hung in the balance, none of the allied governments could claim to have been consulted before the Americans imposed their naval blockade, nor did we have any illusions as to the part we might have played in subsequent decision making had the Soviets refused to give way.

In appreciation of our 'support' during the Cuban crisis, all the permanent NATO delegates were invited to Washington, where President Kennedy, at a White House reception, presented each of us with an inscribed silver tray as a token of his country's gratitude. As a special bonus we were also given a tour of America's nuclear triad, consisting of the Strategic Air Command, the intercontinental ballistic missiles in their silos, and the nuclear submarines off the coast of Virginia. Up till then, this kind of hardware had been shrouded in secrecy and all the information we had consisted of a few selected statistics.

Another effect of the Cuban crisis was to intensify the long-festering debate over nuclear warheads for Canada's armed forces. Even though National Defence Minister Douglas Harkness had given orders for Canadian participation in the continental air alert, this was no more than a gesture so long as our Bomarcs were unarmed. I had been intimately involved in the nuclear issue from the moment I arrived at NATO, where both our air division and our brigade were about to take delivery of equipment designed exclusively for nuclear warfare. Yet so long as our government refused to make up its mind whether or not to accept the warheads, the CF-104 aircraft and the Honest John missile launchers were just as useless as the Bomarcs. In the event of war they would be targets for enemy attacks, without the capability to retaliate.

When I was summoned before the NATO review committee for my annual report on Canada's military contribution to the alliance, I was told that our soldiers and airmen were well trained and highly professional, and their equipment was satisfactory. But a brigade was only one third of the division we were committed to maintain in Europe, and besides, what were we going to do about providing our aircraft and our guns with ammunition? Until we did, the Canadian air division could not be considered battle worthy, and while the brigade did have equipment other than its Honest Johns, it certainly could not live up to its full potential.

I felt like a schoolboy whose examiners are confronting him with his failures. Had I been free to speak my mind, I would have told them that I couldn't answer their questions because the Canadian cabinet was split down the middle on the nuclear issue and therefore didn't know what it was going to do. I might also have told them that, in my opinion, Canada was making a mistake by stationing forces equipped with nuclear capable weapons in western Europe. Our presence there was based on the premise that a Soviet attack, if and when it came, would be launched down the central plain of Germany towards the Rhine, more or less as a continuation of the drive towards Berlin in World War II. This seemed to me a highly dubious assumption. Why should the Soviets attack where NATO's defences were the strongest and where they'd risk destroying much of Europe's industrial base? I thought it much more likely that an offensive might be directed either against Turkey, which throughout history has been a thorn in the side of every Russian government, regardless of political orientation, or in the Arctic, where Soviet troops had a great deal of experience and we were notoriously weak. It therefore seemed to me that, instead of having nuclear capable forces without nuclear ammunition stationed like sitting ducks in western Europe, it would make much more sense to have Canadian troops equipped with conventional weapons and trained for Arctic warfare assigned to the defence of our northern approaches.

But I wasn't authorized to say any of these things. Instead Ottawa provided me with some feeble excuses about the cost of maintaining military forces so far away from home and about the expensive infrastructure a country with Canada's vast distances and severe climate had to maintain. This was perfectly true, but it did nothing to explain the inconsistencies in our defence policies or our failure to live up to our commitments, both of which were rapidly becoming politically divisive issues back home.

In November 1962, on the heels of the Cuban crisis, a parliamentary delegation arrived in Paris to look into Canada's military contribution to NATO. Paul Hellyer, who was the defence critic in the Liberals' shadow cabinet, was part of the delegation along with two other high profile Liberals, Judy LaMarsh and Ross Macdonald; the Conservative members of the delegation were, by comparison, decidedly obscure members of their party. As soon as they arrived, Hellyer asked me to arrange a meeting for him with General Lauris Norstad, the NATO commander. I told him that, as the government's representative, I couldn't set up such a meeting unless it involved the entire delegation, so he went ahead and made his own arrangements to see Norstad. I knew nothing about it until later, though of course I would have had no reason to interfere. In retrospect, I realize that Judy LaMarsh's mission was to divert my attention while Hellyer visited Supreme Allied Headquarters. She had dinner with Alison and me, plus a handsome colonel whom National Defence had assigned as her escort. It turned out to be a thoroughly pleasant and entertaining evening.

Back in Ottawa, Hellyer submitted to Pearson a confidential report based on information given to him by Norstad. The gist of that report was that Canada was not living up to its NATO commitments. While we might have adopted a non-nuclear role at the time our contribution was being negotiated, it was now four years too late to change course and leave NATO with a gaping hole in its defences.

His case was bolstered by General Norstad, who stopped off in Ottawa early in January 1963 on his way home following his retirement as NATO commander. He was being recalled because of unspecified policy differences with the Kennedy administration, and personally I was sorry to see him go. He was a highly intelligent, decisive, civilized person, whom I had always found easy to get along with. I had no idea at the time I said good-bye to him in Paris that he was heading for Ottawa, let alone that he would comment at a press conference on Canada's ineffectual contribution to NATO.

The Norstad statement triggered a chain reaction which was to lead within a few weeks to the demise of the Diefenbaker government. Apparently swayed both by Hellyer's report and Norstad's visit, plus no doubt his reading of public opinion, Pearson announced in mid-January that the Liberals, if elected, would honour Canada's commitments to NATO. In accordance with the requirements of the McMahon Act, they would negotiate a bilateral treaty with the United States for the acceptance of nuclear warheads, albeit only until Canada could define for itself a new role within the alliance. This turn-around in Liberal policy deepened the split between the pro- and anti-nuclear forces in the cabinet, as did the prime minister's somewhat misleading statement in the House of Commons about changes in NATO's defence strategy, promptly followed by a public State Department denial. Early in February, the minister of national defence resigned in protest over the nuclear issue, and two days later the Diefenbaker government was defeated by a vote of non-confidence in the House of Commons.

In the midst of the election campaign I was surprised to be summoned to London by the newly appointed minister of national defence, Gordon Churchill. He was accompanying the prime minister, whose political troubles did not deter him from taking time out to receive the Freedom of the City of London, and they both questioned me about our relationship with NATO. I told them what I had said before, that our position was totally illogical and unacceptable as far as our allies were concerned, that the decisions taken years ago to equip our air division with 104s and our brigade with Honest Johns made no sense so long as the government refused to sign the bilateral agreement with the United States which would give our forces access to nuclear ammunition. Diefenbaker looked up into the air as though waiting for inspiration and said: 'If only the people of Canada could hear.'

Hear what? Presumably he meant that the military had pulled the wool over his eyes, that they hadn't explained to him when they persuaded him to acquire these weapon systems that he was committing Canada to a nuclear role, which was true enough. But it was equally true that he bore the ultimate responsibility for decisions he had made without looking into their implications, and that when it came to extricating himself from the consequences, he was quite incapable of making up his mind one way or the other.

Later that day I was walking with Gordon Churchill when he suddenly turned on me and said: 'You've got us into this mess, you'll have to get us out of it.' I was stunned. 'Mr. Churchill,' I said, 'I wasn't even in the country at the time these decisions were made, and it wouldn't have been up to me to make them even if I had been around.' 'Well,' he said, 'you'd better do some thinking and come up with a solution.'

I flew back to Paris, where I found a telephone message to the effect that I was to return to London at once because the prime minister wanted to see me. So I took the next plane back to London and though the prime minister didn't have time to see me after all, Churchill did. He had been doing some thinking of his own, he informed me, and he had come up with a perfect solution to the nuclear dilemma. His suggestion was that since Canada was one of the governments which had agreed to set up nuclear stockpiles in Europe, all we needed to do was ask the Supreme Allied Commander to release nuclear warheads to our forces; we did not need to sign any bilateral agreements with the Americans. I tried to explain to him that, under the MacMahon Act, there had to be a bilateral agreement before the president of the United States could, in the event of an emergency, release nuclear weapons to an ally for purposes of collective defence. We might not like the legislation, but the fact remained that the supreme allied commander didn't have the authority to release the warheads to us.

He wouldn't accept my explanation, and it soon became clear we were going around in circles. 'Your interpretation of the law is different from mine,' I finally said, 'but I presume you have consulted the judge advocate general and that he agrees with you. So if you'll send him to Paris, I'll be glad to join him in putting your case before the NATO commander.' He obviously wasn't thrilled with my suggestion but he said 'All right' and dismissed me, with another jab about the way I was mishandling my responsibilities. After he had returned to Canada he phoned me from Winnipeg and said: 'Have you arranged it?' I said I was still waiting for the judge advocate general. I never heard from him again.

To the extent that the Liberals came to power in 1963 on the understanding that they would acquire nuclear warheads for our forces, the change of government relieved some of the pressure under which I had operated at NATO. The more relaxed atmosphere was evident during a visit of NATO ministers to Ottawa, which had actually been planned by the Diefenbaker administration. Judy LaMarsh, who was minister of national health and welfare in the Pearson cabinet as well as member of Parliament for Niagara, thought it would be a great idea if the NATO delegates were given a tour of the famous waterfalls, to be followed by a dinner in a local restaurant and a wine-tasting session. Only Niagara wines were to be served. This was before our wine industry had learned how to neutralize the overpowering flavour of Concord grapes, and as we worked our way through the various brands my European colleagues looked increasingly puzzled. The labels said Chablis, Burgundy, and Champagne, but the taste was always the same: Concord grape. 'C'est bien parfumé,' said Couve de Murville noncommittally. In the end the Danish minister saved the day with a speech about Canada's matchless contribution to NATO fellowship.

Yet for all the Liberals' campaign promises, the change of regime in Ottawa did not resolve fundamental questions concerning Canada's role in NATO or the strategy on which that role was to be based. Much though I sympathized with our soldiers and our airmen for being given equipment without ammunition, much though I deplored some of the ill-advised decisions of the Diefenbaker government and the subsequent search for scapegoats, I shared Diefenbaker's concern about an alliance where subordination to

American defence planning and decision making was the price to be paid for huddling under the nuclear umbrella. President de Gaulle clearly felt the same way, but, unlike Diefenbaker, he translated those feelings into decisive action.

Strangely enough, de Gaulle apparently wasn't aware of the existence or implications of an integrated command at the time of the Cuban crisis. It wasn't until a few months later that Admiral Denison, the American head of NATO's naval forces in the Atlantic, came to see him in the hope that his command of a French flotilla during the blockade of Cuba would earn him the Légion d'Honneur. According to Maurice Schumann, who was at the time chairman of the foreign affairs committee in France's National Assembly, the president was dumbfounded. 'Just what French forces were you commanding?' he demanded to know. Denison explained what he considered to be self-evident, namely that under NATO's integrated command, all national units were subordinate to the supreme commander. Did this mean that, had hostilities broken out, French forces might have been involved, without the specific consent of the French government? Indeed it meant just that.

Denison never did get his Légion d'Honneur. Instead de Gaulle announced that never again would anyone other than the president of France be in a position to send French forces into battle. Being an ally did not mean taking orders from the head of another government, and if that was what NATO's integrated command was all about, he wanted no part of it. France would withdraw from the military alliance and build its own nuclear deterrent. As for NATO headquarters, it would have to find a home somewhere other than France.

The decision came as a shock to all of us. Not only did it mean that all the physical facilities of NATO, including the early warning system and all supply depots, would have to be dismantled; equally important from Canada's point of view was the symbolic significance of the move. The banishment of NATO from France represented a body blow to the tripod concept of our foreign policy, based on special relationships with the United States, Great Britain, and France. I tried at the ambassadorial level to speak to my French counterparts, in the hope that they might persuade the government to reconsider, and Paul Martin, the foreign minister in the Pearson cabinet, came over to speak to Couve de Murville. The Quai d'Orsay people were not unsympathetic. But the final decision was de Gaulle's, and he wouldn't budge.

Perhaps we were naïve to think we could exert any influence on a French government whose relationship with Canada was deteriorating visibly under the impact of developments in Quebec. It was the time of the quiet revolution, 'maîtres chez nous' had become the universal slogan for Quebeckers living in Paris, and a French enclave asserting its independence in the midst of an Anglo-Saxon continent was, for de Gaulle, a welcome offset to the 'défi américain.'

Just how welcome became painfully obvious in January 1964, when Pearson came to Paris on an official visit that was designed to heal any rifts in the friendship between the two countries. Everything went well until the banquet at the Elysée Palace which President de Gaulle gave in honour of Canada's prime minister. All the diplomatic niceties were being observed, yet I sensed the underlying tensions as I sat at an angle across the table from de Gaulle and saw him repeatedly glance at his watch. The meal was served with clockwork precision, and at the appointed time de Gaulle got up to propose a toast to his visitor. One of the things that unite our two countries, he said speaking in French, is 'le lien inoubliable avec notre peuple au Canada.' There was no mistaking his meaning: when he spoke about 'our people' he meant Quebeckers, not Canadians in general.

Pearson was so nettled by this reference to a special relationship between France and Quebec that he departed from his prepared text in order to refer, in his speech, to 'our people from all over Canada who lie buried near the battlefields where they died defending France in two world wars.' To reinforce the message, he took off the following day for an unscheduled visit to the battlefields in northern France, where he paid tribute to Canada's dead. But nothing Pearson did or said seemed to have much of an impact on de Gaulle's conviction that there was little common ground between their two countries. 'Enfin vous êtes anglo-saxon,' he said to Pearson at the end of their final encounter, as though to pinpoint an incorrigible flaw in Mike's genetic code.

As time went on and Quebec nationalism assumed increasingly separatist overtones, the French government's apparent determination to treat Quebec as a sovereign country continued to sour our relationship. I don't think de Gaulle was out to break up Canada; as a matter of fact neither he nor his cabinet knew much about Canada, and I doubt whether they were particularly interested. But the president was acutely conscious of his role as the leader who had restored a measure of self-respect and self-confidence to a nation humiliated and deeply divided by the dismal wartime record of its military leaders, its politicians, and many ordinary citizens. What de Gaulle wanted above all else was to turn France once again into a country that could be proud of its place as the centre of European civilization and a counterweight to the homogenizing influence of the United States.

Quebec's quiet revolution seemed tailor-made for this purpose. It underlined the fact that historically, economically, and above all culturally France was a world power to be reckoned with, that the French had established outposts in the new world long before the English arrived on the scene. One of the reasons why we have so much difficulty understanding French foreign policy is that, in our consumer-oriented society, we underestimate the importance the French attribute to culture. I believe more than half of the expenditures of the Quai d'Orsay are devoted to cultural activities of one kind or another, all designed to project the French fact abroad. The French are not out to revive or reconquer a colonial empire. What they do want is to establish a sort of commonwealth based on francophone culture; and in this they have been remarkably successful. Years later, when de Gaulle stood on that balcony in Montreal and shouted, 'Vive le Québec libre!' I wasn't particularly surprised. It was in a sense the finishing stroke in a picture which I had watched taking shape in Paris in the early 1960s.

As ambassador to NATO I wasn't directly involved in the dealings between the French and Canadian governments, though I did attend some of the official functions. But I was determined to take advantage of my presence in Paris not only to improve my knowledge of French, but to acquire an understanding of the forces which were transforming Quebec and, to some extent, Canada as a whole. Back home the Liberal government of Mike Pearson was delving into bilingualism and biculturalism in the hope of finding a solution to the Canadian dilemma, while John Diefenbaker was fighting a losing battle to keep his Conservatives from adopting the two-nation concept advocated by such people as Marcel Faribault – 'that fellow Ferryboat,' as Diefenbaker scathingly described him. But was either party being realistic?

Paris in the 1960s was teeming with Quebec students, virtually all of them ardent separatists. I engaged one of them, a brilliant young man who later became a professor of philosophy in Montreal, to spend three or four hours with me every Saturday morning, discussing everything from Maupassant to politics in French. He was pretty reserved at first – I guess arguing with an ambassador was a novel experience for him – but once he decided he could trust me, he became devastatingly frank. 'You probably think that, because you're an ethnic Canadian, you can mediate between the French and the English,' he told me, 'but this is something we have to resolve directly between ourselves. You ethnics keep out of it.' For me these discussions turned out to be an eye-opener. I came to realize something that has stayed with me to this day, namely that Quebec separatism is not a short-term phenomenon that can be resolved by a compromise. Wanting to be independent is an issue that goes much deeper than language or even culture. People who truly believe in independence won't settle for anything less.

Oddly enough, Quebec's increasingly militant nationalism and the accompanying rhetoric about inalienable links with France had a palpable effect on the way most Canadians reacted to a political and military crisis that was brewing on a distant Mediterranean island. Tension had been building up for some time in the newly independent republic of Cyprus between the Greek majority, which continued to clamour for union with the mother country, and the Turkish minority, which was determined to resist such a union, with outside help if necessary. But no one at NATO seemed particularly concerned about the situation until Christmas Day 1963, when I was summoned to a special meeting of the council to discuss the violence that had broken out between the two factions and its possible consequences should either Greece or Turkey decide to intervene. To most of my fellow NATO delegates, this was a case of two members of the alliance quarrelling over a piece of real estate to which they had equally valid claims. But to many Canadians, there was an added dimension to the confrontation in Cyprus. Perhaps subconsciously, they compared it with the situation in Quebec which Lord Durham had so aptly described some 125 years earlier as 'two nations warring in the bosom of a single state,' and they rejected any union between Cyprus and Greece just as they resented any meddling by France in the affairs of Quebec.

Personally I disagreed with this interpretation. Unlike most of my colleagues and compatriots, I had good reason to be familiar with the historical background of the Cypriot crisis because my grandfather had, in a sense, been a reluctant witness at its birth. To me, what was happening in Cyprus in the 1960s was the logical climax of a story that began during the Russo-Turkish war of 1878. At that time Britain, faced with the prospect of a Russian victory, threatened to intervene on the side of the Turks and subsequently launched a successful appeal against some of the more important clauses of the Treaty of San Stefano, which my grandfather had negotiated and signed on behalf of the tsar. As a reward for all this help, Britain got from Turkey the island of Cyprus, whose predominantly Greek population clearly had no say in the matter. If it hadn't been for that deal, which isolated Cyprus from the rest of the independence movements in the Balkans, the island would presumably have gone its own way long ago, along with the rest of the crumbling Ottoman Empire.

To make matters worse, Britain had panicked when trouble broke out in Cyprus after World War II and had sent Archbishop Makarios, the leader of the militant Greek Cypriots, into exile. As Lord Caradon, the last British governor of the island, later told me, banishing Makarios achieved nothing except to turn him into a national hero destined to come back to a hysterical welcome. Certainly Makarios was a wily, byzantine bishop in the tradition of nineteenth-century exarchs, who used the church to build themselves an impregnable power base and manipulate public opinion. But he personified the aspirations of his compatriots, and somehow he succeeded in preventing Cyprus from becoming another Ireland. In all too many instances, British attempts to decolonize their empire were achieved at an exorbitant cost to the local population and to international stability. In Cyprus, as in Palestine, they hung on until the situation became totally unmanageable, then dumped it in the lap of the United Nations.

Because of my family connection with the history of Cyprus, I explained to my NATO colleagues that I found it difficult to be completely impartial. No way could I equate the Turks' claim to all or part of the island with what I considered to be the outpouring of a Greek independence movement that had been forcibly suppressed for close to a century. On the other hand, there were times when the Greeks seemed to be going out of their way to help me forget my bias.

This was particularly true in the summer of 1964, when intelligence sources reported that substantial Greek forces had landed on the island. Palamas, the Greek delegate to NATO, claimed that there were only a few hundred men sent there to train the population in self-defence. According to our information, the actual number was closer to five thousand, and their intentions appeared far from peaceful. By then, a United Nations peacekeeping force with a sizeable Canadian contingent had taken up position in Cyprus, and there was a grave danger not only that two NATO members might find themselves at war against each other, but that the UN force would be caught in the crossfire. I was selected to raise the issue in council and to challenge the figures Palamas had given us. It was a tough assignment because Palamas was my personal friend, as incidentally was Birgi, the Turkish delegate. Nevertheless I told him that the figures he had given us were not correct; either he had been misinformed by his government or he had chosen to conceal the facts from us.

When I had said my piece Palamas got terribly agitated, said it was not up to the UN peacekeeping force to snoop on friendly nations, and stormed out of the meeting. I went to have a private talk with him and assured him that I was not impugning his veracity, that I assumed he had been misinformed, which I honestly believe was probably the case. Indeed I had the impression that neither he nor his Turkish counterpart wielded much influence with their respective governments. But I also told him that there was a grave danger of war, and that if NATO was to be of any help, we had to have facts, not the subjective claims and counterclaims of the antagonists. He calmed down and we remained friends. He was sidelined from public life during the regime of the colonels but resurfaced later as Greek minister of external affairs.

The armed conflict which seemed so imminent in 1964 never happened. But while we managed to avoid war, we didn't achieve peace. Why, after twenty years, is there still a need for a peacekeeping force in Cyprus? Partly, I believe, because by its presence the UN has relieved the two factions of the pressure to negotiate, to find a permanent solution to their problems. An additional reason is that the military establishments in the United States and in Britain are reluctant to disturb a *status quo* which provides them with important advantages. The Americans don't want a settlement that might offend Turkey, their staunch ally and host to their missile bases, while the British hope Cyprus may allow them to keep their naval installations. In a very real sense, this little island has become a microcosm of many of the tensions and ambitions which make world peace so difficult to achieve or maintain.

My four years at NATO were essentially an initiation into the pressure-cooker atmosphere of international crises and an apprenticeship for the responsibilities I was to assume in 1966 when I was appointed Canadian ambassador to the United Nations. The experience left me as convinced as ever that Canada had to belong to a collective security system, that there could be no question of trying to 'go it alone.' But at the same time, events such as the willingness to play chicken with the Soviets around Cuba and talk about firing nuclear weapons to warn the Soviets we were serious about Berlin reinforced my suspicion that NATO governments were not facing up to the realities of nuclear war.

FOURTEEN

The hot seat in New York

֍֍֍֍֍֍֍֍֍֍֍֍֍֍֍֍֍֍֍֍֍֍֍֍֍֍

I had no idea what to expect when Secretary General U Thant called on 17 May 1967 to summon me to his office for a meeting of the UNEF Advisory Committee. The committee, which consisted of representatives of countries which were contributing troops to the peacekeeping force in Egypt, had not met in the four months since Canada had been elected to the Security Council, or, for that matter, since my arrival as Canadian ambassador to the United Nations the previous fall; and to the best of my knowledge, there was no urgent reason why it should meet now. While there had been a growing number of increasingly serious raids and reprisals on the Syrian-Israeli border, UN observers had found no evidence to support Arab charges that Israel was planning a full-scale war against Syria. Besides, a certain amount of turmoil in the Middle East had, over the past quarter century, become a regrettably constant feature of the international landscape.

No doubt I would have been less complacent had I known that, while our attention was diverted to Syria, there had been a steady build-up of military power in Egypt, or that the Soviets were prodding Egypt's President Nasser to establish by force of arms his leadership of the Arab world. Our intelligence people must have been aware of these developments, as their relationship with their American colleagues was very close. But Canada's permanent representative at the United Nations was insulated from such sensitive information, presumably for security reasons.

I was therefore stunned when U Thant informed us at the 17

May meeting that the commander of UNEF had received a message from the commander-in-chief of the forces of the United Arab Republic (that is, the federation of Egypt and Syria) to the effect that UAR forces were being ordered into the Sinai desert to occupy positions formerly held by UNEF, including Sharm el Sheikh at the mouth of the Gulf of Aqaba. For their own safety, all United Nations forces were to be withdrawn immediately.

Even before his meeting with the UNEF Advisory Committee, U Thant had assured the UAR ambassador that, since UNEF had been stationed in the area with the consent of Egypt, 'if the UAR government withdraws its consent and requests the Secretary General to withdraw UNEF, it is my duty and obligation to comply.' His only reservation was that such a request would have to come from the government rather than a military commander and be addressed to the secretary general, who alone had the authority to issue the appropriate orders.

Since I'd had no advance warning, I had no instructions from our government as to what Canada's reaction to these developments should be. However, having served with Mike Pearson in 1956 when the establishment of UNEF was being negotiated, I felt justified in cautioning U Thant and my colleagues on the committee against precipitate action and its possibly grave consequences. Since no formal request had as yet been received from the UAR government, the secretary general should have the issue debated by the General Assembly which happened to be in session at the time. I said, 'I think it would be an intolerable situation for UNEF to be simply withdrawn without further ado, on the receipt of a peremptory request; it was understood at the time [in 1956] that there would be mutual discussion.' I also urged U Thant to take advantage of whatever time might be left to appeal to Nasser to reconsider his decision. As the Brazilian ambassador pointed out, it might be easier for the UAR president to backtrack before he had issued a formal request rather than after.

When the UNEF Advisory Committee reconvened the following day, U Thant told us that since we had last met the government of the United Arab Republic had officially informed him that it had decided 'to terminate the presence of the United Nations Emergency

Forces from [sic] the territory of the United Arab Republic and Gaza Strip.' The secretary general went on to report that, as soon as the UAR ambassador had handed him the letter signed by his foreign minister, he had once again assured the ambassador that UNEF could not remain in place without the consent of the UAR government. He therefore proposed to order its withdrawal, though his official reply would also express his 'serious misgivings about this action in view of the grave implications it may have for peace in the area.'

Just how grave seemed to me alarmingly obvious. Now that Ottawa had provided me with instructions confirming the stand I had taken the previous day, I felt more justified than ever in urging the secretary general to consult with the other governments in the area before taking a step that would bring two traditionally hostile armies face to face with each other. It was not that I questioned the UAR's legal right to demand the withdrawal of UNEF, but I couldn't accept the interpretation of that right to mean immediate and complete compliance. I was particularly concerned about the consequences of a withdrawal from Sharm el Sheikh, which controlled Israel's lifeline for oil imports from the Persian Gulf to the port of Eilat. As I reminded the committee, Israel had handed over Sharm el Sheikh in 1956 in return for a specific undertaking that it would not be surrendered to Egypt without previous consultation. There was no doubt in my mind that our failure to live up to that undertaking would lead to war.

The ambassadors of Brazil, Denmark, and Norway all supported my argument, but the so-called non-aligned countries which contributed the bulk of the UNEF forces, notably India and Yugoslavia, were absolutely adamant that anything less than complete and prompt compliance would be an affront to UAR sovereignty; and the secretary general's staff, including Ralph Bunche, came down unequivocally on their side.

In any case, it was obvious that U Thant's mind was already made up, and his undertaking to report to the General Assembly 'all the facts relevant to the situation' was little more than a courtesy. As he pointed out several times over, it was an agreement between the Egyptian government and Secretary General Hammarskjold which had paved the way for the development of UNEF, and it was therefore not up to the General Assembly to decide what should be done when one of the parties to that agreement decided to terminate it. In answer to my specific question, he said he proposed to reply to the UAR government first and report to the General Assembly second, not the other way round. Clearly the UN was to be presented with a *fait accompli*.

U Thant did leave for Cairo in a last-ditch attempt to negotiate a compromise settlement, but since he had already handed Nasser the only trump card in his hand, the attempt was clearly fore-doomed. Even while he was winging his way to the Egyptian capital Radio Cairo was broadcasting Nasser's latest speech full of pas-sionate accusations against America, Britain, and Canada for sup-posedly leading 'a big world-wide campaign' to keep UNEF in Egypt and turn it into 'a force serving neo-imperialism.' A few hours later he announced that he was imposing a blockade on Israel's trade through the Gulf of Aqaba.

For a variety of reasons the Security Council, which might be considered the logical agency to deal with such a serious threat to world peace, had remained idle throughout the mounting crisis. The Soviets and their allies had no wish to have the council inter-vene in a situation which, they believed, would end up consolidating their influence in the Middle East. The United States may have been reluctant to engage in lengthy debates of resolutions which were bound to fall victim to yet another Soviet veto. Some of the non-aligned countries, such as Nigeria, were too preoccupied with their domestic problems to worry about what was happening in the Sinai. Finally, the fact that the president of the Security Council in May was the representative of the Chinese government in Taipeh, which almost two thirds of the council members didn't even recog-nize, hampered any initiative that might have been taken.

With the help of Hans Tabor of Denmark, I had been trying to have the Security Council convene from the day the secretary general first informed us of the demand for the withdrawal of UNEF; but it wasn't until Nasser announced the blockade of the Gulf of Aqaba that most of our fellow members acknowledged the need for such a meeting. When we finally met on 24 May, I put forward a deliberately mild resolution, ostensibly in support of the secretary general's peace mission to Cairo. All it did was urge the Security Council to authorize U Thant to send UN observers into the Sinai and Gaza Strip to replace the withdrawing peacekeeping troops.

But even this innocuous resolution was promptly blocked by Nikolai Fedorenko of the Soviet Union, who claimed it was Israel's threat to Syria rather than anything Nasser had done that threatened peace in the Middle East. He dismissed my arguments as those of a neo-imperialist who 'points at the moon but sees his own finger,' which in turn enabled Britain's Lord Caradon to respond that the Soviet representative's motives were as transparent as his proverbs were obscure. Everybody except Fedorenko had a good laugh, but Caradon's wit provided only momentary relief from the futility of the debate and the atmosphere of impending doom. When we adjourned later that day, no vote had been taken on the Canadian-Danish resolution; indeed the council was so deeply divided that it had proved impossible even to agree on an agenda for the meeting.

Meanwhile National Defence had the bright idea of sending Canadian warships through the straights of Gibraltar into the Mediterranean; and Nasser, who had already taken a dim view of the part I played in the UNEF debate, used the appearance of these ships as a pretext for ordering the Canadian component of the peacekeeping force out of the country within forty-eight hours. The official explanation was 'the biased attitude of the Canadian government towards Israel,' plus the danger that the population's 'hatred against Canada,' triggered by the naval flotilla, might lead to hostile incidents against UNEF forces in general. But General Indar Jit Rikhye, the Indian commander of UNEF, put his finger on the true reason. The Canadian contingent, he explained in his book called *The Sinai Blunder*,* consisted mainly of a transport unit, and UAR authorities had resented all along the opportunity the Canadian air crews had to observe their troop movements. The order that they be removed ahead of other UNEF forces merely confirmed

*(Frank Cass 1980) p. 91

the general's suspicions that war was imminent: 'If the Canadians were being asked to pull out earlier, so that the U.A.R. could deploy its forces unobserved by any UNEF eye, it was high time for the rest of us to get out as soon as we could, even though there was no "evidence of hostility" at that time against any other contingent.'

Rikhye pleaded with Ralph Bunche, the secretary general's deputy in New York, to refuse to accept an order which singled out any part of UNEF for special treatment, whether favourable or otherwise. For reasons of morale as well as logistics, he said, he should not be expected to command a desert force whose 'administrative tail' had been cut off. But he was overruled by Bunche, who pointed out that they all had to face 'certain hard realities in connection with an operation such as this.'

Before dawn on Monday, 5 June, the new Security Council president, Hans Tabor of Denmark, was awakened to be told that war had broken out between Israel and its Arab neighbours. Having failed to achieve what the convoluted language of one resolution called 'the forgoing of belligerence,' the Security Council tried frantically to bring about a cease-fire. At first its efforts were blocked by the Soviet Union, whose representative kept insisting that any cessation of hostilities would have to be accompanied by an unconditional Israeli withdrawal from occupied territories. But by week's end, when Egypt and Jordan had acknowledged defeat and Israeli forces were at the gates of Damascus, Fedorenko was as anxious as any of us to put an end to a conflict which had turned into a rout for the Arabs and a major embarrassment for their Soviet allies.

In a series of marathon Security Council sessions which began at noon on Friday, 9 June, and continued almost non-stop until the early hours of Sunday, the council hammered out and adopted a resolution for the cessation of hostilities and the stationing of UN observers along the armistice line. Both Syria and Israel agreed to abide by the terms of the resolution; and though the war of words – the shouting, recriminations, and diatribe – continued to engulf the United Nations throughout the summer and well into the fall, the battle fronts were once again silent.

As far as I was concerned, the Six-Day War had demonstrated

both the strengths and the shortcomings of the United Nations and its agencies. On the negative side, the UN's inability to prevent the war from happening was due, at least in part, to the growing polarization not only between the communist and the western blocs, but between the have and have-not members of the organization. In the twenty years since I had first come to the United Nations as deputy to General McNaughton, the fifty-one founding members had been joined by seventy-five others, virtually all of them newly independent third world countries, with their own set of priorities and concerns. Understandably enough, the delegates of these Afro-Asian countries were profoundly conscious of the unequal distribution of wealth throughout the world and suspicious of anything that smacked of racial discrimination or neo-colonialism. They were also keenly aware of the fact that, jointly, they commanded a majority in most if not all UN agencies.

The two meetings on 17 and 18 May of the UNEF Advisory Committee reflected these divisions, as did subsequent meetings of the Security Council. The non-aligned countries all sided with Egypt and clearly resented any suggestion that Nasser should be dissuaded from exercising what they considered the prerogative of any sovereign government. Even India took this uncompromising stand, in spite of the fact that General Rikhye, the Indian commander of UNEF, was warning the secretary general and, presumably, his own government of the danger to which a confrontation between UAR and Israeli armies would expose his troops.

Because of these divisions and deep-seated suspicions, my role as the representative of a western country was extremely delicate. There was a great deal I would have liked to say when the Security Council met to discuss the withdrawal of UNEF. I would have liked to tell the members that, in his report to the United Nations, U Thant had chosen to ignore completely the objections which three members of the UNEF Advisory Council had raised to unconditional compliance with Nasser's demand. There was nothing in that report to suggest that anyone had pleaded for the issue to be brought before the General Assembly. Yet I knew only too well that, if I were to challenge the words or actions of a Burmese secretary general, I would be branded as an imperialist and all the third world countries would band together with the Soviet bloc to defeat any proposal I might put forward.

Indeed U Thant himself was a product of these divisions, a compromise candidate chosen to succeed Hammarskjold partly because he symbolized the UN's multiracial identity, partly because none of the permanent Security Council members had any particular reason to object to his appointment. He had been a school principal when the prime minister of newly independent Burma, whom he had known at university, persuaded him to join the public service as an official in the ministry of information. A few years later he was included in the Burmese delegation to the United Nations and, in due course, became Burma's permanent representative. In 1961, following Hammarskjold's mysterious death during the UN peacekeeping operation in the Congo, it soon became apparent that no strong successor would prove acceptable to all four permanent members of the Security Council. After a few weeks of backroom manoeuvring, U Thant was elected to step into what one of his predecessors had described as 'the most impossible job in the world.'

During the two years I represented Canada on the Security Council I saw a good deal of U Thant, and I came to admire the serenity and self-discipline which were clearly the result of his Buddhist upbringing. I was also impressed with the complete impartiality with which he treated the great powers. While he dispensed, to my way of thinking, more than the required dose of indulgence to non-aligned countries, he did not hesitate to lash out at the United States for its military involvement in Vietnam, the Soviet Union for its suppression of freedom movements in Hungary and Czechoslovakia, or France for its policies in Algeria.

Nevertheless, I found U Thant a difficult man to either understand or get along with. The UN charter allows the secretary general a great deal of latitude in the discharge of his responsibilities, and a more statesmanlike personality such as Hammarskjold would have known how to use that power to defuse the UNEF crisis. In my opinion U Thant lacked the qualities of dynamic leadership, and his legalistic reaction to Nasser's request for the withdrawal of peacekeeping forces seemed to me designed to result in exactly the kind of armed conflict which we were so desperately trying to forestall.

Yet when I tried to reason with him, he just smiled in his gentle, enigmatic way, without any indication whether or not I was getting through to him. Being an emotional Slav, I found this attitude exasperating. I would have been much happier had he told me to shut up and said that he disagreed with me and would go ahead doing what he thought was best. But he never showed any reaction, not even impatience, and never said yes or no. For a while it got so bad I could hardly bear to speak to him.

On the positive side, the UN did eventually prove to be the one forum where representatives of different countries, ideologies, and historical backgrounds could meet and come up with compromise solutions. The public, which identifies the United Nations with endless debates replete with grievances, self-glorification, and vitriol, tends to assume that it is all a tedious exercise in futility. To be perfectly honest, there are times when the delegates feel the same way. During the Six-Day War, when the Security Council sessions were all being telecast and when some of the Arab delegates indulged in interminable recitals of grievances past and present, I got a typically Pearsonian piece of advice from my prime minister. 'Keep your head up, George,' said the message from Ottawa. 'With your head down, you look bald and asleep.'

But most of the time these characters who lambaste each other in public are also meeting in private, possibly over a drink in the delegates' lounge or in the UN restaurant (the 'poison palace,' according to its critics) or in each other's quarters; and it's there that the real efforts are made to resolve seemingly insoluble problems. One of my first decisions when I came to the UN was to move the Canadian delegation from its remote location on Third Avenue as close as possible to the centre of activity, so that we could participate more easily in this kind of behind-the-scenes diplomacy. I found a perfect place within walking distance of the UN, and as a result, many of the consultations during our term on the Security Council took place at the Canadian mission.

The effectiveness of an ambassador to the United Nations depends, to a large extent, not so much on the eloquence of his public pronouncements as on the channels of communication and friendship developed at these informal meetings. In that respect I was

particularly fortunate in my rapport with the United States representative, Arthur Goldberg, and with Hugh Caradon of the United
Kingdom. Goldberg, generally known as 'The Justice' because he
had given up his seat on the Supreme Court to accept the UN
appointment, was a former secretary of labour whose expertise in
labour relations and propensity to quote from *Alice in Wonderland*
endowed all his pronouncements with substance as well as humour.

Hugh Caradon had earned his spurs as British colonial adminis-
trator and last governor of Cyprus, where he had presided over the
transfer of power to Makarios. Though he consistently impressed
his Security Council colleagues with his wisdom, wit, and oratory,
there was at least one occasion when he managed to run afoul of
George Brown, Britain's foreign secretary, who was visiting New
York. At a luncheon the Caradons gave in his honour, Brown was
holding forth on some pet topic when he absent-mindedly reached
for a cluster of ceramic fruit which adorned the centre of the table.
He picked up a grape and just about cracked a tooth on it. 'Don't we
pay you enough so you can f . . . well afford real ones?' he exploded.

Goldberg, Caradon, and I met many times during the weeks leading up to the Six-Day War, and because of Canada's direct involvement in UNEF, we agreed that I should carry the ball for the three of
us in the Security Council. After the war, when both the General
Assembly and the Security Council were deadlocked for months
over a formula for a more permanent settlement of the Middle
Eastern crisis, we continued our discussions and our contacts with
delegates of non-committed countries. The Soviets, who had
prodded the Arabs into the war and then abandoned them to their
fate, were trying to recover some of their lost prestige by clamouring once again for an unconditional withdrawal of Israeli forces
from occupied territories. Most of the third world delegates supported this demand, but eventually the Latin Americans decided to
opt for a compromise proposal.

This breakthrough paved the way for Resolution 242, which
stipulated that the withdrawal from territories acquired by Israel in
the recent conflict should go hand in hand with the negotiation of
'secure and recognized frontiers' between the belligerents. Intro-

duced by Lord Caradon, Resolution 242 was adopted unanimously by the Security Council in November 1967 and has remained, in principle if not in fact, the basis of a permanent peace settlement in the Middle East ever since.

Behind the scenes negotiations also proved helpful in defusing the potentially explosive *Pueblo* incident. A small American naval vessel with a crew of eighty-three men, the *Pueblo* was engaged in what the Americans called 'surveillance' off the North Korean coast when it was captured by the North Koreans. At a Security Council meeting two days later, the Americans presented what to them was irrefutable evidence that the *Pueblo* had been seized outside territorial waters, contrary to international law, and they demanded that both the ship and its crew be returned promptly. The Soviets, on the other hand, supported the North Korean claim that territorial waters, as measured from the outcroppings of the coast and its adjacent islands, extended well beyond the point where the *Pueblo* was captured. In other words, the council was faced with two irreconcilable interpretations of international law.

Meanwhile, American public opinion was clamouring for the president to use the armed forces in a bid to free the *Pueblo* and its crew, and Lyndon Johnson responded by moving warships into the area. Quiet diplomacy was clearly called for to prevent the incident from escalating into full-scale war. A major problem, however, was how to put out feelers towards a country which was not represented at the UN, and which had let it be known that it would neither appear before the Security Council nor abide by any resolution the council might pass.

As a first step to overcome this difficulty, a member of the American delegation asked me could I find out how to get in touch with the North Koreans. I said I'd see what I could do and made an appointment to meet with the deputy head of the Soviet mission, but we got absolutely nowhere. They sat me down in a chair which was obviously hooked up to a tape recorder and proceeded to tell me they had no idea who was in charge of North Korean affairs at the United Nations. As for the *Pueblo*, all I got was the official party line that the Americans had been operating a spy ship in territorial waters, and that getting caught red-handed was exactly what they deserved.

My next step was to ask a number of friends at the UN whether they happened to know who picked up the mail for the North Koreans. Someone mentioned that if might be the Hungarians, so I took a chance and invited the Hungarian ambassador for lunch at the University Club. He was a rather nice man and we were on friendly terms, so the invitation didn't come as too much of a surprise. During our lunch, I simply put it to him that the *Pueblo* incident could conceivably provoke a major war, and that some way had to be found for the Americans to negotiate directly with the North Koreans. Could he suggest a way in which this might be arranged?

Unlike the Soviets he didn't bother lecturing me about American sins and iniquities. He simply said he would make some enquiries and let me have a reply as soon as possible. Two days later he asked me to meet him at the United Nations and informed me that the North Koreans were willing to negotiate with the Americans at Panmunjom, on the border between North and South Korea, on such and such a date. I passed the message on to my American colleague, and that was the end of my involvement in the *Pueblo* affair. The Panmunjom negotiations went on quietly for many months, and the Americans never did recover their ship or the secret papers and equipment that were on board. But they did secure the release of the crew, and though they were forced to offer an apology, they revoked it as soon as their men were safe.

As far as the public was concerned, there was no indication that the United Nations had played any part in defusing the incident. This is a role of the UN which is not widely understood – that it is a sort of caravanserai of conflicting interests and ideologies and therefore can act as a catalyst in negotiations and settlements which, ostensibly, have nothing whatever to do with the organization. As we have often seen in recent years, arranging a summit meeting is a major undertaking which takes months or years of planning and suffers, in the event that it does finally take place, from the glare of publicity and exaggerated expectations. Yet these

same heads of state or their high-level representatives come to the
UN General Assembly almost as a matter of routine, and often take
advantage of the opportunity to confer with each other about matters of war and peace. Soviet President Alexei Kosygin, for instance,
came to New York in the wake of the Six-Day War, ostensibly to
harangue Israel and its allies at the 'emergency' UN assembly but
more importantly to meet with the president of the United States
in Glassboro as well as a number of delegates (including Canada's)
in New York and quietly grope for a way out of the Middle East
impasse.

The only other occasion during Canada's two-year term on the
Security Council when I was called upon to take some sort of
initiative was in August 1968, when the armed forces of the Soviet
Union and its Warsaw Pact allies occupied Czechoslovakia, arrested
the leading personalities in the country's government, and whisked
them off to Moscow. Over the previous few months, the Kremlin
had watched with growing apprehension as the Czechoslovaks lib-
eralized the economy, released political prisoners, and relaxed press
censorship. But when the spectre of free elections loomed on the
horizon, the Soviets decided that the attempt to create 'socialism
with a human face' was going too far. True to the Brezhnev Doctrine, they were not prepared to face the risk that one of their
European satellites might choose to leave the fold.

For me, watching the television news and seeing Soviet tanks
roll into Prague was like reliving a bad dream. It was almost exactly
twenty years since the Kremlin had masterminded the *coup d'état*
that put an end to democracy in Czechoslovakia; and then as now,
there was little the United Nations could do to stop it. From the
Soviet point of view, keeping Czechoslovakia within the communist
bloc was clearly an issue which was not negotiable. Short of risking
a nuclear war, the best the western powers could do was to settle
for a cosmetic, face-saving formula which would at least put the
facts on the record.

Goldberg had by then been replaced as United States representative by George Ball, who, for all his brilliance, was very new to the
job and not exactly an expert on UN matters. He and Hugh Caradon

therefore decided that, once again, I should co-ordinate western initiatives in the Security Council. The strategy we agreed upon was that we should start out by introducing a resolution condemning the invasion of Czechoslovakia and calling upon the Warsaw Pact forces to withdraw from its territory. This was obviously going to be vetoed by the Soviets, at which point I would call upon the Security Council to send an observer to Prague to find out what had happened to the secretary of Czechoslovakia's Communist party, Alexander Dubček, and his colleagues. By describing this second motion as procedural and humanitarian rather than substantive, we hoped that it would not be subject to a veto.

My job as co-ordinator of this game plan was twofold. First, since nine votes constituted a majority in the Security Council, I had to find nine delegations which were willing to vote for our resolutions. My second objective was to locate a credible Czechoslovak spokesman who might tell the Security Council and the world at large that the Soviets were lying when they claimed they had been invited into his country to perform an act of 'fraternal assistance,' that they were in fact guilty of the forceful overthrow of a legitimately constituted government.

The Danish ambassador, Otto Borch, helped me canvass the third world delegations whose support was essential, not only because we needed their votes, but also to ensure that the debate could not be interpreted as yet another squabble between east and west, and that it should clearly express a universal indictment of a brutal and illegal act. We succeeded to the extent that nine countries from four continents – Brazil, Britain, China, Denmark, Ethiopia, France, Paraguay, Senegal, and the United States – joined us in condemning the invasion of Czechoslovakia. Algeria, India, and Pakistan abstained. The only negative votes were cast by Hungary and the Soviet Union.

Since the Soviet 'nyet' constituted a veto, I proceeded according to plan to move that a UN emissary be sent to Czechoslovakia to find out what had happened to Dubček, President Svoboda, and several ministers whose fate was still a closely guarded secret. This suggestion triggered an outburst of rage on the part of Yakov Malik, the Soviet Union's deputy foreign minister, who had replaced

Fedorenko as ambassador to the UN. He called Canada a second-rate imperialist power and me a stooge of the United States and Great Britain. As for my resolution, it was just a transparent attempt to meddle in a socialist family quarrel. The way he put it, 'imperialists should not stick their noses into socialist and communist affairs, otherwise they might lose their nose.'

Britain's Hugh Caradon tried to soothe Malik's temper by suggesting that all the Security Council wanted to know was whether Dubček and the other arrested Czechoslovak leaders were safe. If Malik could reassure the council on that score, perhaps there would be no need to debate the Canadian-sponsored resolution. But Malik refused to give any such assurance, which enabled me to point out that sending a fact-finding mission to Prague was simply a humanitarian gesture. What was at issue, in my mind and the minds of an overwhelming majority of Security Council delegates, was not whether Czechoslovakia should or should not have a communist regime. The issue was the removal and arrest, by the armed forces of a foreign power, of the legally constituted government of a sovereign country.

As for finding a spokesman of that government, the acting Czechoslovak delegate at the United Nations, Jan Mužik, laid his career and possibly his life on the line when he told the Security Council that, far from threatening anyone, all his country had done was try 'to retain the human rights and liberty which are an integral part of any truly socialist system.' The Warsaw Pact forces, he said in a carefully worded statement, had no reason for invading Czechoslovakia and should therefore be withdrawn. A more forceful and authoritative denunciation of recent events came from Jiří Hájek, Czechoslovakia's foreign minister, who happened to be in Yugoslavia at the time of the invasion and therefore escaped the fate of his government colleagues. Hájek headed straight for New York and the Security Council, where he branded the Soviets and their allies as insensitive, and their actions as illegal. On behalf of Czechoslovakia's legitimate government, he demanded that the invaders 'grasp the enormity' of their mistake and leave his country without delay.

Having tried and failed to prevent Hájek from appearing before the council, the Soviets retaliated with an editorial in *Pravda* which attacked me personally as an imperialist, the son of an imperialist, and a 'marksman for the western plotters.' This at least had the effect of turning me into an instant celebrity. The *Pravda* attack made news all over Canada, as did its repudiation by Mitchell Sharp, recently appointed foreign minister in the Trudeau cabinet. His initial reaction to the invasion of Czechoslovakia, which he described as 'very disappointing,' had been almost incredibly mild. But an official Canadian government statement issued the following day used much stronger language, and when the Soviets tried to mount a vendetta against me, Sharp did come to my defence. 'The Soviet propaganda attacks via the press on Canada and on Mr Ignatieff personally,' he said, 'are clear demonstration of the sensitivity of the USSR to world reaction against their invasion and military occupation of Czechoslovakia.'

On the face of it, the Security Council debate ended up accomplishing little or nothing. The Soviets made it abundantly clear that they had no intention of allowing a UN emissary to visit Prague, and when the council adjourned shortly after Hájek's appearance, the best we could claim by way of tangible result was that, maybe, we had persuaded the Soviets to allow Dubček and his colleagues to return home, admittedly stripped of all power but at least unharmed.

Yet I have reason to believe that the Soviets were genuinely dismayed by the extent to which world opinion rose in protest against the rape of Czechoslovakia. At the United Nations, the near-unanimous condemnation included third world countries traditionally friendly to the Soviets; in western Europe, the Communist parties denounced the invasion; in Yugoslavia, defence policy was henceforth based on the assumption that any threat to the country's territorial integrity would come from the Soviet Union. As the Yugoslav ambassador told the Security Council, no socialist principles could conceivably justify such a gross violation of a nation's sovereignty.

Shortly after I became president of the Security Council in September 1968, Malik came to see me and said he had something confidential to discuss with me. Frankly I was surprised; I had known him for twenty years and never before had he approached me with a similar suggestion. However, I asked my advisers to leave us alone, upon which he turned on me and said, in Russian: 'Why have you gone back to the worst of the cold war attitude you displayed in 1948?' What he was talking about, of course, was my reaction to the Soviet-inspired overthrow of the Czechoslovak government headed by President Beneš. Coincidentally, I had also represented Canada in the Security Council on that occasion – McNaughton who was our ambassador happened to be away – and then, as twenty years later, I was determined to have a legitimate representative of Czechoslovakia refute the Soviet claim that their interference was a response to the will of the people.

So what Malik was trying to tell me was that, true to my ancestry, I had throughout the years played an anti-Soviet, counter-revolutionary role in recurrent Czechoslovakian crises. I replied that surely he must know that my background had absolutely nothing to do with the case. I was the spokesman of the Canadian government which was deeply shocked by the Soviet Union's display of imperialism and use of naked military power. 'You claim,' I said, 'that because Czechoslovakia is a socialist country, you have the right to march in and remove by force a government which doesn't happen to suit you; what do you think Canadians would say if the Americans took the same attitude towards a democratically elected government in Ottawa?' The Soviets, I told him, had violated the most basic principles of non-intervention and respect for the territorial integrity of other countries; instead of indulging in personal attacks against their critics, they might be well advised to worry about the conclusions other governments and other nations were going to draw from their actions.

Suddenly he dropped his belligerent attitude and said, almost plaintively: 'What should we do?' This sort of volte-face is typical of the way the Soviets operate: they try to bully you, then if you stand your ground they become unsure of themselves. I said it was for him and his government to figure out how they were going to convince the world that the invasion of Czechoslovakia was not symptomatic of a return to Stalinism, that it didn't mean they proposed to embark on a series of military conquests. He asked whether I had any suggestions and I said yes, I did. In the growing number of incidents which were once again threatening the armistice in the Middle East, the Soviets invariably backed the Arabs just as the Americans sided with the Israelis. As president of the Security Council, I proposed to call the council into session every time there was such an incident; and if he wanted to prove that his objective was really the pursuit of peace rather than imperialist expansion, he would support the council in its call for an unconditional adherence to the terms of the cease-fire. He said he would, and throughout the month he remained on his best behaviour.

Later that fall Pierre Trudeau came to New York for the first time in his new capacity as prime minister of Canada. We had met before when, as a freshman member of Parliament and legislative assistant to Mike Pearson, he came to New York to spend three months as an observer at the UN. But at that time he had seemed determined to remain in the background, and though we saw each other at official functions, we didn't really get to know each other.

The main reason for the November 1968 visit was a private meeting with the secretary general, which was held in my apartment and attended by a handful of officials. A major item on the agenda was the civil war in Nigeria, and the possibility that Canada might bring the issue up for discussion at the United Nations. The war, which pitted the central Nigerian government against an attempt by Biafra to secede from the country, had become a tremendously emotional issue in Canada and throughout much of the western world. Faced with daily newspaper reports and televised evidence of starvation, disease, and atrocities, many Canadians including members of Parliament were baffled and angry about our alleged indifference and failure to ask the United Nations to intervene.

The NDP was particularly vocal on the subject, and several of their members came to New York to tell me that I was not exerting myself sufficiently on behalf of the Biafran people. Ed Broadbent, who was then a junior member of Parliament, informed me in a very aggressive tone that I was abdicating my responsibility by failing to raise the issue in the UN, that he had taken a count and found that eleven or twelve African countries would support a Canadian resolution to debate Biafra.

I told him that I had done my own survey and had reached the conclusion that, if the chips were down, we couldn't count on the support of more than six African delegations, seven at the most. In any case it was no use playing the numbers game, because much more fundamental issues were involved. Andy Brewin, a veteran NDP member and an old friend of mine, intervened to ask, didn't I have trouble squaring my passive stance with my conscience? This really upset me. I said, 'Anyone can clear his conscience by putting on a mantle of righteousness; it's much more difficult to face the realities of African politics day in, day out. You come and try it!' Broadbent was outraged: 'Why do you allow a civil servant to talk to you like that, Andy?' he asked. But Brewin assured him that he had known me since I was in kneepants and that he was used to my ways.

I then tried to explain to them what the prime minister was told by U Thant and his staff during his New York visit, and what Mitchell Sharp had been told on several previous occasions, namely that the situation was considerably more complicated than the news media, the churches, the NDP, and all the other people who were clamouring for action had been led to believe. To begin with, it is a sad but uncontestable fact of life that, because of the way the newly independent countries were carved out of colonial empires without regard to tribal constituencies or natural barriers, practically every African state has a potential separatist movement. In the eyes of the Nigerians and most of their neighbours, what was happening in Biafra was not the emergence of a legitimate independence movement but rebellion, pure and simple; and any move on our part to raise the issue in the UN would have met with the determined opposition of all but a small handful of delegations. All we could expect to accomplish would be to sour our relations with most African countries and cause irreparable damage to our friendship with Nigeria.

If I felt I had a reasonably good insight into the African point of view, it was largely thanks to my friendship with Chief Simeon Adebo of Nigeria, one of the most interesting and colourful members of the UN community. He was invariably referred to as 'The Chief,' though no one dared enquire whether this was a tribal title or a carry-over from his days as chief of Nigeria's civil service during the days of colonial rule. Having been educated at British universities and with six years' experience as delegate to the UN to look back on, he knew how to explain African concerns to me in terms I could understand. Though Adebo had left by the time the Biafran crisis reached its peak, our close personal ties stood me in good stead with his successors. Unfortunately some of his equally admirable colleagues, such as Makonnen of Ethiopia and Marouf of Guinea, proved far less durable than the Chief. Both were recalled in the wake of changes of government in their respective countries, where firing squads put an end to their promising careers.

As a result of my talks with the Nigerians, I came to understand that one of the reasons why they were so firmly opposed to any United Nations involvement in Biafra was that they knew only too well what had happened in Kashmir, in the Sinai, and in Cyprus. In each of these instances, a peacekeeping force had become more or less a permanent fixture, and the armistice line had evolved, to all intents and purposes, into an international frontier. So the net result had been partition, which was exactly what the Nigerians were determined to prevent. As some of the African delegates put it to me, 'How would you like it if there were an armed uprising in Quebec and the United Nations decided to send a peacekeeping force to separate Quebec from the rest of Canada?'

The most the Nigerians would agree to, albeit reluctantly, was that food and medical supplies should be flown into Biafra. No doubt this was a help, but it didn't prevent the war from turning into a terrible massacre. For me personally, this was one of the most devastating experiences in my career. My instincts were all on the side of those who wanted to put an end to the killings, the maiming, and the starvation, no matter what the political consequences might be. Having witnessed the horrors of civil war in my childhood, I knew only too well that the main victims, whether in Africa or anywhere else, are always the most innocent and helpless members of society. If Ed Broadbent thought I was being cold-blooded, he was dead wrong. But it is one of the quandaries of public service that you have to follow the requirements of *realpolitik* as dictated by the interests of your country and the likely effectiveness of any proposed course of action. It was clearly in Canada's interest to stand by Nigeria in its struggle against separatism. As for the chances of helping the people of Biafra by raising the issue in the General Assembly, U Thant made it clear to Prime Minister Trudeau at their meeting in November 1968 that the United Nations had always opposed secession and would continue to do so, regardless of anything Canada might try to do about it.

Biafra was not the only reason why, towards the end of 1968, I felt increasingly frustrated and isolated in my New York post. Another source of aggravation and personal embarrassment was the Canadian government's ambivalent attitude towards South Africa's policy of racial discrimination and its refusal to pull out of Namibia. On the one hand we were vocal in condemning apartheid and voted, along with an overwhelming majority of the General Assembly, that Namibia should be freed from South African rule. But even while I was being called upon to express these noble sentiments, our Department of Industry, Trade and Commerce was urging Canadian companies to increase their investment in Namibia and circulating brochures which extolled the wonderful opportunities for developing its invaluable natural resources.

I tried to tell Ottawa that we couldn't have it both ways, that by saying one thing and doing another we were forfeiting the trust of African countries such as Nigeria and Tanzania. Either we should put our money where our mouth was and work towards a gradual disengagement from a South African-ruled Namibia, in which case the least we ought to do was warn Canadians that they were investing in the country at their own risk; or else we should stop confusing our African friends by supporting their resolutions in the United Nations. I spelled out these options in the United Nations chapter of the government's foreign policy review, which I was asked to write after I left New York and before I took up my next posting. It wasn't until a year or so later that I discovered that this particular recommendation had been edited out of the published report.

Security Council delegates cannot be effective unless they know that the suggestions they put forward and the positions they adopt have the full backing of their political masters. At the time of the UNEF crisis and the Six-Day War, what made the rapport between Goldberg, Caradon, and myself so meaningful was that all three of us had ready access to the highest echelons of our respective governments. Goldberg, who was the personal nominee of President Johnson, attended cabinet meetings whenever UN matters were to be discussed. Caradon enjoyed the confidence of the British government to the extent that he was elevated to the House of Lords and given the title of minister before being sent to New York.

While I didn't operate on quite as exalted a plane, I did get a phone call every morning from Paul Martin, Canada's foreign minister, so we could discuss any issues that might come up that day in the Security Council. He was incredibly well informed, more so even than Mike Pearson or any of his officials. By the time he phoned me around 7.30 a.m., he had read all the morning papers as well as every confidential document and probably a book or two on the outstanding issues, so I didn't have to fill him in on the background. He either told me right away what position he wanted me to adopt, or else he'd say that he wanted to consult the prime minister and the cabinet before calling me back. Either way I was never in any doubt, by the time I opened my mouth in the Security Council or at informal meetings, that I was expressing the wishes or viewpoint of the Canadian government.

These phone calls stopped abruptly when Martin went to the Senate and Mitchell Sharp became foreign minister. Sharp was extremely knowledgeable about international trade, but the world of diplomacy was alien territory to him, and not particularly interesting at that. Though he visited me from time to time in New York, I think it is fair to say that the Trudeau government was not UN-oriented; the emphasis was on developing relations with the People's Republic of China and building a 'just society' at home rather than cultivating traditional channels of international relations. The net result, as far as I was concerned, was that I found myself without instructions from Ottawa, and I was left to explore for myself what our response might be to such events as the Soviet invasion of Czechoslovakia.

If I had not enjoyed a different kind of relationship with Paul Martin and Mike Pearson, I might not have been so acutely aware of what I was missing. As it was, and given the fact that Canada's two-year term on the Security Council was due to expire in December 1968, I was glad when I was told that I was to be transferred to Geneva as Canada's permanent representative on the Disarmament Commission.

FIFTEEN

The cool seat in Geneva

I had been in Geneva less than two months when I found myself playing host to the Standing Committee on External Affairs and National Defence, which was touring Europe in search of new approaches to Canada's foreign and defence policies. The thirty members of Parliament were primarily interested in two issues. One was the desirability of Canada's membership in NATO. It's no secret that Trudeau was at that time far from enthusiastic about the Atlantic alliance, to the extent that he was giving serious consideration to opting out of it. The committee's other major concern was the policy Canada should adopt with regard to arms control and disarmament.

In order to give the visiting parliamentarians some idea of the price a neutral country, with no ties to any power bloc, pays for its territorial security, we started off with a working luncheon to which I had invited a number of Swiss politicians and government officials. Most of the Canadians were surprised to learn that all adult Swiss males must put in annual periods of military service, that those who are too old for combat duty get called up for civil defence exercises, and that Switzerland, with a population of five million, can mobilize an army of some 800,000 men within less than forty-eight hours.

This information served as useful background for the afternoon program, which consisted of a private briefing followed by a discussion period in the council chamber of the old League of Nations building. When I was asked what would happen if Canada were to withdraw from NATO, I replied that, in so far as such a withdrawal would diminish our ability to influence situations that affected our security, the consequences could be very serious indeed. As two world wars had surely shown, Canada could not dissociate itself from events in Europe, and any attempt to do so would leave us isolated not only in terms of collective security but also in international trade. Given all the benefits Canada derived from being part of the alliance, I thought our membership dues were remarkably modest.

Another question dealt with disarmament: was there any way Canada could show greater initiative in this area? I suggested that legislation should be passed to establish an advisory panel of experts from the worlds of science, law, defence, and diplomacy. By asking pertinent questions, relating disarmament to national security, and suggesting a range of available options, such a panel could provide Parliament and the government with something that was sadly lacking, namely an objective, non-partisan, thoroughly researched basis for disarmament debates and policy decisions. No doubt bits and pieces of the expertise required to choose weapons or new approaches to disarmament issues did exist within individual departments, but a mechanism was needed to co-ordinate this expertise, give it continuity, free it from departmental prejudices, and open it up to input from non-governmental sources.

To me and to many members of my audience it seemed like a sensible and far from revolutionary suggestion. After all, the Swedish Peace Research Institute was founded on a similar concept, and other countries had indicated they were planning to follow suit. But External Affairs was not pleased, particularly when my statement prompted questions in the House of Commons and a *Globe and Mail* editorial referred to my call for 'some sort of co-ordination of weapons technology' within the various departments of the Canadian government. Clearly stung, Marcel Cadieux, the under-secretary of state for external affairs, fired off a telegram in which he rapped my knuckles for 'implying inadequate interdepartmental coordination.' He realized, he went on to say, that I'd had no intention of precipitating criticism and that I hadn't had time before leaving for Geneva 'to become thoroughly familiar with interdepartmental working liaison arrangements in this field.' Never-theless, it would be extremely unfortunate if the parliamentary committee were to take my remarks at face value.

Cadieux was wrong when he said I had 'implied' lack of co-ordination. I had spelled it out to the best of my ability, if not to the parliamentarians, then certainly in my correspondence and previous discussions with the hierarchy of the department. The government's ambivalent policy with regard to South Africa – condemning apartheid out of one corner of its mouth and encouraging improved trade relations out of the other – was a case in point. As for Cadieux's remark that I wasn't sufficiently familiar with inter-departmental co-operation, the truth of the matter was that, having spent a few weeks in Ottawa helping to draft the United Nations chapter of the Trudeau foreign policy review, I was only too familiar with the mind-numbing futility of these so-called liaison meetings. Interminable hours were spent discussing competing or overlapping jurisdictions and responsibilities, and on the rare occasions when a decision was reached, it invariably represented the lowest common denominator among divergent points of view. The net result was that recommendations on arms control and disarmament which were being drafted before I left for Geneva in February 1969 reached me in June, presumably after running the gauntlet of inter-departmental brickbats. In the meantime, the conference for which they were intended had adjourned in May.

My predecessor, General E.L.M. 'Tommy' Burns, had not run into the same problem because way back in the Diefenbaker era Howard Green had insisted that Canada's representative to the Disarmament Conference should have the status of adviser to the government, with his own research staff and direct access to the cabinet. When I was appointed to succeed him, I assumed that my position would be the same, until a peremptory note from Cadieux set me straight. Unlike Burns, said the under-secretary, I was not of deputy minister rank; I would therefore report through 'normal' channels and receive my instructions from an interdepartmental committee of External Affairs and National Defence. To say that disarmament did not rank as a high priority with either department would be an understatement.

If the need for a Canadian contribution to the disarmament debate nevertheless received a fair amount of attention throughout the rest of 1969, it was largely because of the importance the prime minister personally seemed to attach to the issue. To my pleasant surprise he invited me to spend an evening at 24 Sussex Drive while I was in Canada for a brief visit, and I found that we were in fundamental agreement on the need to do whatever we could to slow down or preferably reverse the nuclear arms race. The government's throne speech that fall singled out disarmament as an issue of prime importance, and for a while, I had high hopes that Trudeau might speak on the subject either at the General Assembly in New York or at the Disarmament Conference in Geneva the following spring. As I pointed out to Ivan Head, Trudeau's chief adviser on external affairs, a throne speech delivered in Ottawa did not exactly arouse rapt attention in the international community; if Canada was really to be counted as a participant in the crusade for arms control, then the most effective way of delivering that message would be for the prime minister to appear before the United Nations or one of its major agencies.

In reply I was told that if I came up with a good topic for a speech, something really new and exciting, the PM would consider it. Nobody actually used the word 'sexy,' but that's what it amounted to. I suggested a number of possible topics, including an agreement to develop the Arctic for exclusively peaceful purposes, similar to the Antarctic Treaty signed in 1954. But either they were not exciting enough or else their implications were overly sensitive. When Trudeau finally decided that he had too many pressing engagements back home to attend either the General Assembly or the Disarmament Conference, I began to suspect that his concern about the nuclear arms race didn't run as deep as I had hoped.

Indeed, by the end of the sixties it was becoming increasingly obvious that the Canadian government was essentially inward-oriented, too immersed in bilingualism, national unity, and the country's economic woes to spare much time for any international activities that weren't trade-oriented. To begin with, there had been the prime minister's appearance on a national television program, when he described the concept of diplomacy as 'a little bit outmoded.' In an age of telecommunications, he said, a good news-paper provided the government with as much useful information about events and conditions in foreign countries as did ambassadors' reports. Then came an austerity drive which was to lead to the recall of some twenty-five per cent of foreign service officers from abroad and the dismissal of many of them; and this was followed by the formation of an interdepartmental committee to study the inte-gration and possible amalgamation of all government departments with foreign operations.

Finally, in December, while announcing the appointment of Ed Ritchie as the new under-secretary of state for external affairs, the prime minister went out of his way to emphasize Ritchie's qualifi-cations as 'a good economist, very able on the trade side.' Not a word about his distinguished diplomatic career in a number of highly sensitive posts. Indeed, Trudeau confirmed rumours which had been circulating in Ottawa for months before the appointment was announced, that he had seriously considered choosing someone from outside the department. Apparently he either didn't realize or didn't care about the devastating effect such an appointment would have had on the already eroded morale of the foreign service.

What it all added up to, in the opinion of many if not most External Affairs people, was a deliberate and systematic down-grading of the skills and expertise which to us were the essence of diplomacy. Clearly we were henceforth to be appraised according to our salesmanship rather than our ability to analyse international problems, negotiate under pressure, make tactical decisions con-cerning strategy and timing, know whose advice to trust and whose to reject, when to insist and when to concede a point. External Affairs was to become a stable for efficient administrators, people adept at reading computer printouts and skilled in managerial techniques, who could be transferred at a moment's notice to other departments and replaced with instant diplomats from the four corners of the public service.

It was symptomatic of this technocratic approach to diplomacy that Mitchell Sharp sent a circular letter to all heads of mission, inviting them to identify target areas for possible expenditure cuts. The avalanche of paper which descended on Ottawa from its diplomatic outposts was to be singled out for special attention. The minister's request for suggestions provided me with a welcome opportunity to unburden myself of some of the thoughts that had been on my mind for some time. As I told him in a long letter I composed while attending the General Assembly in New York, far too much time was being spent telling foreign service officers *how* to do things rather than telling them *what* it was they ought to be doing. Personally I welcomed the government's economy drive. But the best way to save money was not to cut staff or impose quotas on the number of telegrams, but rather to define the objectives and priorities of each mission, work out an action plan, and supplement it with periodic instructions. Heads of mission would then know exactly what information Ottawa wanted, instead of flooding the department with all kinds of more or less relevant reports on the off chance that some of them might arouse the interest of a mandarin or a politician. 'In short,' I wrote in conclusion, 'I am suggesting that economy must be related to function, and to the relevance of what the department and missions are doing.'

A reply of sorts arrived in the form of the government's preamble to the Foreign Policy Review which had been in the making for well over a year. Clearly inspired by the prime minister, this document set out to summarize the directions which the government intended Canada to pursue in the international arena. It pointed out that the country had many difficulties of its own – difficulties which called into question the desirability of Canada's continued participation in peacekeeping operations or, for that matter, the advantages of our membership in NATO. In the words of the authors, it would be risky and misleading to assume that Canada could or should continue to play the role of 'helpful fixer' in international affairs; such a reactive approach to world events was out of keeping with the realities of the day and with the government's policies.

Mike Pearson told me when we met at The Hague to attend a conference of the Institute of Strategic Studies how deeply hurt he was by this explicit repudiation of the kind of internationalism he had stood for and by the contemptuous 'helpful fixer' label which Trudeau had affixed to Canada's role as conciliator and advocate of collective security during the post-war era. He particularly resented the implication that there had been something self-serving about activities which, in his opinion as well as mine, represented nothing more or less than the discharge of our responsibilities as a member of the United Nations and of NATO. He foresaw, correctly as it turned out, that apart from weakening international institutions at a time when they were in particular need of strengthening, excessive preoccupation with domestic issues would undermine the very national unity to which the government claimed to be so totally committed. Under the leadership of St Laurent and Pearson, Canadians had found a sense of collective pride in their country's contributions to peacekeeping and its assistance to the world's underprivileged countries. Perhaps Trudeau came to the same conclusion some ten years later when he began promoting the north-south dialogue.

Now that Pearson was no longer prime minister, we were able to resume the personal friendship which had meant so much to me ever since our wartime days in London. He and Maryon announced in the spring of 1970 that they were coming to stay with us, obviously on the assumption that we were living in the beautiful villa which the Canadian government had purchased for its representative on the United Nations agencies in Geneva. During the previous winter, when the incumbent had suffered a nervous breakdown apparently brought on by overwork, I was asked to take on his responsibilities on top of mine. But since my predecessor refused to vacate the villa that went with the job, we continued to live in a rather seedy two-bedroom apartment which wasn't exactly designed for visiting VIPs.

Once the Pearsons had got over their initial surprise, they seemed perfectly at home in our unprepossessing quarters. The very first morning Mike got up early to make himself a cup of coffee, then settled down to sip it on the porch and announced that he didn't know what we were complaining about. Alison told him that he was no use to her at all; she had hoped he would phone his former colleagues in Ottawa and tell them that their failure to provide decent accommodation for their ambassador was a disgrace, instead of which he seemed as happy as could be. We ended up by taking Maryon away to our house in southern France so Mike could work, undisturbed, on his report to the World Bank about international aid.

The next time I saw Mike was when he came to my installation as provost of Trinity College, a few weeks before he died. He didn't look at all well, and though I didn't realize how ill he was, I made a point of going to Ottawa to thank him for coming. During my visit I found that his quarrel with Walter Gordon was very much on his mind, so I urged Walter to go and make his peace with Mike before he died, which he did.

The Pearsons' stay in Geneva was one of the few bright spots in an otherwise frantic and generally frustrating year. My new responsibilities cast me in the role of Canada's spokesman in some eighteen United Nations agencies – things like GATT, the WHO, UNESCO, and the ILO, which was actually an offshoot of the old League of Nations. Some of these were meeting concurrently or right after each other, so that the best I could do was to rush in and read some prepared statement which I'd barely had time to scan beforehand, let alone study or interpret. As a result, I was painfully aware of my inability to make worthwhile contributions to discussions of some extremely important problems.

In addition, Geneva was the headquarters for close to two hundred international organizations ranging from the Red Cross and the World Council of Churches to agencies dedicated to the protection of human rights, the survival of wildlife, the allocation of radio frequencies to telecommunication satellites, and the administration of patents. The year I arrived in Geneva there were 3326 meetings which, theoretically, I should either have attended or at least monitored in case Canadian interests were involved. The following year the number went up to 4049.

As though all this were not enough, I found myself occasionally cast in roles which were clearly outside the limits of my responsibilities. Education, for instance, is a provincial jurisdiction, and I therefore didn't expect to be involved in the activities of the World Education Conference even though it was taking place in Geneva. But when the deputy ministers of all Canadian provinces turned up for the meeting, it turned out that the deputy minister from Saskatchewan who headed the delegation couldn't speak any French while his counterpart from Quebec refused to speak anything else, particularly in a city where the language of communication was French. 'C'est impossible,' she protested indignantly. 'Nous voici à

Genève et le monsieur du Saskatchewan ne parle pas un mot de français. Pas un mot!' The long and the short of it was that I was asked to preside over their meeting and see if I could restore some semblance of peace. Had I refused there would have been allegations that federal officials were being unco-operative, so I figured I'd better say yes.

In spite of my absurd workload, I think I would have been content had I felt that we were making headway in the Disarmament Conference, which, to my way of thinking, outranked all my other responsibilities in importance. Unfortunately its accomplishments were far from impressive. Because the two superpowers which acted as co-chairmen determined not only the agenda we had to follow but also what within that agenda was or was not negotiable, we spent an incredible amount of time discussing peripheral issues which neither the United States nor the Soviet Union considered vital to their interests. The seabed arms control treaty was a case in point. After months of debate about jurisdiction and verification, we announced with a flourish that we had succeeded in prohibiting the use of underwater platforms as launching pads for nuclear weapons. Yet we had not even discussed let alone reached an agreement to limit the movement of nuclear submarines, which constituted a much greater menace. It was almost like saying that a submarine armed to the hilt with lethal missiles was engaged in legitimate pursuits so long as it remained mobile; but should that submarine stall, it could no longer use its arsenal against a potential enemy. It didn't seem to me like much of an accomplishment.

Similarly, our attempts to prohibit chemical warfare dealt with substances which the major belligerents had stockpiled during World War II, but steered clear of the more lethal techniques scientists had come up with in the mean time for possible use in a future conflict. By 1970 the military had access to the so-called binary process whereby apparently harmless chemicals are packed inside a shell where, by process of implosion, they become a paralysing nerve gas. The only antidote to such horrors, as I saw it, was to outlaw chemical warfare in all its hideous manifestations.

During discussions I'd had with the head of the External Affairs disarmament division, we agreed that Canada should take a lead in advocating such an unconditional ban. But, once in Geneva, I found that my superiors had suffered a change of mind. Presumably at the behest of National Defence, I was told that I'd have to tell the Disarmament Conference that the Canadian government reserved for itself the right to use chemical weapons such as tear-gas in defence of law and order at home. In my opinion this reservation was utterly irrelevant since all we were discussing in Geneva was a ban of chemical weapons in wartime, not some hypothetical intervention that might be required for domestic purposes. I also pointed out that, by qualifying our position in any way whatever, we would open the door to other reservations and controversies. The only sensible course was to ban the stuff outright.

Predictably enough, I was overruled, and with a heavy heart I made the statement National Defence had inspired. My one comfort was that the conference did follow up by outlawing biological warfare, without any ifs or buts. What happened was that American scientists, who knew what their research could lead to, came to Geneva and pleaded with us to stop the world from becoming engulfed in a deadly epidemic. President Nixon, to his credit, ordered the unilateral destruction of America's stockpiles of biological weapons, at which point we quickly put together a treaty that was signed by all the members of the Disarmament Conference. Though the Soviets never followed up with a certificate of destruction of their stockpiles, the treaty was at least a measurable step in the right direction.

As for the chemical warfare debate, it confirmed my suspicions that External Affairs was rapidly losing whatever influence it formerly had on foreign policy decisions. Even while the Interdepartmental Committee on External Relations was supposedly labouring to integrate Canada's foreign services, it was becoming increasingly clear to me that economic and commercial policies were being determined by the Departments of Finance and Industry, Trade and Commerce, environmental issues by the Department of the Environment, and defence by National Defence, while such key issues as Canada-US relations and commonwealth affairs were being handled by the prime minister and his foreign policy adviser.

The net result, as far as I was concerned, was not co-ordination of plans and policies, which I would have welcomed, but utter confusion. Wearing my twin hats as Mr Disarmament and Canada's representative to the United Nations agencies in Geneva, I found myself at the receiving end of so many conflicting signals that I never knew whether any particular instructions represented the views of an individual department or a consensus, or whether a policy had been cleared with those provincial governments whose interests might be involved. One day I would be told, presumably on the initiative of External Affairs, to inform UNCTAD that we had decided to remove or relax restrictions on imports of shoes or textiles from third world countries. A week or so later, along would come instructions to say the exact opposite in GATT, no doubt because the Ontario or Quebec governments had protested against having their market flooded by cheap imports.

On one occasion the deputy minister of industry, trade and commerce flew into Geneva in the morning, made a major policy speech (whose contents were complete news to me) in the afternoon, and buzzed off the same evening, leaving me to field the questions and explain the discrepancies with my previous statements, made in accordance with instructions I'd had from Ottawa. If I hadn't already been aware of the futility of my role, this incident would surely have brought it home to me. So long as I was supposedly my country's spokesman in all these international organizations, it seemed to me that I was entitled to know what the government's policies were and what contribution I might be able to make towards their implementation. Instead, ambassadors under the Trudeau regime were expected either to carry out routine administrative duties or, whenever anything important was in the offing, act as professional greeters for the dignitaries who had been dispatched from Ottawa to speak for Canada. More and more of my time was being spent meeting these VIPs at the airport, arranging hotel accommodation and entertainment, and making sure the compulsory limousine was at the visitors' disposal. Under the circumstances, I suppose I shouldn't have been surprised when, in answer to my pleas for reinforcements to help me carry my work load, External Affairs sent me a man previously employed as assistant manager at the Château Laurier. I had asked for someone with experience in economics or modern technology, in international law or the problems associated with relocating millions of refugees, and I got a hotelier. All things considered, it may have been an appropriate choice.

What made life even more frustrating was the realization that Canada was by no means the only country whose government was reluctant to play the role of 'helpful fixer.' In the United States as well as Europe, the winds of isolationism were once again blowing strong and threatening to undermine the spirit of international co-operation which the United Nations agencies in Geneva were supposed to represent. As a Pearson disciple I was a firm believer in the interdependence of nations and the need to tackle collectively such global problems as the escalating arms race, the depletion of scarce or irreplaceable resources, the threat to our environment, the growing incidence of violence and terror, and the possible breakdown of the post-war economic order. Yet as the UN agencies failed to come up with acceptable solutions, their options were being rapidly pre-empted by unilateral government decisions and actions. Instead of the international, non-discriminatory trading system envisaged by the founding fathers of the General Agreement on Tariffs and Trade, the nineteen-sixties and early seventies saw the emergence of rival trading blocs, rampant protectionism, and an OPEC crisis that plunged the entire world into recession. At the same time, the focus of arms control and disarmament talks shifted away from the Disarmament Conference towards the bilateral Strategic Arms Limitation Talks (SALT) between the superpowers. After three years in Geneva, it all made me wonder what exactly was the purpose of my mission.

While attending the General Assembly in New York in the fall of 1971, I got a phone call asking whether I would allow my name to go forward as a candidate for the position of provost of Trinity College at the University of Toronto. I didn't think for one moment that anything would come of it, but the prospect intrigued me, and after discussing it with Alison, I decided I had nothing to lose by throwing my hat in the ring. Back in Geneva, I had almost forgotten the conversation when I got a transatlantic call asking me to go to Toronto for an interview. I warned the selection committee that an Anglican college which, throughout its history, had always been headed by distinguished clergymen might look askance on a provost who wasn't even an Anglican, let alone an ordained minister; but they recommended me for the job just the same.

Though I had little reason to think that External Affairs would miss me, the resignation of a senior official and the likelihood that this would be interpreted as an expression of dissatisfaction with the *status quo* did apparently cause a bit of a stir in Ottawa. I got calls from both Ed Ritchie and Mitchell Sharp, plus an indirect message from the prime minister, all saying in effect that surely this didn't mean the end of my association with the public service. One of several suggestions was that I be appointed chairman and chief operating officer of the National Museums – a hybrid position which the government proposed to create for my benefit. But I said I had accepted the provostship at Trinity and I intended to devote all my time and energy to it. Besides, I didn't think that the chairman of the National Museums should be on the government's payroll; to the extent that he was responsible to the people of Canada, he ought to be totally independent. In the end, just to show that I was leaving without any hard feelings, I did accept a five-year term as volunteer chairman of the National Museums board.

Some time after I had been installed as provost of Trinity College, I was surprised to get a request from External Affairs to fill out a questionnaire, so as to enable the computer to compile my personality profile. I protested that I had filled out altogether too many of those things during my years as ambassador, that I was no longer a member of the department, and that the government ought to have a pretty complete profile of a person who had spent thirty-three years in the public service; but having been assured that this was truly necessary, I agreed to comply. One of the questions was: 'What if any of your talents have not been fully utilized by the government?' I put down 'cooking,' but the computer rejected my answer and opted for 'food processing' instead. The next box read:

'State experience.' I left that one blank, but a lady from Ottawa phoned and begged me to reconsider, because they simply had to have the information.

A small incident, no doubt, but one which to me was symptomatic of the erosion of a foreign service that had once been the envy of the English-speaking world. There had been a time when foreign service officers were professionals who were expected to think, to initiate, to weigh all possible options and come up with creative, carefully documented recommendations. At that time, External Affairs had been permeated from top to bottom with an *esprit de corps*, a desire to contribute to Canada's stature in the world, a determination to live up to the department's traditions of excellence. Joining External Affairs had been the ambition of many of the brightest, most promising young people in the country.

Not any more. By word and by deed, the prime minister and his entourage had made it clear that they considered professional diplomats an obsolete and essentially redundant breed. Members of the department, from ambassadors down, had been reduced to glorified hoteliers and administrators readily interchangeable with other public service officials.

Though leaving External Affairs after so many years of total immersion was a bit like severing one's umbilical cord, I felt exhilarated at the prospect of starting a new, challenging career. Ironically I was renewing, at the age of sixty, my association with the institution which had welcomed me as a new Canadian and had propelled me, in a sense, into the foreign service more than three decades before. If it hadn't been for the Rhodes scholarship I earned as a Trinity College student I wouldn't have gone to Oxford, wouldn't have met Mike Pearson, and wouldn't have been persuaded by him to enter the External Affairs competition at Canada House in London. In retrospect, I had few regrets. My life as a diplomat had been stimulating and rewarding. I'd had a ringside seat at some historical events. I had met an incredible number of fascinating people and formed friendships I shall cherish as long as I live. Above all, I'd felt privileged in being allowed to participate in the search for world peace and understanding among nations.

But now it was time for a change. The more I thought about it, the more I realized that, by leaving the public service, I was trading the protective but confining cocoon of bureaucracy for the free world of academe, where my opinions would not be homogenized in a hierarchical cauldron, where I'd be expected to generate ideas rather than data for the government's electronic wizards, where I could speak my mind about some of the most important issues of our time. With the benefit of hindsight, I am convinced it was one of the best things that ever happened to me.

Index

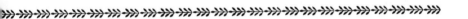